DAVID RICHA[_]
Ashe & Deane
1968 Metchun

History of the Book

by

SVEND DAHL

Second English Edition

THE SCARECROW PRESS, INC.

Metuchen, N.J.   1968

Copyright 1968
by The Scarecrow Press, Inc.

Preface

This book comprises a series of lectures given at the beginning of the 1920's and considerably expanded for publication here.

Most of the existing works on the history of the book present its various phases: manuscripts, printing, binding, illustration, the book trade and libraries separately. In this work I have attempted to present them all in a unified account so that their interrelationship will become apparent and the history of the book will appear in perspective as an essential factor in the history of culture.

The earlier editions of this work have been out-of-print for many years. This new edition incorporates the results of recent research, and brings the acount down to the present day.

I wish to thank those specialists who have so kindly examined various parts of the book: Dr. J. Christian Bay, former Librarian of the John Crerar Library in Chicago; Palle Birkelund, State Librarian of Denmark; Ejnar Philip, printer; and H. P. Rohde, Librarian at the Danish Royal Library.

I also thank Otto Andersen, bookdealer, for various helpful suggestions and for the warm interest that he has shown in this new edition.

1957

This second edition in English has been revised extensively and includes an index prepared by Mrs. Lena Y. de Grummond, Professor of Library Science, University of Southern Mississippi.

1968   Scarecrow Press, Inc.

Table of Contents

Chapter 1. Antiquity

The history of the book extends over more than five thousand years. There are, however, only a few scattered facts from the first two-thirds of this period to guide us in forming a picture of books and their place in the ancient world. Archeological investigations of the last generation have led to many new discoveries in this field, but there is still much that is unknown or uncertain. The classical Greek and Roman writers, usually our best source for the history of culture, provide very little information about books.

Hence we must use a great deal of caution in venturing on this uncertain ground; it is all too tempting to draw general conclusions from isolated finds, conclusions that may be completely refuted by later discoveries.

Egyptian Papyrus Rolls

When seeking the earliest available evidence for any phase of cultural history one will seldom seek in vain in ancient Egypt. Productive literary activity, to judge from archeological finds, developed to a high degree in the kingdom of the Pharaohs; not only were religious texts produced, but scientific and literary works as well.

In the still, swampy waters of the ancient delta of the Nile there grew large quantities of a plant which the Greeks called papyros, a word of uncertain derivation. The Egyptians used it for many purposes, but we are concerned here only with the use they made of the stalk, which is triangular in shape and may reach a height of 10-15 feet. The pith of the stalk was cut into thin strips, which were dried and laid out in a row with the edges overlapping slightly. Over these strips another row was laid crosswise and the two layers were then moistened with water and pounded together into an integral unit (see Fig. 4). This gluing process was extremely stable and the two layers are still firmly bonded in most of the

7

papyrus sheets that have been preserved.

After the strips had thus been combined into a sheet, the sheet was presumably sized so that the ink would not run. It was then dried in the sun and glazed to produce a glossy surface. The finished sheet, when it was of good quality, was very supple and flexible and this flexibility has generally been retained amazingly well through the centuries. The sheets were glued together side by side to form long sections. The production of papyrus seems to have become an industry at an early period. The product was sold in large quantities in the form of bales or rolls from which sheets could be cut as needed. Ordinarily the sheets used were 6 to 7 inches high, but later we find sheets up to three times this size. The better grades of papyrus were light in color, being yellowish or almost completely white, while the poorer grades were brownish in tone.

The manufacture of papyrus was well developed as early as the third millenium B.C., when it reached a stage of technological perfection that was not to be surpassed later. It is possible that there were some differences of detail in the methods used in different periods, but nothing definite is known about those. There are a number of uncertainties about the manufacture of papyrus; the description that is usually given is not based on Egyptian writings but is derived from painted reliefs found at Thebes and from an account by the Latin author Pliny the Elder, supplemented by the investigations of modern Egyptologists.

One characteristic of all papyrus, regardless of quality, was that there was a difference between the two sides of the sheet because the two layers of strips lay at right angles to each other. The side on which the strips run horizontally was called the recto side, and this was the side usually preferred for writing; the side with the strips running vertically was called the verso and was less frequently used. A material as pliable as papyrus was eminently suited to being rolled, and when this was done the recto became the inner side and the verso, with no writing on it, the outer side.

The Egyptian book was in the form of a roll. In reading it was unrolled gradually so that the writing appeared little by little.

As a rule, the writing was divided into columns, thus making the
lines quite short and dividing the book, in a sense, into "pages,"
which came successively into view as the roll was unwound. One
famous papyrus roll now in the University Library at Leipzig is
about 65 feet long and is divided into 110 "pages." The text begins
at the extreme right of the roll, and the pages follow one another
from right to left.

The system of writing that was used was not, except in certain religious books, the original hieroglyphic seen in inscriptions,
but a more rapid and easier form of writing that had been developed
as early as the middle of the third millenium B.C. for use on papyrus and was, like the fine grade of papyrus, called hieratic (priest-
ly). In a later period we find papyrus sheets with another type of
writing, the so-called demotic (popular), which is further simplified.
The oldest papyrus known dates from about 2400 B.C., but papyrus
evidently is even older, dating back to the time when hieroglyphic
was in use, because there is a hieroglyphic symbol for the papyrus
roll.

The writing tool used by the Egyptians was a reed stalk cut
at an angle, with one end frayed by chewing to form a soft brush.
By turning it, thick or thin lines could be produced. In the third
century B.C., however, a stiff, pointed reed, the calamus, came
into use, making it possible to write a finer line. This became the
common writing tool; like the ruler for making straight lines, it was
part of the equipment of every scribe. The ink used was made from
lampblack or charcoal by adding water and an adhesive. It was superior to our present-day ink--the writing has often preserved its
deep black sheen through the ages. Red ink was also used, especially for titles and chapter headings. The scribe kept his pens and
ink on a sort of palette, a thin oblong piece of wood with a slot to
hold the pens and two or three depressions for ink. The papyrus
rolls were kept in clay jars or wooden boxes. Since the outer part
of the roll would be subject to wear it was often made of better material or protected by a covering, and the edges of the roll might be
reinforced by gluing on strips.

The fact that papyrus has been preserved down to the present

1.   Papyrus roll with Greek text in columns.

day, and in considerable quantities, is not due to any inherent characteristics of the material.   From statements made by ancient
writers we know that when a roll lasted a couple of hundred years
it was considered to have reached an honorable old age.   We often
find complaints about the fragility of the material and its poor keeping qualities.   Destruction by insects was quite common, and attempts were made to counteract this by dipping the papyrus sheet in
cedar oil.   The worst enemy was moisture.   It is, of course, impossible to estimate how many papyrus rolls have been destroyed;
but what is now preserved must represent only a small fraction of
what originally existed.   An indirect proof that moisture must bear
the major part of the blame for this destruction is seen in the fact

that by far the greater part of the papyri that have been found come
from excavations in Egypt.   While the Graeco-Roman world used
more papyrus than did the Egyptians for almost a thousand years,
only a very few papyrus finds have been made in these countries.
The reason lies primarily in the destructive effect of the climate.
For this same reason only a few finds have been made in the humid
Nile delta; the major finds are from the dry sands of middle and
upper Egypt.   Egyptian graves have been excellent repositories for
this fragile material.   In the last centuries B.C. it became the custom to make mummy coffins of discarded papyrus sheets glued together and covered with a layer of plaster; several papyrus texts
have come to us in this manner.   A far greater number, however,
have been preserved through the general religious custom of placing
various sacred texts, prayers, etc., in the grave as protection during the soul's journey into the realm of the dead; among these the
"Book of the Dead" was especially common.   This book is known
from about 1800 B.C.; it gradually acquired a conventional content,
and copies were apparently made by priests on a production basis,
with spaces left for the name of the deceased--an industry of the
same type as that which later developed for the letters of indulgence
issued by the Catholic Church.

The trade in Books of the Dead was probably the only book
trade that existed in ancient Egypt.   Some of these books were extensively illustrated, and the illustrations were presumably drawn by
an artist before the scribe wrote the text.   In most instances the
pictures formed a border that ran the entire length of the roll above
the text.   Their artistic value varied greatly, but all exhibited the
stylistic features so well known in Egyptian relief carvings.   A few
Books of the Dead had colored illustrations or other special treat-
ments.   These were presumably intended for persons who had been
very prominent or very wealthy.   The ordinary man had to be content with smaller and more modest productions.   From all indica-
tions papyrus was expensive, even more so after it had become a
large-scale export product, and consequently it was not the only
writing material used in Egypt.   Leather was popular, and for short-
er notations wooden tablets, pieces of limestone and potsherds were

2. Fragment of an Egyptian Book of the Dead, intended for a person of rank. Above the text there is a colored pictorial frieze with artistically drawn figures. (British Museum). Most Books of the Dead, however, were less elaborate, many having no illustrations. Since the text was not intended to be read it was often full of errors.

used.

We have almost no information about libraries in classical
Egypt. There was no separation between book collections and archives; books and documents had the same outward appearance and
required similar methods of storage. In Egypt, as well as in other
countries of the ancient world, libraries were attached to religious
centers or temples. The temple of the sun god Horus, which is
still preserved at Edfu in southern Egypt, has a room whose walls
are decorated with the titles of 37 books that the library had received as a gift. In the vicinity of Thebes two graves have been
found with inscriptions in which the word librarian appears as a
title; buried here are a father and son, who presumably belonged to
the priesthood and had accordingly been teachers of learning and
writing.

Early Chinese Books

While the papyrus sheet became the prevailing writing material in the Nile valley and thus determined the outer form of the
book in Egypt, a simultaneous development in far-away China took
a different form. China possessed the art of writing and produced
literary works as early as the third millenium B.C. During the
next thousand years or more we know that the country had imperial
historians; the great philosopher Lao-tze, who lived about 500 B.C.,
was said to have been archivist at the imperial archives.

The materials used for writing at that time were bone, tor-
toise shell, split bamboo stalks; later came wooden tablets on which
lines were drawn with a stylus. The writing began in the upper
right-hand corner and ran vertically downward, the lines following
one another from right to left, just as in Chinese books of the present day.

Almost no wooden manuscripts are still in existence. One
major reason for this was an edict to destroy all books, issued by
the Emperor Chin Tain Shihuangti in the year 213 B.C. This was
done to punish authors who had dared to criticize his political ac-
tions. Only a few books escaped the burning, and most of the
wooden books that were produced thereafter proably were destroyed

by rot.

This book-burning incident was followed by a period of great literary activity; efforts were made to replenish the supply of books by seeking out and reissuing the surviving works of classical literature from the time of Confucius. Writing was no longer restricted to wooden tablets but was also done on silk cloth, either with a bamboo pen or a camel's hair brush. The ink used was a black substance obtained from the varnish tree; later, india ink was made from lampblack mixed with glue. Silk possessed several of the properties of Egyptian papyrus--it was pliable and had a smooth surface--but it was more expensive.

Cuneiform Tablets of the Near East

In addition to Egypt and China, a third region that had a highly developed culture in ancient times was the Near East, Mesopotamia in particular. In the fourth millenium B.C. at the latest, a people called the Sumerians migrated from the east into the southern part of the country between the Tigris and the Euphrates and then gradually spread northward. The culture they developed is known to us through the excavations at Ur, Lagash, and especially at Nippur, which obviously had been a great religious center. There is no doubt that the Sumerians had a system of writing and an increasingly significant literature, and they are generally considered to be the originators of cuneiform writing, an original pictographic form that early changed to a phonetic system.

True cuneiform characters were first introduced by the Semitic Akkadians who, toward the close of the third millennium B.C., put an end to Sumerian rule as they gradually adopted the Sumerian culture. These peoples included the Babylonians and together with the Assyrians, a Semitic people of northern Mesopotamia, they attained a dominant position in all of the Near East. In the 15th century B.C. their language became the diplomatic language of the time; even in the royal archives of the Egyptian city El-Amarnas many cuneiform tablets in the Assyrian-Babylonian language have been found.

At Nippur, parts of a large temple library and archives containing clay tablets have been discovered; these date partly from the Sumerian period and partly from the Babylonian and Assyrian period. The temple of Nippur had several rooms, some of which undoubtedly were used for the library and others for the archives. When the clay tablets were found they were in unorganized piles and many were broken; but originally they must have been contained in clay or wooden boxes or in woven baskets set on clay bases or on wooden shelves along the walls. To protect them against moisture these boxes were coated with asphalt and the same was probably also done with the baskets. In other instances, the tablets had merely been tied together and placed directly on the shelves or in niches in the walls; these as well as the boxes and baskets were undoubtedly marked with small clay labels.

In tablet-writing, the characters were impressed in soft clay by a blunt triangular instrument of metal, ivory or wood, thus giving the characters their wedge-shaped form. After the writing was completed the tablet was dried in the sun or baked in an oven and became as hard as brick. Some of the larger tablets had small holes in the surface to permit steam to escape during the baking process. Some of the tablets that have been found, however, were not adequately baked; consequently it has been difficult or impossible to separate and decipher them.

Nearly half a million tablets, including fragments, have been excavated to date from the ruins of the Near East and Mesopotamia, and many of them are now in European and American museums. The tablets are rectangular and vary greatly in size; some are 12 inches wide by 16 inches long but the majority are only half that size. The tablets were written on both sides; the back was slightly concave while the face was flat or convex. The back of the tablet that lay on the top of each stack was turned up; it bore the title of the work and often the names of the owner and the scribe, as well as an admonition to treat the tablets with care. The latter might well be necessary, for if a tablet fell to the floor it was easily broken. It was customary, when the contents were no longer of interest, to use the tablets as material for roads and floors, or to stack them in solid piles.

3. Cuneiform tablet containing a hymn to the Babylonian
king Dungi (University Museum, Philadelphia).

Literary activity flourished among the Babylonians and the
Assyrians and there was plenty of clay in the country between the
two great rivers.   There were undoubtedly writing rooms in conjunc-
tion with every temple.   The period of Assyrian greatness, which
follows that of the Babylonians, falls in the 8th or 7th century B.C.,
and the archives and library of King Ashur-bani-pal (Sardanapalus?)

in the Assyrian capital city of Nineveh are famous. This site was
excavated a hundred years ago by British archeologists and more
than 20,000 complete tablets and fragments are now preserved in the
British Museum. The clay of the tablets found here is finer and
more carefully baked than that found elsewhere, and the writing is
generally clearer and more elegant, for which credit must go to the
large staff of calligraphers at Ashur-bani-pal's court. This king
evidently gathered texts from all places, both inside and outside his
kingdom; these were then reworked and copied, just as was later
done at the library of Alexandria. Babylonian-Assyrian literature is
extensively represented in the library of Ashur-bani-pal, but there
are also Sumerian texts. A large part of the library was destroyed
when the Medes, allied with the Persians, conquered Nineveh in 612
B.C. Two or three private Assyrian libraries have also been found.

We also have collections of clay tablets with cuneiform writing from two other Near East civilizations. The Hittites, who flourished between 1900 and 1200 B.C., have left us about 15,000 unusually large clay tablets in their capital, Boghazköl, which lies east of
Ankara. Catalogs that have been found give the titles and the number of tablets in each work. In Ras-Shamra, an important trade
center of northern Syria in the time of the Hittites, clay tablets
have been found with texts in the Ugaritic language, which is closely
related to Phoenician. They are written in a kind of cuneiform with
only 29 signs, representing an alphabet somewhat similar to the
Phoenician alphabet, the progenitor of the Greek and all later alpha-
bets. This Ras-Shamra alphabet, as well as the Phoenician, must
be considered to have been inspired by Egyptian writing.

Other Early Writing Materials

Among the several kinds of writing material that were in use
at various times and various places during the first two or three
thousand years of historical time, bast fiber was in use perhaps
earliest of all. Both the Greek and the Latin words for book, byb-
los and liber, originally denoted bast. Palm leaves, dried and
rubbed with oil, were used for writing in India for many centuries
(and are still used there to some extent). Hence there is nothing

remarkable in the fact that a related material such as bast was
used in the same manner; the characters could be scratched in with
a pointed instrument just as was done on palm leaves.   Linen also
was used for books since Livy mentions linen book rolls.   Leather
was used to an even greater extent; some of the recently discovered
Dead Sea scrolls are of leather.   Even in Mesopotamia, where clay
tablets were dominant, other writing materials were also used.   In
the ruins of a city near Nineveh cuneiform writing has recently been
found on tablets of wood and of ivory coated with a layer of wax.

Greek Papyrus Rolls.   The Alexandrian Library

The papyrus roll apparently reached the Greeks in the 7th
century B.C.   Export of this material from Egypt to Greece then
increased steadily and by the 5th century the use of papyrus appears
to have been general.   The fact that Herodotus does not mention
papyrus rolls in his description of Egypt may be an indication that
they were in common use in his own country.   The Greeks called
the blank papyrus sheet chartres, which became the Latin charta
and produced our words chart and card.   The written sheet was
called byblion, or biblion, in Greek.   The Greeks called the papyrus
roll kylindros while the Romans called it volumen, a word that is
still used in many languages to denote one book of a set.   Another
word with the same meaning, tomus, (Greek tomos) was originally
used for a roll consisting of a series of separate sheets pasted together.

The oldest known Greek papyri date from the 4th century
B.C.   The letters have the primitive and severe form found in inscriptions, but there are too few rolls preserved from this period
to justify general conclusions.   Not until we come to the 3rd century does our knowledge become somewhat more complete and certain, supported by the numerous finds of Greek papyri that were
made in the 19th century, particularly in Egypt and Asia Minor, and
largely from the Alexandrian period.

The more extensive finds in this period are due to the flowering of Greek culture and religion after Alexander the Great incorporated Egypt into his far-flung empire.   From then on the papyrus

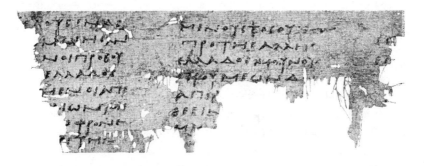

4.   Papyrus fragment from the first half of the 3rd century
B. C. , containing a text of Herodotus.

book became a part of the Greek world.   The connection between
Egyptian and Greek culture was strengthened still further when Ptolemy I, after the fall of Alexander's empire, established his powerful kingdom in the Nile valley and devoted himself to giving his new
capital, Alexandria, a position of leadership in culture as well as in
politics and commerce.   He, and especially his son Ptolemy II, invited Greek scholars, offering them a carefree life as members of
a sort of religious brotherhood or academy.   This academy had its
quarters in the new temple of the muses, the Museion, patterned after Aristotle's famous peripatetic school in Athens.

In the Museion there was both study and teaching; the library
that was assembled during the third century B. C. was quite comprehensive, even containing translations of Egyptian, Babylonian and
other early literature.   This library was the larger of the two collections that made up the Alexandrian library.   The other collection
was located in the temple of the national deity Serapis and was
called the Serapeion.

The primary object of the Alexandrian library was to collect
the whole of Greek literature in the best possible editions, and to
arrange them and provide them with commentaries--a task to which
a phenomenal amount of labor was devoted.   The poet Callimachus
was one of the many outstanding scholars who worked in the library.
On the basis of its subject catalogs (pinakes was the word for cata-

log) he compiled a sort of author catalog of the entire Greek literature of that time.   The existing fragments of his work indicate his
excellent qualifications as a cataloger.

We know practically nothing about the library quarters at the
Museion, but those at the Serapeion have been excavated.   The size
of the Alexandrian library is not definitely known, but it is estimated at about 700,000 rolls in the larger division and about 43,000
in the smaller.   If these figures are correct there must, in many
instances, have been several copies of the same work.   Large sums
of money must have been available for purchases, and a great deal
of work was certainly expended on copying poorly preserved manuscripts and in preparing new critical editions to supersede more or
less doubtful texts.   Long works were divided up into several rolls
of approximately the same length and several short texts were combined into a single roll--all presumably done to make the rolls a
standard, practical, length.

No complete roll has been preserved.   The usual length was
probably about 20-23 feet; when rolled this would make a cylinder
2-2.5 inches thick, which was thus easy to hold in the hand.   Rolls
over 30 feet long were certainly exceptional.   The height of the rolls
also varied, although here again we note a tendency toward standard
measurements.   Only a few of the rolls that have been preserved
are over 12 inches high, the majority being between 8 and 12 inches
or between 5 and 6 inches.   The portion of the papyrus sheet used
for writing also varied considerably; the more elaborate manuscripts
have wider margins than the plainer ones.   The length of the columns could be from 2/3 to 5/6 of the height of the roll, and the
space between columns and the distance between lines varied.   The
space between lines might vary within a given manuscript; the width
of a column was generally somewhat less than its length (see Figs.
1 and 4).

The instrument used for writing literary works was a thick
hollow reed stalk, cut to form a pointed pen.   Only capital letters
were used (the small Greek letters did not evolve until the Middle
Ages) and no space was left between words, which makes the texts
difficult to read.   On the other hand, it was customary to mark the

end of a unit in the text by placing a line, the so-called paragraph-os, under the beginning of the last line of the unit, and this word has continued in use to denote divisions of the text. The script was a formal type of calligraphy which the scribes were taught, but each scribe developed individual characteristics in his writing. For ordinary daily use there was a more rapid cursive script with less definite lines and with combined letters. About four-fifths of the papyri that we have are in cursive script; these represent mainly public and private documents and letters.

The scribes who wrote the literary manuscripts constituted a sizable professional class with considerable education. They were paid partly by number of lines, presumably of standard length, and partly according to the nature of the text. When the scribe had finished his work the manuscript was proofread either by himself or by a corrector, who corrected the errors and might also make critical notations in the margin to clarify the text (the so-called "scholia") or insert signs (asterisks, etc.) to call attention to linguistic peculiarities.

The title of the roll, when there was one, was usually placed at the end of the text, probably because it was best protected there, being innermost as the book lay rolled up. The use of specific titles was undoubtedly a relatively late practice. Greek papyri of the earlier period probably had no titles, but were identified, as Callimachus did his work, by the name of the author and the initial word or words of the text. To tell the rolls apart as they lay or stood in their containers, a sort of label did gradually come into use. It was attached to the upper edge of the roll. The word title itself comes from this label, which the Romans called titulus or index, and the Greeks sillybos. The wooden or stone jar in which the rolls were kept was called bibliotheke by the Greeks, but the meaning of this word was extended quite early to include a collection of books in general; in Latin the jar was called capsa or scrinium.

Illustrations were probably not unusual in papyrus rolls, even though few, mainly of a mathematical or similar nature, have been found. In a number of instances a portrait of the author was reproduced, and the suggestion has been made that the columns of Trajan and Marcus Aurelius in Rome are to be interpreted as large-scale reproductions of picture-rolls.

The amount of papyrus used by the Greeks and later by the Romans must have been considerable. A number of varieties, or brands, came on the market, some named for Roman emperors (charta Augusta, Claudia, etc.). In the later Roman Empire factories were established in Rome to make papyrus sheets from material imported from Egypt.

It appears likely that the Ptolemys imposed a tax on the exportation of papyrus and the papyrus trade later became a government monopoly. The top sheet in a bale was called protocol and received a sort of official stamp. This monopoly continued even after the Arabs conquered Egypt.

Among the oldest papyrus finds is that found during the excavation of Herculaneum in 1752. About 1800 carbonized rolls were found in this town, which had been destroyed by the eruption of Vesuvius in 79 A.D. These are now preserved in the National Library at Naples. There are also famous papyrus collections in the National Library at Vienna (Archduke Rainer's collection of about 80,000 pieces), the British Museum in London, the Bodleian Library at Oxford, the Staatliche Museum in Berlin and the Egyptian Museum in Cairo. The University of Copenhagen has a small collection of Greek papyri.

But to return to the library at Alexandria, it is obvious that such a great literary center would also be important in the development of the book trade. There is indirect reference to the existence of publishers in Athens as early as the 5th century B.C., and from Xenophon's Anabasis we know that there was trade in books with the Greek colonies. With the rise of the Alexandrian library the opportunities of the book trade were expanded, partly because the library itself became a large-scale customer and partly because the library made available an outstanding collection of manuscripts from which copies could be made for sale.

Among the books acquired by the library at Alexandria were some said to be from the collection left by Aristotle. He had willed his library to one of his pupils, but it was later broken up and part-

ly destroyed; a few of the books were said to have been brought to
Rome by Sulla.   Beyond this we know very little about Greek private
libraries, but that of Aristotle must certainly have been outstanding.

When Caesar conquered Alexandria in 47 B. C. part of the
larger division of the library was burned.   The final destruction of
the Alexandrian library presumably came in 391 A. D., when the
Christians, under the direction of Archbishop Theophilus of Antioch,
destroyed the temple of Serapis.

The Library at Pergamum

The library at Pergamum in northwestern Asia Minor was
founded by Attalus I and was expanded by Eumenes II.   It may be only legend that the latter tried to kidnap Ptolemy's competent librarian and put him to work in the Pergamum library and that Ptolemy
put his unfortunate librarian in prison to prevent this, and there is
probably no basis for the statement by a Roman writer that the Egyptian king at the beginning of the second century prohibited the export
of papyrus in order to prevent the library at Pergamum from expanding and overshadowing the one at Alexandria.

The Pergamum library very likely used the Alexandrian library as a model in matters of organization and cataloging.   We
have some idea of the library's quarters through the excavations of
German archeologists in 1878-86.   When they excavated the temple of
Athena in Pergamum they found four rooms, the innermost of which
contained a colossal statue of Athena and was presumably a sort of
meeting or reception room, while the three adjoining smaller rooms
may have been used for books; all four rooms opened into a colon-
naded archway--an arrangement that we find in many other library
installations of ancient times.

Pergamum and its library probably never attained as illustrious a position in the scholarly world of the time as that held by
Alexandria and the library there, and it is possible that the Pergamum library was actually incorporated into the Alexandria library by
Anthony's gift to Cleopatra.

Leather had undoubtedly been used for writing at various
places in the ancient world even in very early times.   Among the

Egyptians and the Jews as well as the Assyrians and Persians and
the Greeks, animal skins were so used.   The Greeks called them
diphthera, a name that was later applied to other writing materials
as well.   It was not until the third century B.C. , however, that
leather was subjected to a special treatment to make it better suited
for writing and the development of this process is usually asso-
ciated with Pergamum.   The processing of leather for writing pur-   .
poses was done on a large scale there and the word parchment,
charta pergamena, is presumably derived from the name of the city.

As a rule, sheep, calf or goat skins were used.   The hair
was removed, the skin scraped thin was soaked in lime water to remove fatty substances, dried, and then, without any other tanning,
it was rubbed with finely ground chalk and was polished smooth with
pumice stone or a similar material.   The final product produced by
this method was excellent for writing; it presented a smooth and
firm surface and was usable on both sides.   Its durability exceeded
that of papyrus, though it was by no means resistant to all types of
destructive action.   One factor that contributed greatly to its extended use was that, in contrast to papyrus, it permitted erasures to be
made easily.   This is the reason that among vellum manuscripts--
especially from the Middle Ages and other periods when the material was expensive--we find palimpsests, that is, sheets on which the
original writing had been rubbed out and new text written over it
(Fig. 8).   Palimpsest means 're-smoothed." The manufacture of
parchment was not restricted to a single country and for this reason
it was, at least in the early period, not so expensive as papyrus
came to be.   Nevertheless, at the beginning it was mainly used for
letters, documents, and other small items; it was only gradually
that parchment, which the Romans called membrana, was raised to
the status of a book material, and it had to compete with papyrus in
this field for three centuries before it finally attained supremacy.
From the fourth century A.D. papyrus gradually went out of use. It
is true that in the papal chancellery there are rolls or sheets of papyrus from as late as the 11th century, but these were rare exceptions.

Although we do not possess a single Greek or Roman vellum

roll there is evidence that the roll form was used for vellum books.
The Jews used parchment rolls and use them even today for their
sacred book, the Torah. The length of a roll was generally limited
by the length of the animal's hide, though when necessary several
pieces were sewed together to make longer rolls. Parchment was
also used as a covering for papyrus rolls--representing the very
first stage of bookbinding.

The Roll Superseded by the Codex

However accustomed the people of antiquity may have been to
the roll they must have felt that it had disadvantages for ordinary
daily usage. One important disadvantage was that when the roll had
been read it had to be rewound before it could be read again; in the
case of a long roll this might involve some difficulty. Even though
a stick (called umbilicus) was customarily used, some wear was
caused by this operation when the rolls were used frequently. As
long as papyrus was the standard material the roll was the most
natural form; with vellum, however, the situation was different.

From very early times the Greeks had used small writing
tablets of wood, sometimes with a coating of wax, on which brief
notations could be scratched with a metal stylus. School children
used them for writing their exercises. Two or more tablets of this
kind were often bound together to form small booklets (those made
of two tablets were called diptycha) and such notebooks were used
extensively by tradespeople or by scribes for temporary notations.
When vellum came into regular use for writing it was very easy to
adopt the form of these tablet books for vellum books, and this step
was taken in the first period of the Roman Empire. This form was
called a codex and it has remained essentially unchanged since its
adoption. A few codex sheets have been preserved from about the
end of the first or the beginning of the second century A.D. Vellum
codices were certainly in use at that time, although they were probably considered less respectable than papyrus rolls. They were
used for small and less expensive editions because vellum could be
used on both sides and a text that would require a large roll or several rolls could be contained in a relatively small codex. In recent

years a number of codices from the second, third and fourth centuries have been found in Egypt--proof of the rapidity with which the codex form had penetrated into the very homeland of the papyrus roll. Attempts were made to apply the codex form to papyrus, perhaps as early as the first century A.D., and a number of papyrus codices date from the 3rd-5th centuries A.D. The older material did not lend itself to the new form, and the papyrus roll continued to exist alongside the codex until both the papyrus material and the roll form were finally abandoned.

Archeological finds show that parchment codices were in the majority by the fourth century and by the fifth century they had taken over the field completely.

It is quite interesting to note that the oldest writings of the Christian Church were nearly all in codex form; only a few were in rolls. One reason given for this is that the early Christians were not wealthy enough to afford papyrus, but had to content themselves with the less expensive vellum.

A certain special respect has been attached to the roll as the most ancient book form even in our own day, as we see, for instance, in the custom of giving documents a distinctive and formal appearance by making them in rolls--festival speeches, honorary diplomas, etc. In expressions like honor roll we have a reminder of the time when such documents were still in roll form, and the word control really is "contra-roll," i.e. a roll that the tax office kept as a safeguard along with the regular tax roll.

There are several old codices in which all the sheets have been laid inside one another in a single fold; such a procedure naturally made the book awkward, and also made the inner pages narrower than the outer ones. The idea of dividing a book into several folds, with a few sheets in each and tying these folds together with string, much as is done with the signatures in books today, developed quite early.

The format of books in the first four centuries of our era was rather small; the ratio of width to height was usually about 2:3. Just as today, there were undoubtedly certain standard sizes of sheet, and the various formats were obtained by folding the sheet

once or twice. From the fifth century on larger formats became
more common. As in papyrus rolls and modern books, the finer
codex manuscripts show a tendency to wider margins, while the inferior ones have their pages filled with writing almost out to the
edge; nearly always, however, more space was left at the outer
edge of the sheet than at the top and bottom, probably as protection
against wear. In its general features the codex was basically similar to the roll in design. Even the practice of placing the title at
the end of the text was transferred from the roll to the codex, even
though it was of no practical significance in the latter. It was not
until the fifth century that it became the regular practice to place
the title at the beginning of the work as well. One new feature that
was introduced along with the codex was pagination. This device
was unnecessary in the roll, where the columns were necessarily
maintained in their proper order, but in the codex it became of
practical importance. In the beginning, however, it was often used
only on certain pages or on the front side of each sheet; hence it
cannot actually be called pagination, but rather foliation (pagina =
page; folium = sheet).

As mentioned earlier, only a few rolls with illustrations are
known, but we have a considerable number of codices from the first
centuries A. D. with some sort of pictorial embellishment, including
illustrations that actually represent the contents of the text (Fig. 7)
as well as purely decorative designs. The pictures are colored but
have practically no shading and the figures and faces are reminiscent
of those on monuments, coins or wall paintings. As early as the
4th century there were Greek and Coptic manuscripts in which the
first letter of each section was enlarged and decorated with various
flourishes in color, usually red, thus introducing the initial (initium
= beginning). The script used in the earliest codices was a special
form of calligraphy, just as in the rolls, and it gradually became
more and more fixed in its form. There is a series of Greek and
Coptic manuscripts from the 4th and 5th centuries, of quite different
content but all written in an almost identical, beautiful hand with
broad rounded lines, indicating a growing tendency toward uniformity
in style of writing.

The implement used for writing on vellum was the hollow part of the shaft of a feather, preferably from a large bird such as the eagle, raven or goose. From these ancient pens developed the later goose quill and our metal pens. The ink was of the same composition as that used on papyrus; it was not until the 12th century A.D. that the ink that we know today, made of copperas and tannic acid, came into use. How the early codices were bound is not known with certainty. In most instances a simple parchment cover was probably all that was used, but there is a codex from the 3rd century in which six blank sheets at the front and back were pasted together and covered with leather. There are examples of Egyptian leather bindings from the 6th-8th centuries that show traces

5. Coptic binding in red and yellow leather with tooled geometric designs. (Egyptian Museum, Berlin.)

of handsome intaglio work on the covers (Fig. 5). These bindings were made by the Christian Egyptians, the Copts, and because of their professional quality they must have been preceded by a long period of development.

Book Trade and Book Collecting Among the Romans

When the Romans conquered the world and appropriated the
fruits of Greek culture, the Greek tradition in the realm of books
was continued on Roman soil. Roman military leaders brought Greek
book collections back to Rome as spoils of war--direct evidence of
the high value placed on books.

Gradually a book trade developed in Rome, presumably conducted in large part by immigrant Greeks. The book dealer, called
bibliopola, used specially trained slaves (servi literati or librarii)
for copying texts; they were paid by number of lines, the standard
line consisting of 34 to 38 letters.

In the time of the Republic the book trade was very limited
and publishing was even more limited. An exception was the large
publishing business conducted by Cicero's friend Pomponius Atticus;
his editions of Cicero's works and of the classics were famed for
their accuracy.

With the coming of the Empire the book trade began to flourish in Rome as well as in other cities; book stores were located on
the busiest streets and were often meeting places for writers and
scholars. Lists of new books were posted on the walls or on door
columns. Booksellers were, as a rule, also publishers; the book-
buying community had grown so large and widespread that there was
need for an intermediary between the author and his readers. Not
without reason did Horace boast that his verses would be read on the
shores of the Black Sea and on the banks of the Rhone and the Ebro.
The Roman publishing industry differed from that of our day in important respects. The author received no payment; on the other
hand the publisher did not have a monopoly on the publishing of a
book but merely undertook the production of a certain number of
copies. The author was free to arrange with other publishers to issue the same work, and anyone who wished could buy a book and
have it copied; there were no legal regulations protecting the literary property of the author, and he did not count on any financial return from his writing. Only by dedicating a work to some wealthy

patron could he expect pecuniary reward.

It was the general custom for the author to gather a group of his friends and to read aloud to them from his latest work in order to arouse interest in it. The great historical work of Herodotus was first made known through his own reading aloud from it in the towns that he visited on his travels. In time, however, this custom developed into something of a nuisance, especially since the less talented authors were often the most eager to recite their own product. In the last centuries B. C. it was the publishers who began to invite the literary public together to hear new works read.

We know the names of several prominent publishers from the period of the Empire. There were the Sosii brothers, who were publishers for Horace among others, and Tryphon, who issued the writings of Quintilian and Martial. These publishers had philological scholars on their staff as proofreaders, who went through every single copy and corrected any errors. Nothing definite is known about the size of the editions, but works in demand could attain wide distribution within a short time. Neither do we know a great deal about the prices of books beyond the obvious fact that the price depended on the size of the book and the style in which it was published.

Wealthy Romans with literary interests had their own slaves to copy the books that they wished to possess, though it is doubtful that they did this because it was cheaper than buying the books from a dealer. There is no doubt, however, that important books or beautifully executed copies brought high prices; this applies especially to the original manuscripts of those authors who were most in demand among Roman collectors.

The number of private Roman collectors contined to increase throughout the later years of the Republic and during the Empire and gradually the bibliophile came into fashion; a sizable book collection was an essential part of a prominent Roman's house, preferably arranged in an elaborate setting that would add to the owner's prestige. We have accounts of such collections comprising several thousand rolls. They were usually divided into a Greek and a Latin section. Wealthy persons also had libraries at their country villas

and charred remains of the collection in the villa of the Pisos,
mainly Epicurean writings, were found at Herculaneum. By no
means did the owner always care about the contents of his books;
there must have been some basis for Seneca's complaint about the
many collectors who did not know even as much as their slaves.
The Roman luxury libraries can be visualized as follows: In a room
of green marble tiles the book rolls were arranged on shelves, in
niches or in open cabinets along the walls; the rolls either lay enclosed in purple leather cases or stood upright in elaborately decorated containers. In the room stood busts or relief portraits of
famous authors, a custom that Pliny the Elder says was introduced
by Asinius Pollio when he founded the first public library in Rome.

Public libraries were also found in the Roman Empire. With
Alexandria as a model, Caesar planned to set up a similar library
in the capital of his empire but he did not live to see the idea realized. After his death, Asinius Pollio established the first public library in Rome in the Libertas temple, in the year 39 B. C. Under
the Emperor Augustus two other large libraries were added, the
Palatine library in the temple of Apollo on the Palatine Hill, established 28 B. C. in commemoration of the battle of Actium, and the
Octavian library in the hall of Octavian in the temple of Jupiter on
the field of Mars. At each of these libraries there was a librarian
with several assistants; the library workers were called librarii and
belonged to the slave class. The person in charge, however (pro-
curator bibliothecae) usually belonged to the equestrian class or was
one of the Emperor's freedmen. The salary of such a public serv-
ant in the first century A. D. was the equivalent of about $2500 per
year today. Both of the libraries founded by Augustus were largely
destroyed by fire as were so many others of that time: the Palatine library in 191 A. D. and the Octavian library presumably in 80
A. D. The library in the temple on the Palatine Hill was rebuilt by
Domitian. There were also public libraries on the Capitoline Hill
and at the magnificent baths built by Caracalla about 215 A. D.

All of these collections were overshadowed by the library
that Trajan founded about 100 A. D. , the Bibliotheca Ulpia, which also served as the archives of the empire. In 370 A. D. there were

    6. Ruins of a Roman provincial library (the Celsus Library at Ephesus) founded 110 A.D. At the back of the large hall is an apse for a statue; along the walls are two rows of niches for book cases. The outer walls are double as protection against moisture.

said to have been no less than 28 public libraries in Rome, and similar institutions had gradually grown up in the provinces as well (Fig. 6). Literary and archeological sources record a large library founded by Hadrian in Athens. The public libraries were, like most of the private libraries, divided into a Greek and a Latin section. The rolls lay in wooden cabinets set in niches in the walls. The long colonnades found in most libraries were coveted places of retreat for students, who could sit here and read or carry on their learned discussions. There is evidence that home loan of books was permitted in special cases. As the 4th century A.D. drew to a close, however, the interest in libraries declined sharply and many of them deteriorated.

    Latin literature began in earnest in the second century B.C., and it was not long before there developed a style of handwriting for use in literary works that differed from the ordinary cursive writing.

The earliest Latin book script was stiff and formal and like the
Greek script it consisted very largely of capital letters. The oldest
known example of this form appears in a papyrus from Herculaneum;
the letters are jagged and have many corners. In the so-called
capitalis quadrata style the letters are almost square, while in capitalis rustica (Fig. 7) they are slimmer and more elegant. Along
with these styles of writing there was another with broader and more
rounded shapes, the so-called uncial script. By the 4th century uncial was fully developed and it was the standard book script until
the end of the 8th century (Fig. 8). Both styles, as well as the
Greek style, used some abbreviations.

Invention of Paper in China

While the papyrus roll and the parchment codex were thriving
side by side in the libraries of the Roman Empire, a significant discovery was being made in China.

After the great book burning of 213 B.C. the Chinese began
using silk cloth for writing. But silk was expensive and they began
making an entirely new material, of silk rags that had been cut up
in pieces and soaked to form a pasty mass that was then dried and
became a sort of thin paper. This material was still too expensive
to be widely used, so attempts were made to find something less
expensive. According to tradition this search came to an end in
the year 105 A.D. when Ts'ai Lun invented paper. Instead of silk
cloth he used much cheaper substances as raw material: plant bark,
especially bast fiber from the paper mulberry tree, discarded cotton cloth, old fishnets, etc. His invention soon met with general
acceptance and in the next two or three centuries many manuscripts
must certainly have been written on paper, though practically none
are preserved from this early period. In a small oasis town at Lop-
nor in the desert of Tibet, Sven Hedin dug up several pieces of paper that may be the oldest in existence--they are assumed to be
from the second or third century A.D. A number of paper manuscripts have been found in the walls of a temple at Tun Huang in
Turkestan; some of these are now preserved in the British Museum,
some in the Bibliothèque Nationale, and a few in the Royal Library

7.   An uncial (capitalis rustica) Virgil manuscript of the 4th
century.   (Papal Library in the Vatican.)   The illustration shows
the smithy of the Cyclops and is typical of Roman painting of the
classical period.

in Copenhagen (one of the latter is dated 1016).   Like the papyrus
books these manuscripts were in the form of rolls.

For almost 700 years the Chinese were able to keep their
method for producing paper a secret, but when Chinese papermakers
were captured by the Arabs in the middle of the 8th century, the
process was discovered.   From then on paper started its journey

8. Uncial manuscript that once belonged to the monastery of Bobbio. The large writing is from the 4th century and is a text of Cicero. This text was later erased and the parchment was used for a text by Augustine, written in the 7th or 8th century in small uncial hand. (After Franz Steffens.)

through the Arab empire, reaching Europe about 1100. Before this took place, however, great changes of another nature had taken place and had set their mark on the history of the book in Europe.

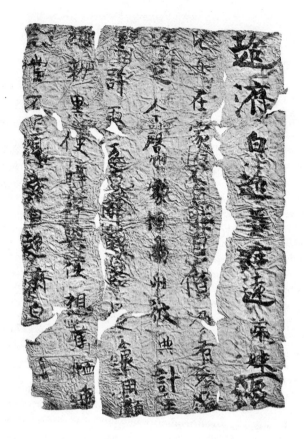

9. One of the fragments of paper documents excavated by
Sven Hedin in a monastery ruin in the desert of Tibet. The paper
is from the 2nd or 3d century and is perhaps the oldest paper known.
The characters were probably made with a hair brush.

Chapter 2.　The Middle Ages

Early Monastery and Church Libraries

When the Roman Empire gave way and Italy was laid waste
by plundering expeditions of the barbarians, Roman book collections
fared ill.　A great many of them were certainly destroyed during
the fifth and the beginning of the sixth century A.D., when the death
struggle of the Roman Empire took place.　Christianity had already
begun to make its influence felt before this time; Christian literature was taking its place along with Greek and Latin literature.　The
churches had collections called bibliothecae sacrae or bibliothecae
christianae, containing the books of the Bible, the writings of the
church fathers and the liturgical books that were used in the church
services.　Many of these libraries were destroyed during the perse-
cution of the Christians that began under Diocletian in 303 A.D.

Outstanding among these libraries was the one at Caesarea
in Palestine.　Founded by the church father Origen and later reorganized by his pupil Pamphilos (who died 309 A.D.), its importance
for the Christian world was similar to that of the Alexandrian library in the world of Hellenic culture.　The Bibles produced at the
writing schools in Caesarea were widely esteemed.　The library was
destroyed in 637 when the Arabs conquered Palestine.

Little information is available about book collections of other
church fathers.　Books were collected in the monasteries of Coptic
Egypt, where the first communities of monks were formed as early
as the second century.　Knowledge of hieroglyphic writing was dying
out and Greek script was used by the Christians.　The Coptic language, which constituted the last phase of the ancient Egyptian language, was written in Greek letters and continued to be used by the
church even after Egypt was conquered by the Arabs in the seventh
century.　There was considerable literary activity in these Coptic
monasteries.　From a number of them, especially those in the Nit-

rian desert, the British in the 19th century brought home many Coptic manuscripts and a number of Syrian manuscripts.   These manuscripts included Christian and other texts going back to the fifth century.

Following the barbarian invasions the importance of the Christian Church, and especially of the Church of Rome, in the world of books continued to increase.   Throughout the medieval period the church performed a work of decisive significance in preserving that part of the classical literature of the ancient world that had escaped destruction in the great political upheavals.

Byzantine Libraries

Ancient Greek culture found a special place of refuge in the Byzantine Empire.   Just as the Ptolemys had done in their time with Alexandria, so the emperor Constantine the Great in the fourth century sought to make the capital of the eastern Roman Empire, Byzantium (Constantinople), a cultural center.   Some two generations before the Alexandrian library was burned by the Christians, Constantine, with the aid of Greek scholars, founded a library in which Christian as well as secular literature was represented.   Under Julian the Apostate another library for non-Christian literature was formed.   Constantine's library burned in 475 and was reestablished, but its subsequent fate is uncertain.   At the time of the capture of Constantinople in 1204 it was damaged considerably but there was still an imperial library in existence when the Turks captured the city in 1453; many of the books were burned at that time or carried away and sold.

At the academy founded by Constantine in Byzantium the study, and hence also the copying, of the Greek classics was eagerly pursued; the same was true of the Byzantine monasteries, which continued to be strongholds of Greek learning throughout the Middle Ages.   The most famous of all these was the Studium monastery in Byzantium, where the abbot Theodore in the 9th century compiled rules for the conduct of copying rooms and libraries; but there were also some twenty famous monasteries located in the mountains of the small peninsula Athos by the Aegean Sea, which had their flour-

ishing period in the 10-15th centuries. Even today these contain
about 11,000 manuscripts along with some musical texts. The monastery of St. Catherine on Mt. Sinai and several others also possessed very valuable collections of manuscripts; in the Sinai monastery was found the famous Biblical manuscript, Codex Sinaiticus,
which later came to Russia and is now in the British Museum.

The Byzantine monastery libraries, as well as those in Byzantium itself, became veritable mines for the book collectors of the
Renaissance. In spite of this and the vandalism they have suffered
throughout the ages these libraries today still contain great treasures
from the early Middle Ages. They preserved the Byzantine cultural
tradition, which was later continued by the Greek Catholic Church in
the monasteries at Kiev and Novgorod and in the Balkans; this applies particularly to the monasteries of Athos, where the libraries
became prototypes for those in Russian monasteries.

Among the Byzantine scholars whose names are still known
was Photius, who lived in the 9th century. He gave us valuable in-
sight into the literature of classical antiquity through his bibliography, Myriobiblon, in which he describes the contents of the approximately 280 works in his collection.

Arabic Interest in Greek Literature

Interest in Greek literature flourished in areas entirely outside the realm of the Christian Church. When the Arabs were forming their great empire that extended from Central Asia through Asia
Minor and North Africa to Spain, creative contact was also established between Greek and Arabic literature and science. In this
great Islamic empire there were large libraries attached to seats of
learning, mosques and especially to the courts of princes and rulers;
there were also private collections of importance. The art of writing was highly respected and early assumed a decorative character.

In the first phase of the development the center for the transfer of Greek literature to Arabic culture was the library of the famous Caliph Harun-al-Raschid and his son Al-Mamuns in Baghdad.
Greek manuscripts were used, and later Iranian and Syrian transla-

tions were made from the Greek.

The next phase of Islamic culture was connected with the large collections of books in North Africa and Spain. Among these the library of the Fatimite family in Cairo became especially famous. It is said to have contained several hundred thousand volumes before it was plundered by the Turks in 1068; its final destruction did not come until the 12th century. Some material from the Fatimite collection is preserved in Yemen. The contents were primarily manuscripts of the Koran and other religious books, but there were also works on mathematics, astronomy, medicine, philosophy, law and linguistics. Jewish scholars played a considerable role at that time in the transmission of the literature of ancient Greece.

This literature acquired a new seat at the library of the Umajjades in the Spanish town of Cordova. Al-Hakam II in the 10th century had books brought in large numbers from all parts of the Islamic empire, and in his palace he kept numerous scribes, editors and bookbinders. This library suffered great damage through plundering and fire, and with the fall of the dynasty in 1031 it ceased to exist. In the days of its glory it had been especially active in the translation of Greek classics into Arabic. These Arabic translations were later translated into Latin, and several famous classical authors, including Aristotle, Hippocrates and Galen, were, in part at least, made known to European scholars of the Middle Ages in this roundabout way. After the fall of the Umajjades this translating activity moved to Toledo.

Widespread destruction of books accompanied the storming of Samarkand and Baghdad by the Mongolians in the 13th century. After that period the various ruling dynasties of Islam paid more attention to Persian literature and history, and under the Sefavids in the 16th century Persian book production reached a high point.

The Islamic world was able to develop such great literary activity partly because in paper it had a writing material that was cheaper and better than papyrus or vellum. The Chinese papermakers taken captive in the 8th century and brought by the Arabs to Samarkand in Turkestan made paper of linen rags and flax, and the manufacture of paper soon spread throughout the entire caliphate.

In the time of Harun-al-Raschid, at the close of the 8th century, there were paper factories in Baghdad and in Arabia.

Linen rags were used especially, along with pieces of cordage, and the paper produced in Islam can accordingly be called rag paper. The raw material was shredded, soaked in lime water, dried in the sun and thoroughly rinsed with clear water. It was then spread on a netting stretched over a frame and was rubbed with fine flour and wheat starch. To make the sheets suitable for writing they were dipped in wheat flour paste or in a pasty residue of cooked rice, and then smoothed with a burnishing stone.

The art of papermaking came to Europe about 1100, when the Arabs introduced it into Spain. One of the first places where paper was made was the current literary center, Toledo, though the earliest known place was in the vicinity of Valencia.

Libraries of the Roman Church

In general, the Church of Rome, through its monastic orders and ecclesiastical institutions, continued the care and use of books after the fall of the Roman Empire and the triumph of Christianity. A peculiar figure in this period of conflict between the old and the new was Cassiodorus, a Roman of distinguished ancestry who lived at the end of the 5th and beginning of the 6th century. He had been in the service of the Ostrogoth king Theodoric the Great, during whose reign the reading of the ancient authors had its final flourishing. In his old age Cassiodorus withdrew from the life of the world to found a monastery, the Vivarium, in southern Italy. There he established a sort of Christian academy. In the rules laid down for its conduct he admonished the monks to serve God also by diligent study and careful copying of texts; he meant not only ecclesiastical texts but secular literature, both Greek and Latin, as well. Cassiodorus was the first to specifically charge the monastic communities with the task of transmitting learning and the scholarly tradition. After his death part of his monastery library is said to have come to the papal seat at Rome. There, as early as the 5th century, books were being collected as part of the papal archives in the Lateran, but almost nothing is known about this first papal library.

In this troubled period there were also instances of concern
for literature among prominent ecclesiastical and civil officials outside of Italy. The archbishop of Clermont, Sidonius Apollinaris, in
his letters, provides a glimpse of several libraries in southern Gaul
in the period following the invasion of Attila; he describes in particular the beautiful collection of the prefect of Gaul, Tonantius Ferreolus, in his villa Prusiana near Nimes. This collection the bishop considered as good as any in ancient Rome. With the supremacy
of the Franks, however, a period of cultural decline began in this
region; there was no revival until the end of the 6th century. It was
at about this time that the learned Spanish bishop Isidore collected
his extensive library in Seville and used it in writing his works, one
of which, the Etymologiae, a sort of encyclopedia, was widely used
as a textbook for several centuries.

Books Among the Benedictines and the Irish Monks

No other monastic order was more interested in working with
books than the Benedictines. Benedict had had in mind pious literature, but in the many Benedictine monasteries that sprang up throughout Europe in the latter half of the 6th century, the study and copying of classical authors were pursued along with that of religious
works. Knowledge of Greek and Latin was necessary for the reading of church literature and the monks developed proficiency in these
languages by working with the classical authors. They thus created
an international literary culture, primarily religious in character,
but maintaining a connection with the intellectual life of classical antiquity. The Catholic Church of the Middle Ages must be given
credit for the continuing influence of classical civilization down to
our own day.

The work done by the Irish monks was particularly interesting. Although Ireland was far removed from the countries of the
classical world, this island became the chief refuge for classical
culture in the early Middle Ages. Ireland had been Christianized
in the 5th century by the holy Patrick, who came from Gaul, and
one century later there were said to have been about 300 monasteries in Ireland and Scotland. In these there developed a literary

culture that far surpassed that of the monasteries on the mainland.
The Irish monks, who had a knowledge of Oriental and Byzantine
culture as well as of the Greek language, were eager practitioners
of the arts of writing and bookmaking.   They evolved a special national style of script and decoration, which will be considered later.
The originals for their manuscripts were obtained on pilgrimages to
Rome and by exchanges with French and Italian monasteries.   In the
9th and 10th centuries all the monasteries of Ireland were destroyed
by the Vikings.   The old Irish manuscripts that remain are nearly
all from the monasteries that the Irish had established on the European continent.

Missionary zeal was characteristic of the Irish monks; it
brought them at an early period to both England and the continent.
Around the year 590 the famous Irish abbot Columban, together with
twelve other monks, founded the first monastery in Gaul (France) at
Luxeuil, bringing along manuscripts to start a library.   For more
than a century Luxeuil was one of the chief centers of French intellectual life.   St. Columban later became the founder of a no less
famous monastery in Italy, at Bobbio, bringing the distinctive Irish
manuscript tradition to the fatherland of the Church.   Some of his
monks, among whom was Gallus, founded the present monastery of
St. Gallen in Switzerland; its library later attained great repute.

The influence of the Irish monks was felt in England as well.
At the monastery Lindisfarne in northern England, for instance, envoys from the papal seat were also laboring as missionaries.   The
monastic libraries in England, among which Canterbury's took the
leading position, did in part escape the ravages of the Viking period.   Most famous among the English ecclesiasts of that time were
the church historian Bede, Bishop Benedict, who journeyed to Rome
six times and brought back books, and Boniface, who traveled to
Germany and introduced Christianity there.   One of the monasteries
that Boniface founded, Fulda, later had a considerable library and a
famous school of writing and painting.   A pupil of Bede, Egbert, became archbishop of York and there founded a library; Alcuin later
became librarian there, before he was called to the continent.

Luxeuil gave rise to another famous monastery, in Corbie in

Picardy, and from the latter came in turn the Saxon monastery Kor-
vey, in whose library Widukind in the 10th century wrote his chronicle. Many more examples could be given of the propagation of
monasteries, and genealogical tables could even be worked out for
the monasteries of the various orders; the daughter institutions usually received a collection of manuscripts from the parent monastery
as the basis for a library.

Evolution of Book Script

As this great literary culture developed in the monasteries,
with Latin as its linguistic form of expression and Latin literature
as its special field of study, handwriting also underwent evolution.
It began with the Latin cursive form, which had taken its place in
the first centuries A. D. alongside the capital and uncial forms mentioned earlier. This cursive style was the ordinary, everyday script
used in ancient Rome, and it consisted almost entirely of small letters (minuscules). The two other forms consisted mainly of capital
letters (majuscules). Little by little the cursive script found its
way into books, and in the early Middle Ages it developed into individual national styles at the various monasteries (Fig. 10a). The
West Gothic form was common in Spain from the 8th to the 12th century. The French or Merovingian form was originally used by the
Merovingians in their documents; it has a number of variant forms,
as seen in the Luxeuil and Corbie manuscripts. The Italian style
appears in many manuscripts from Bobbio, and the Beneventan form,
developed at Monte Cassino, reached its high point in the 10-11th
centuries.

Both the Italian and the French forms of handwriting were
partly influenced by still another national style, the Irish-Anglo-Sax-
on, or the insular form as it is also called. The Irish form did
not, like the others, develop from Roman cursive but from another
Roman form, the half uncial (Fig. 10b), a broad rounded style that
the Irish monks gradually revised into a more angular and com-
pressed minuscule hand, while adopting features of the still current
runic alphabet. This special Irish style was disseminated by the
monks on their missionary journeys and was used in the monasteries

that they founded (Bobbio, Luxeuil, St. Gallen, etc.) along with a more fluent Irish minuscule. English monasteries likewise used both an Anglo-Saxon half uncial and a minuscule form, and these were brought to the continent by English monks.

A common feature of all these styles of writing was the use of abbreviations, or abbreviatures as they were called. In the manuscripts of the ancient period a few constantly recurring words or syllables were shortened, but in medieval manuscripts, first in ecclesiastical and then later also in secular texts, abbreviations became more common. They did not become very frequent until the 12-14th centuries, when they gradually became systematized. Originally, quite different abbreviations were used in the different types of handwriting--the insular manuscripts, for example, had several peculiar abbreviations of their own. Later the system became more fixed and uniform. Considerable practice was required to master this system, and regular lexicons were compiled of the abbreviatures and their meaning. At first abbreviation consisted of condensing the word, so that only a few of its letters were written; i.e. DS = deus (God), DNS = dominus (lord), EPS = episcopus (bishop), etc. In ecclesiastical manuscripts this was done to emphasize the words rather than to save space, as was the case later. Besides these condensations, there also came into use a series of fixed symbols for frequently recurring words--a sort of shorthand that had its origin in old Roman legal documents: *3* = eius (his), *7* = et (and), *ƥ* = pro (for), *ƿ* = per (through), etc. Still another type of abbreviation was superscription; the latter part of a word was shortened by writing a single letter above the first part of the word, as *ǧ* = ergo, *m̂* = mihi, etc.

When a monk had to write a manuscript he first cut the vellum to size, squaring it with the aid of a knife and a ruler; then the surface was smoothed and lines were ruled on the sheets, the distance between the lines being marked by small holes punched in the margin with a divider. The lines were scratched with an awl or drawn in red ink, later often with a graphite pencil. When he was finally ready to begin writing, the scribe (calligrapher) sat down at a sloping desk fitted with two inkwells, one for red and one for black

West Gothic script of the 10th century.

Merovingian script of the 7th century.

Beneventan script of the 11th century.

Irish script of the 7th century.

10a.   National forms of Latin minuscule script of the 6th
century.   (After Franz Steffens.)

10b. Half-uncial script in a manuscript of the 6th century.
(After Franz Steffens.)

ink; equipped with his quill pen and his erasing knife he started to work. The red ink was used to draw a red vertical line through the initial letters of the text; this was called rubricating (rubrum = red).

When the scribe had finished copying a text he added a few lines at the end (subscription or colophon) in which the title of the book was included. These lines usually began with the words explicitus est, or simply explicit, a reminder of the time when manuscripts were in the form of rolls, meaning that the manuscript has been unrolled. The title could also be found at the beginning of the manuscritp, in the words hic incipit (here begins) followed by a statement of the text involved. At the end the scribe also frequently noted when and where and for whom the work had been done, etc., and he sometimes added his own name.

Manuscript Decoration

Illustrations were used even in the manuscripts of the ancient period, mainly in works on natural history and medicine. In the Hellenistic period there must certainly have been entire books of pictures with explanatory text only. Papyrus was not as good for book paintings as vellum. Ancient vellum manuscripts did, in fact, display the beginnings of artistic book decoration, which continued its vigorous development in the medieval period.

Until the 12th century illustration was found mainly in Gospels (evangeliaries). They were ornamented with pictures of Christ surrounded by the four Apocalyptic beasts and by the four evangelists, Matthew, Mark, Luke and John, each with his own symbol. The so-called canonical tables--compiled to show the inner harmony of the Gospels--were arranged in columns and surrounded by a colonnade with arches. Another major object of decoration in manuscripts was the letters (initials) at the beginning of the various sections or chapters. Even in Roman times these letters were made larger and were often set off by the use of red lead or cinnabar. This custom developed rapidly in the medieval monasteries; the initial letters were made larger and larger and were adorned with scrolls and borders of greater and greater artistry. The large decorative letters were painted in various colors, and gold or silver was often used. A further step was sometimes taken by painting an entire scene within the outline of the letter.

Besides these splendid initial designs many manuscripts from the later Middle Ages have a number of independent illustrations called miniatures, from the Latin word minium (red lead). If gold was used in addition to the other colors they were called illuminations (lumen = light), and the manuscripts thus adorned were often designated as "golden books." The paints were either opaque colors or water colors. Gold was used in the form of very thin leaves or as a powder; in the early period it usually had a yellow brass sheen, later it was more reddish.

The monk or nun who wrote the text seldom made the initials or the illustrations. The scribe simply left space for the latter, often writing directions in the margin in a light hand that could be erased. The "miniator" or the "illuminator" then took over, equipped with his supply of colors, his brushes and his gold. The outline of the picture was drawn in fine lines with a pen, then the colors were painted and the gold laid or sprinkled on.

Varying styles can be distinguished in the decoration of initials, the execution of miniatures and illuminations, and in the handwriting itself. The so-called Merovingian ornamentation, for instance, which was general throughout western Europe in the 8th century, was characterized by initials showing fishes and birds and by

11. Canon tables in a manuscript of the 12th century, made either in the Helmarshausen monastery near Diemel or at Lund for the cathedral there. (University Library, Uppsala, from "Golden Books.")

the use of red, green and yellow. This standard pattern was varied
in different ways depending on whether the paintings were made in
German, French or Spanish monasteries.

Byzantine book decoration, which reached its highest development in the 11th and 12th centuries, was characterized by extensive
use of gold, of purple, and of other dark colors. This produced a
rather somber and mystical effect at times and it showed the influence of Syrian and other Oriental art. The Byzantine style in turn
affected some western European book painting, as seen in manuscripts from Ireland and northern England. Here book artistry
flourished in the 8th and 9th centuries, and is recognizable by its
Celtic braided work and ribbons, often embellished with heads of
birds, dogs and various mythical beasts; gold and purple occur frequently. In southern England in the 10-11th century book decoration was characterized in particular by borders of profusely branched
foliage and other special features.

Among the famous manuscripts executed in the styles described above are the Gospel produced at the Irish monastery Kells
about 800 A.D. (the Book of Kells, now in Dublin; Fig. 14), also
the Gospel from the northern England monastery Lindisfarne, about
700 A.D. (now in the British Museum). Another is the manuscript
with silver and gold letters on purple vellum, called Codex Argenteus (the silver book), which is now in the University Library at Uppsala in Sweden. It contains part of the translation of the Bible into
Gothic made by Bishop Ulfilas in the 4th century. It was written in
Italy in the 6th century and later disappeared, to reappear in the 16th
century in a German monastery. It was then taken to Prague and
from there the Swedes carried it home as booty in the Thirty Years'
War.

Alongside these and other illustrious manuscripts were many
that had only a limited amount of decoration or none at all. Not
all the monks or nuns who executed the decorative work were equally gifted. Nevertheless, in general, decorative art in the Middle
Ages found one of its most significant expressions in book painting.

12. Byzantine book painting made in Constantinople in a manuscript around the end of the 10th century. It is presumed to represent Solomon seated on the throne; behind him is a woman symbolizing wisdom, at the left Jesus Syrach. (Royal Library, Copenhagen, from "Golden Books.")

13. Miniature from the Codex Aureus, the work of a southern Eng-
land miniature school, probably at Canterbury, about the year 750.
The decoration combines English-Scandinavian features with strong
Byzantine traits   (Royal Library, Stockholm, from "Golden Books.")

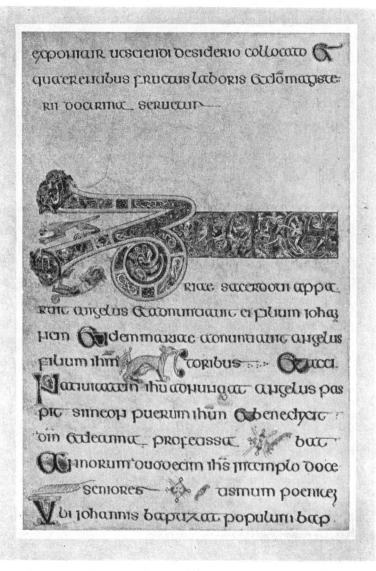

14. Page from the Book of Kells, the book of the Gospels made at the Irish monastery of Kells about 800, in Irish script with Celtic features in the decoration.

Charlemagne's Attempt at Centralization

It was an event of great significance for the entire literary
world when Charlemagne, in the 8th century, invited foreign scholars to his court in the interest of promoting knowledge and scientific activity in his empire.   From Italy came Paulus Diaconus.
From York in Northumberland came Egbert's pupil Alcuin, whose
work has left its mark at the Abbey of St. Martin in Tours; the
school that he established there became the model for many other
monastery and church schools.   One of Alcuin's pupils, Hrabanus
Maurus, became a leader in the monastery library of Fulda.   Charlemagne maintained a staff of scribes at his court in Aachen and
collected a sizable library.   The scholars attached to the court were
assigned to working up philologically correct editions of classical as
well as theological works, just as had been done in the library of
Alexandria.

15. Carolingian minuscule script in an Augustine manuscript
of the 11th century.   (After Franz Steffens.)

Charlemagne and his circle also instituted reforms in the
style of writing and gradually the Carolingian (or Caroline) style was
established as the standard form (Fig. 15).   It was a minuscule
hand, probably evolved from the Merovingian, and it gradually superseded the various national forms.   Although it did, of course, take
on certain special features in the writing rooms of the individual
monasteries, in general it maintained a uniform character.   It had
club-shaped vertical lines, reminiscent of the contemporary style

in art, and was called Romance script. In the course of the 12th
and 13th centuries it underwent a transformation; the letters became
narrower and more angular and the contrast between thick and thin
lines became more pronounced--the result was Gothic script (Fig.
16), corresponding to the contemporary Gothic style in art. Writing
thus evolved from the round Roman arch to the pointed Gothic arch.
The letters were written so close together that two adjoining ones
were often run into one (e.g., the d and e). In large liturgical
manuscripts the letters were usually made quite large and heavy and
given a rather decorative appearance; this style was called missal
script (from the mass books, or missals); the name lattice script
was also given it because the crowded letters made it resemble lattice work (Fig. 17). For more ordinary use there was a Gothic
cursive, which was the ancestor of the script that is still used in
Germany and until a generation or two ago was also in general use
in Denmark ("old Danish" script).

16. Gothic minuscule script in a manuscript from 1339.
(After Franz Steffens.)

The Carolingian movement affected the field of illumination
as well. An attempt was made to fuse the various regional charac-

teristics of the manuscripts. In the history of the book, as well as
in the history of art as a whole, the Carolingian period or the "Carolingian renaissance" was influenced by the earlier national styles,
especially the Irish. It also took many of its motifs from the plant
world as well as from Roman decorative art.

Following a period of decline around the year 900, the book
arts blossomed forth anew. A development called the Ottonic renaissance, after the emperor Otto the Great, took place mainly at
the monasteries in Fulda, at St. Emmerau in Regensburg and on the
island of Reichenau in Bodensee. Book ornamentation in this period
represented a mixture of Carolingian and Byzantine elements, along
with a tendency to exaggerate the form and movement of the figures.
At the same time, book illustrations in England, especially at Win-
chester, featured flowing drapery and ornaments in which acanthus
friezes were prominent.

In the 12th and 13th centuries the embellishment of the
Psalms of David became the most important function of book painting. About 100 psalters, as they were called, have been preserved
from these two centuries; many of them, especially the French and
English, have both large and small initials and a charming series
of scenes from the story of David or the life of Jesus. Often these
psalters were made for royal personages. The beautiful psalter
that belonged to Ingeborg, the daughter of Waldemar the Great, is
now in the Condé Museum at Chantilly. The pictures in it show
Byzantine influence, but their dress and the beautifully rounded
curves of the figures are typically French.

Manuscripts and Monastery
Libraries in Scandinavia

Alphabetical writing came to Scandinavia, as well as to the
other countries north of the Alps, with the introduction of Christianity. Ansgar, the Apostle of the North, taught his disciples to read
and probably also to write. As the church became more and more
firmly established the art of book production followed. The oldest
preserved books that can with certainty be said to have been written
in Scandinavia do not, however, go back farther than the 11th

century.   The oldest Old Norse or Icelandic writing shows the influence of Carolingian as well as Irish and Anglo-Saxon styles; the latter in particular set its mark on Norwegian manuscripts, where
runic forms are found.   Icelandic writing was mainly under the influence of the Carolingian style.   Both Norwegian and Icelandic
manuscripts show extensive use of abbreviations.   Through Norway,
Swedish medieval writing received a definite Anglo-Saxon influence,
while Danish medieval writing was influenced by the Carolingian style
and later followed the same transition to the Gothic style that took
place everywhere on the mainland during the 13th century.   The
oldest Danish manuscripts that we have were written in Gothic
script: the Laws of Skania Zealand and Jutland, Henrik Harpe-
streng's Book of Medicine, etc.

17.   Missal, or canon, script.   The pointed, close-set letters give the page the appearance of latticework.   From a French
missal of the 14th century.   (Royal Library, Copenhagen, Thott Collection.)

In the Scandinavian countries monastic culture and monastery
libraries developed as in other countries, and the churches also had
more or less extensive book collections.   In Denmark there were libraries in Øm monastery (Cara Insula) at Ry, in Sorø (there is still
a Justinus manuscript in the Royal Library that was presented to the
monastery of Sorø by Absalon), also at Herredsvad, Naestved, etc.
The cathedrals in Lund, Roskilde, Ribe, Aarhus, Slesvig and other
places also had relatively large collections.   The ordinary parish
churches, of course, had much smaller collections, perhaps only a

few volumes.   In Norway, where the oldest Latin book was written about the middle of the 11th century and the oldest books in the native language toward the end of the same century, there were book collections at the bishop seats of Bergen, Trondheim and Stavanger, and in Munkeliv monastery in Bergen.   In Sweden all other monastery collections were overshadowed by the library of the Birgittiner monastery in Vadstena, which contained some 1500 volumes and was the largest medieval library in the Scandinavian countries.

When Scandinavian medieval manuscripts are compared with those of other countries they are clearly inferior in workmanship and appearance.   The initials and miniatures that were produced in the Scandinavian countries did not come up to the contemporary level of book art elsewhere.   In addition, especially in the case of Icelandic manuscripts, they have been transmitted to us in a poor condition.   Many are discolored by smoke or spotted by fat and dirt almost completely covers the text in some places.   A glance at the two famous Edda manuscripts and the Flatey Book, the largest medieval manuscript from Scandinavia, all three of which were written in the 13th and 14th centuries, gives the general impression that they were made and kept in a society whose esthetic sense was not highly developed.

Not many of the monastery libraries had more than a few hundred volumes.   The library of the Bobbio monastery, which in the 9th century had about 700 volumes, was one of the largest of its time.   Of course, many of the volumes contained more than one text.   Two of the brothers functioned as librarian and director of the scriptorium (armarius or librarius and scriptuarius they were called).   They took care of the cataloging and shelving.   The catalogs were simple inventories, containing only brief information for finding particular manuscripts.   The books were placed in cabinets; only in the later part of the Middle Ages were these partly replaced by sloping desks (Fig. 22).   In the shelving arrangement, the Bible and the Church Fathers came first, then followed theology and classical literature, and finally came the other subjects, such as history, law, medicine, etc.   One of the librarian's duties was to supervise the use of the books.   Among the Benedictines books were

18. Page of the Elder Edda (Saemundar Edda), written at the end of the 13th century; presented to King Frederik III by the Icelandic bishop Brynjólfur Sveinsson. (Royal Library, Copenhagen.)

exchanged once a year, while the monastery regulations of Augustine and Isidore of Seville provided for books to be loaned to the brothers each morning and returned in the evening.

Early Medieval Bookbinding

One of the monastery brothers (ligator) took care of the binding of the books. The oldest type of binding from the Middle Ages, however, was quite different from what we now understand by bookbinding. It was goldsmith's and jeweler's work. In the time of the Empire the wax tablets (diptycha) used by the Romans for short notations were made of ivory for festive occasions and their outer sides were artistically decorated. There are also several examples of such diptycha from the Middle Ages, when they served as bindings for ecclesiastical manuscripts. They are considered the progenitors of the gem bindings of the early Middle Ages, which consisted of flat wooden boards embellished with reliefs in ivory or in hammered silver and gold and sometimes with precious stones, pearls and enamel work. These bindings were made chiefly for the so-called altar bindings. Often the front side, which lay uppermost, was more richly decorated than the back. The motifs for the reliefs were usually taken from pictures in the manuscript itself and represented episodes from Bible stories, with perhaps a crucified Christ as the central figure. In the surrounding border stylized flower and leaf ornaments were often used.

These fine bindings, in common with the miniatures in the manuscripts themselves, exhibit various styles according to the time and place where they were made. Thus there are characteristic Byzantine enamel bindings, silver and bronze bindings with the easily recognizable Irish dragon patterns, ivory bindings that show the marks of Carolingian art, and others that are just as clearly in the Romance style. There are bindings in which the borders set with precious stones are the most conspicuous feature, others in which the central panel, with its high relief in hammered gold, dominates. A multitude of artistic fantasies is represented in these bindings, which are still preserved in quite large numbers in libraries and museums, though many have been robbed of their gold and precious stones.

19. Jeweled binding from the 10th century, containing the
Echtenach Gospels (Landesbibliothek, Gotha).

Leather Bindings

In contrast, ordinary monastery manuscripts had either a
plain parchment cover or a leather binding. In the course of the
14th century, jeweled bindings became scarcer. Many liturgical
books were made of velvet or leather, with metal limited to the corner pieces and the bosses that came into use in the late Gothic period. The book could rest on those bosses when it lay flat and the
face of the binding would not be scratched.

Leather binding, although known in ancient times, did not
come into general use in Europe until the Middle Ages. The covers
of books, were usually made of beech, oak or maple wood, across
which leather was stretched. Dark brown calfskin was commonly
used and it could be decorated in various ways. There is evidence
that deerskin and the skins of other wild animals were used.

From the older medieval period there are a number of bindings embellished with leather tooling: a pattern was drawn on the
damp leather and the lines cut into the leather with a knife and then
spread or punched out with a blunt tool. The technique of leather
carving was used in the Coptic monasteries, but its flourishing came
in the 15th century, when its home seems to have been primarily in
southern Germany and Austria. The decoration usually consisted of
plant designs and grotesque late Gothic animal figures, but included
representations of angels and saints, and later of knights hunting or
of love scenes.

Far more common, however, are the pressed leather bindings, which did not require as fine a touch as did leather carving.
Hot stamps with the designs engraved on them were pressed down
on the leather to make the ornamentation stand out in relief. No
gilding was involved in the process, called blind stamping. Blind
stamping is also found in the early bindings from the Coptic monasteries. The basic pattern consisted of a series of borders composed of small square, triangular, round or heart-shaped figures.
As a rule there was a difference in the design of the outer borders
and of the middle section, where the stamps were either arranged
in small geometric groups or in less formal patterns. In the Carolingian period the variety of stamps was rather limited, but in the

20. Tooled leather binding made in Nuremberg about 1470.
The decoration consists of noble personages with flower garlands; the
binding has bosses and clasps.   (Stadtbibliothek, Leipzig.)

Romance period the number increased considerably, with the sides
of the binding filled with plant and animal designs, figures of saints,
knights and other human forms.   In the gothic period the trend was
back to simpler decoration.

The corners of the binding were, as before, usually protected by brass mountings with bosses, and the book was kept tight-
ly closed by metal clasps.   In the later Middle Ages, iron chains
were attached to the upper or lower edge of the binding to fasten
the book to the desk or the shelf, so that it could not fall down or
be removed.   No importance was attached to decorating the spine of
the book; the books usually lay on a desk.   If they stood on shelves
it was with the spine toward the wall; our practice of placing them
with the spine forward dates from the 17th century.   The title of
the book was therefore often written in ink on the bottom edge,
where it could be seen when the book was lying down, or on the
fore edge, where it could be seen when the book was standing on
the shelf.

It should not, of course, be assumed that all the bindings
made in the monasteries were as artistically executed as those described here; many were quite plain, and not all the monks that
acted as ligators were above the level of dilettantes.   But in just as
many instances the artistic sense and precise workmanship exhibited
in the use of the stamps seem marvelous.

Libraries of the New Monastic Orders

The Rise of Universities

As has been noted, the Benedictines placed special emphasis
on literary activity and in the 12th century the oldest of their monastery libraries, Monte Cassino, attained high renown.   Other monastic orders also made their contribution.   Among these was the Cluniac offshoot of the Benedictine order, among whose principle seats
were Canterbury and the Abbey of St. Albans in England.   The new
monastic orders of the later Middle Ages, the Carmelite brothers
and the mendicant friars, the Franciscans and the Dominicans, also
took part in this work.   In England, where the mendicants came in
1224, they built up large collections of books at London and Oxford;

they did likewise at Annaberg in Saxony, in Venice, Basel, and at
other places.   It is interesting to note that the device now known as
a union catalog was compiled at that early time by the Franciscan
monks.   At the end of the 14th century requests were sent out to
no less than 186 English monasteries for information concerning
their book stock, and on the basis of the replies there was formed
the Registrum librorum Angliae (catalog of books in England), which
is now in the Bodleian Library at Oxford.   It is the oldest known attempt at compiling a common catalog.

The Franciscans and the Dominicans also exerted an important influence on the formation of the first universities.   Universities began to arise in the 13th century, in close connection with the
churches.   The best known of the early universities were in Paris,
Padua and Bologna.   In Paris the first collegium was founded by a
churchman, Robert de Sorbona (it is still called the Sorbonne), and
Bologna became a famous center for the study of Roman law.   All
these universities had their book collections or libraries, which differed greatly in size and content.   The largest seem to have been
those attached to the various collegia in Paris; Robert de Sorbona
presented his own collection to one of them.

The establishment of the universities made it possible for a
book trade to develop.   Bookdealers were usually called stationarii
(the word stationer is still used in England) and they and their
scribes were appointed or at least controlled by the university.
They had to agree to keep in stock correct editions of the books that
were used for instruction and to rent them to students for a fixed
fee.   They could sell books only on commission.   Bookselling was
thus a strictly limited and regulated business, yet it must have paid
well, to judge from the large number of stationers that quickly gathered at the new seats of learning, particularly in Paris.   Rules for
stationers appeared in 1259 in Bologna and in 1275 in Paris.   Privi-
leged bookbinders were similarly attached to the universities.   A
stationer at a university could sell manuscripts to other universities
and to scholars in foreign countries; books on medicine came primarily from Salerno and Montpelier, scholastic literature from Paris, and law books from Bologna.

21.   Late gothic binding: blind-stamped squares and circles inside rhomboids; corner bosses and chain. (Royal Library, Copenhagen.) The decoration shows that it was made by a rather un-
skilled monastery binder.

As in the monastery libraries, the books of the university collections were chained to their places (Fig. 21). If a book was borrowed, another book had to be left as security. Additions to the collections came through gifts by royal persons or other prominent individuals, from high ecclesiastical officers or from professors. The college at Paris was especially fortunate in this respect. As more universities arose in the course of the 14th century, at Oxford and Cambridge, Prague, etc., libraries developed along with them.

22. Late medieval library interior at Zutphen near Arnheim in Holland, showing books chained to desks.

Private Book Collections of the Middle Class

In the Middle Ages literary culture belonged to the upper classes, and the practical reason was the high cost of books. Vellum had gradually become expensive--often several texts were written in a single codex in order to use all the sheets. Copying was a tedious task that could not be performed by cheap labor, such as the slaves of ancient Rome. In the 10th century a countess of An-

jou is said to have given 200 sheep, three barrels of grain and some
marten furs for a single book of sermons; at the end of the 14th
century a prayer book in two volumes was bought by the Duke of
Orleans for 200 gold francs.

23.   German paper mill, run by waterpower.   The waterwheel drove the stamping mechanism on the lower floor.   There
the rags were ground to a soft pulp, which was then treated in the
vat on the upper floor.

It was not until the 14th and 15th centuries that the middle
class attained a cultural, social and economic level that made it
possible for them to own books.   These bourgeois book collections
were not predominantly Latin as were those in the churches, monasteries and colleges.   Books in the national language of the country,
law books, medical and herb books and the emergent poetical literature were by no means unknown in the institutional libraries, but
they predominated in the bourgeois collections.   With the flowering
of the middle class, bookbinding began to develop into a craft outside the monasteries.

The introduction of paper contributed to the wider distribution
of books in middle-class circles.   The Arabs had brought papermaking to Spain in the 12th century, and in 1276 the first paper

mill was established in Italy. A mill of this type was driven by
waterpower. The waterwheel operated a number of heavy beaters
that tore up the raw material--linen and cotton rags, cordage, etc.
--under water and mashed it to a thin pulp, which was then poured
into a vat. A frame made of wood with brass wires stretched
across it was dipped into the vat and on this frame the paper sheet
was formed. Felt pads were used to draw off the water from each
sheet; the sheets were then pressed, dried, and finally sized to
make them suitable for writing. The sizing liquid was made from a
boiled extract of animal hides, bones, etc. The brass wires in the
frame left lines in the paper that were plainly visible when it was
held up to the light, and the idea soon developed of bending some of
the wires to form various designs. These so-called watermarks
could contain the initials or the name of the papermaker. The oldest known watermark dates from 1282. For the first hundred years
or so, the marks were rather crude but later they became more
artistic. The motifs used were flowers, animals, fish and birds.
Often an ox head was the symbol of the papermaker. In Holland one
of the marks used was a beehive. In England a jester's head with
cap (foolscap) appeared. Several of these marks have continued to
the present day and they are now also used to indicate specific formats. From Europe the custom of inserting watermarks extended
to the Orient.

In the 14-15th centuries Italy became the principle producer
of paper. The new art was brought to France by Italians and the
oldest known paper mill in France dates from 1338. From there it
spread to Germany, toward the close of the 14th century, and then,
in the course of the 15th century, to England and Holland, where it
later made great progress. In 1690 it came to America. The
Scandinavian countries got their first paper mills in the 16th century,
by way of Germany. The first one was started in Stockholm about
1540, followed by others in Scania and on Zealand (at Hvidøre) and
one on Tycho Brahe's island Hven.

Manuscripts on paper began to appear in the 14th century
and in the course of the 15th century they became more and more
common. Paper was considerably cheaper than vellum--at first

about one-third the cost, later one-sixth. Handmade paper (or vat
paper as it was called, from the method of manufacture) was of excellent quality, even though it was not entirely white in appearance
and had a slightly rough surface. It is well preserved in the old
books that are extant, except where it has been attacked by book-
worms.

Royal Book Collections

Many of the great bibliophiles of the 13-15th centuries were
royalty. These included Otto III in Germany, Frederick II of Ho-
henstaufen and King Wencelaus of Bohemia. In France, which
throughout the entire later Middle Ages was the leading country in
book illumination, the outstanding collectors were Philip the Good
and other Burgundian lords, as well as a number of the kings of
France: Charles the Bald, Louis IX (Saint Louis), and Charles V
(the Wise). The last is considered the real founder of the French
royal library, the present Bibliothèque Nationale. The catalog of
his library, dated 1373, lists about 1,000 volumes, which were
housed in the Louvre. A bibliophile on an even grander scale was
Charles' brother, John of Berry.

By now the art of miniature painting was no longer confined
to monasteries; a class of independent illuminators had arisen.
They did, it is true, sell part of their work to churches and monasteries, but primarily they worked for royalty and other men of
worldly importance. For the most part, the manuscripts that they
decorated were prayer books (breviaries), particularly the excerpt
from the official ecclesiastical prayer book intended for the laity.
This abbreviated prayer book was called hora in Latin, livre d'-
heures in French, tidebog in Danish, Book of Hours in English, because the prayers in it were to be read at certain times of the day.
These books were usually in a small format (octavo or small quarto); the pictures in them represented not only scenes from the life
of Christ but also landscapes, hunting and battle scenes, festivals,
incidents from civil and peasant life, and other subjects of no relation to the contents of the book.

The names of only a few of these lay illuminators are known.

24. Various watermarks from early handmade papers. At left of second row from top, the ox head, one of the oldest and most common marks in early paper. At lower left, the foolscap, which was much used in Italy and France at the beginning of the 14th century, and later came to England, where it is still in use.

The greatest of them in the earlier period was Jean Pucelle, who
painted flowers, animals and men in fine detail and in true natural-
istic style.   At the end of the 14th century and the beginning of the
15th a group of Flemish book artists moved to Paris; several of
them--Jacquemart de Hesdin, Jehannequin and Pol from Limbourg,
and the latter's two brothers--worked for John of Berry.   Among
other things, they produced one of the most famous Books of Hours,
known as Les très riches heures de Jean duc de Berry.   The miniatures made by these artists give a true-to-life record of Flemish
life and costumes of the time.

After the French-Flemish period the Paris artisans continued
to produce Books of Hours in large numbers, but as time went on
most of these became competent traditional products.   In the second
half of the 15th century the art experienced a revival with the painter
Jean Foucquet of Tours.   Among the many books that he worked on
was one executed for Étienne Chevalier, the most beautiful of all
known Books of Hours.   Foucquet's pictures were not merely decoration, but illustrations related to the text.   He was influenced by
Italian art and was partial to monumental compositions with many
figures, landscapes, pictures of towns and battle scenes, all of which
he executed with superior craftsmanship.

The prevailing style in book artistry of the late Middle Ages
was Gothic.   This is indicated in the frequent use of pointed arches.
The figures were not, as in Romance book painting, part of the
background but stood out boldly.   In older periods the human figures, as in the glass paintings in Gothic churches, were tall and
slender, with narrow shoulders and long hands and feet.   Later the
figures became more true to nature as did the flowers, leaves, insects and birds that adorned the margins against a background of
pale gold.   They were not tied in with the initials but formed independent borders.

The Gothic style in its several variations characterized not
only the Books of Hours but also the Bibles in small handbook format that were produced in large numbers at the universities and distributed far and wide.   It likewise characterized the many late medieval manuscripts of chronicles, tales of knighthood, minnesongs

and other secular literature in the vernacular. In addition there
were the large folio choir books (antiphonaries) with notes, which
were produced mainly in Italy. Finally, Gothic style appeared in
the realistic Dutch book paintings that were so beautifully executed
in the Books of Hours and other devotional books. Gradually this
literature became a profitable trade item, produced by professional
scribes and book painters who sold their illuminated prayer books at
markets or from stalls at or even in the churches. In the small
German town of Hagenau, for instance, a school teacher named Die-
bold Lauber ran a large shop where he kept numerous scribes, illuminators, rubricators and bookbinders busy. The Dutch and German "Brothers of the Common Life" became very active in the production and sale of illuminated devotional books. However, as more
manuscripts were put on the market their illustrative material became more and more routine and lost a great deal of its earlier
artistic value. During this period easel painting was coming into
fashion and diverted attention from book painting.

Decline of Monastic Culture

Prayer books were often, particularly in Germany, bound in
such a manner that the leather of the binding extended beyond the
lower edge of the book and ended in a knot by which the book could
be carried or hung from the belt. These "bag bindings" (Fig. 26)
must undoubtedly have been very common, but only a score of them
have been preserved, five of which are in Scandinavian collections.

It is tempting to ascribe the origin of these bag bindings to
a desire on the part of the monks to make life as easy as possible.
Like the small brackets that were attached to the underside of
church seats to provide something to lean against when the seat was
turned up, these bindings might be considered an expression of the
monks' growing love of comfort. It is well known, of course, that
monastic life declined at many places in the latter part of the Middle Ages and drew far away from its original ideal. This process
of degeneration also affected the literary activities of the monasteries and the private studies of the brethren. From various sources
there is evidence of how book learning deteriorated, how the monks

25. First page of the Mass for the Dead in a Book of Hours that belonged to Count Philip of Bethune. The picture of the funeral procession, in the initial letter, was made by Jean Foucquet of Tours, or at least in his workshop. (Royal Library, Copenhagen.)

neglected their reading and how the monastery libraries stood unat-
tended, the books covered with dust or piled away in some corner.
The French statesman and book collector De Thou found such conditions in the Corbie monastery in the 16th century. Several bibliophiles of the Renaissance period described the sorrow they experienced at the sight of the brethren's indifference toward their book
treasures. Boccaccio, who was also a great booklover, wrote that
he had tears in his eyes at the sight of the library at Monte Cassino
when he visited that monastery in the 14th century.

De Bury's name has come down to our time through the treatise that he wrote in his later years under the title Philobiblon. It

The English bishop Richard de Bury expressed himself even
more dramatically about the decline in book culture and respect for
books. He lived from 1287 to 1345, and was a great favorite of
Edward III, whose teacher he had been, and held important civil and
ecclesiastical positions, becoming both Royal Chancellor and Bishop
of Durham. An ardent desire to collect books had early taken hold
of him, and on his diplomatic missions in Europe he had ample opportunity to satisfy this desire. Paris, with its many book treasures, was for him an earthly paradise. As bishop he received many
gifts of books from monasteries throughout England, and as chancellor he likewise received valuable additions to his library. It was
known that he would rather have a valuable old manuscript than a
sum of money: "decrepit folios and old quartos came creeping to
me instead of the usual fees and New-Year's gifts."

De Bury's name has come down to our time through the treatise that he wrote in his later years under the title Philobiblon. It
was published for the first time in 1473 and since then has appeared
in various editions. In it the bishop gives expression to his love of
books in clever and picturesque language. Philobiblon is primarily
a paean in praise of the book, but it also tells how De Bury collected his books and thus provides a sort of guide to the methods of
the bibliophile. It is here that he makes his pointed comments
about those who mistreat books. In one of the chapters he has the
books accuse the "degenerate race of monks;" he attacks particularly the students in the monastic schools who use the books with dirty
hands, let their "vile nose drippings" fall on the pages, and use
grass straws as bookmarks. Maybe bibliophilic fanaticism colored

26. Left, bag binding, half-opened. (Royal Library, Copenhagen.) Right, the apostle Jacob holding book in bag binding; figure
from the 1435 altarpiece in the church of the Benedictine nuns in
Preetz (Holstein), now in the National Museum (Copenhagen).

the old bishop's words, but decadence in the book culture of the
monasteries certainly was spreading rapidly in his time.   In the 15th
century, however, a reform movement sprang up among the Benedictine orders, with the aim of bringing monastic life back to its earlier ideals and restoring book study and writing to a place of honor.
This revival of activity in the monastery libraries and writing rooms
was not of long duration.   Only the Carthusians continued their copying very long after the invention of printing.

Dawn of the Renaissance

This was the threshold of that period in the history of culture called the Renaissance, the rebirth of the spirit of antiquity in a new form, a movement that affected all phases of intellectual and cultural life. While the study of ancient writers had, on the whole, been considered an auxiliary discipline in the monasteries, the Italian humanists and their successors now cultivated the ancient writers for their own sake, in order to learn their art, their philosophy and their view of life. Along with this there developed interest--one is tempted to say a fanatic interest--in collecting the works of these old authors, tracking down what still remained from ancient times and striving to reach as far back to the sources as possible. Thus at the close of the Middle Ages the Italian humanists and their followers played as large a part in the preservation of Greek and Roman literature as the men of the church did at the beginning of the period.

Although the humanists first directed their attention toward the texts themselves, they did not lack appreciation for the exterior features of a book. Among the most beautifully executed manuscripts that we have, several are from the quattrocento; the beautiful bindings of the Renaissance period will be treated below. The miniatures in Renaissance codices are recognized by the antique motifs--playful cupids, columns, vases, cameos--used in borders and initials. The handwriting is in imitation of the Carolingian minuscule; it is from this humanistic bookhand that the "Latin script" of later periods is descended; today the Latin script has displaced the Gothic style everywhere, except in German-speaking countries.

The man who has been called the "father of humanism" or the "first modern man," the Italian poet Petrarch, has also with some reason been called the father of modern bibliophilism. From his earliest youth he was a passionate lover of books and on his many journeys he bought and copied all the manuscripts that he could. He was active in this pursuit in Holland and Belgium as early as 1329, and on several occasions he was fortunate in discovering hitherto unnoticed texts, such as Cicero's letters to Atticus and others, which he found in the cathedral library of Verona.

Friends in France, England and Germany sent him books. He was particularly devoted to the writers of the Golden Age of Latin literature and applied himself to their works, correcting the many errors that repeated copying had introduced. He could not read Greek, and Greek literature was known to him only through Latin translations. He had Homer translated, and the Bibliothèque Nationale has the copy of the Iliad and the Odyssey that belonged to him and contains his notes in the margins. Petrarch was also interested in ecclesiastical literature. Despite the devotion of humanism to pagan antiquity, it was not an anti-Christian movement, and there were many church people among its representatives. Petrarch's favorite authors included Augustine as well as Cicero.

It was Petrarch's intention that his library should become the property of the city of Venice and be made accessible to the public, which would have entitled him to be called the father of the modern public library. That this idea was not realized and the books were scattered was not his fault.

The Medici and Their Circle

The centers of the Renaissance book world were the large commercial cities of Venice and Florence. In the latter city, in particular, the humanistic movement had one of its mainstays in the person of Cosimo de Medici. He and his successors were supported by the untiring work of Niccolo de Niccoli, who through his enthusiasm for collecting had gotten into debt to Cosimo and had then gone into his service. With the aid of the great financial resources of the Medici, collection of manuscripts was undertaken on an impressive scale. Manuscripts were bought in the countries north of the Alps, where the monks were glad to deal with the affluent Italian collectors. The most eager collector of all was the papal secretary Poggio Bracciolini. During his stay at the great church council in Constance, 1414-18, he made several journeys to St. Gallen and to various German monasteries where he uncovered hitherto unknown ancient works. Expeditions were sent to Greece, to Constantinople and to Asia Minor, where the Byzantine monasteries and libraries provided an abundant supply of Greek manuscripts. Byzan-

27. Italian Renaissance manuscript of the Annals of Tacitus,
with antique designs in the decoration, made in 1448. (Royal Library, Copenhagen, from "Golden Books.")

tine and Greek scholars fled before the Turks to Italy and became
guides and instructors in Greek literature and they took part in the
work of collecting. In 1490 Johannes Laskaris came back from a
trip with 200 Greek manuscripts, many of which contained new texts.
The envoys of the Medici often had instructions to look for books on
their travels, and back in Florence there were many copyists and
illuminators busy in the service of these lords of commerce. Here
lived also the great dealers in manuscripts, chief among whom was
Vespasiano da Bisticci. He knew how to produce correct texts and
how to give his codices an elegant outward appearance. Once he de-
livered to Cosimo a collection of 200 volumes that was produced in
the course of two years by 45 scribes. He also possessed copies
of the catalogs of a number of large libraries and could provide his
customers with valuable bibliographical information.

The Medici carried out Petrarch's idea of a public library--
an idea that was obviously in the air at that time. Another Floren-
tine, Palla degli Strozzi, had had the same idea but he was banished
by Cosimo. Cosimo, in 1441, with the books left by Niccolo de
Niccoli as a basis, established the Biblioteca Marciana, so called
because its quarters were in the Dominican monastery of San Marco. Another Medici collection, developed by the famous Lorenzo il
Magnifico, was called the Biblioteca Laurenziana. In the years following 1525 Michelangelo erected a building for this library at the
cathedral of San Lorenzo. This building is still famous for its elegant reading room, one of the most beautiful rooms of the Italian
Renaissance. The two libraries, Laurenziana and Marciana, were
combined in 1808 and they now form one of the outstanding sights of
Florence, the Biblioteca Mediceco-Laurenziana.

In his work with the Marciana library Cosimo had sought the
assistance of one of the most learned men of the time, Tommaso
Parentucelli, who on this occasion compiled a sort of model catalog
of what a humanistic library should contain. Parentucelli later became Pope Nicholas V and he founded a new papal library in Rome
after the one in Avignon had been dissolved. He gathered a collection of over 1200 codices, presumably the biggest library of that
time. The large sums of money that were taken in by the papacy

in the jubilee year 1450 were used for book purchases.   Pope Nicholas paid particular attention to the acquisition of Greek manuscripts, which he had Poggio and other famous humanists translate
into Latin at princely fees. Pope Sixtus IV housed the collection, now
numbering over 3,500 volumes and apartly accessible to the public,
in handsomely furnished quarters in the Vatican.

Several of the papal cardinals also attained renown as bibliophiles, though none more than Cardinal Basilios Bessarion. He
made a point of collecting Greek manuscripts, particularly after the
fall of Constantinople in 1453.   These he obtained from Athens,
Crete and the Orient.   He is said to have spent 30,000 gulden on
his library, which he willed to the city of Venice.   It now forms
the core of the Library of St. Mark.   Bessarion was not the only
Italian humanist who offered up nearly all his resources on the altar
of the book.   Poggio, Nicholas V (who before he became Pope had
been heavily in debt as a result of his large book purchases), and
others had done the same.

Renaissance bibliophiles also spent large sums on the bindings of their books; the books in Pope Nicholas' library in the Vatican, for instance, were nearly all bound in crimson velvet with silver mountings. The true Renaissance bindings will be considered
later, but it should be noted here that in the 15th century the great
majority of bindings were still of the standard late-Gothic blind-
stamped type.   The material used was calfskin, deerskin, pigskin,
or the more elegant goatskin from Cordova (cordovan leather).   The
stamps used for impressing the decorative work show great variation, though certain ones, such as the Gothic rose and the lily, li-
ons, eagles and deer are met again and again.   A great deal of artistry was often expended on the large engraved brass mountings on
the corners and in the center of the sides of the covers, as well as
on the clasps.   The engraved lines were sometimes colored yellow
or green, less often red.   Many such bindings can still be seen in
libraries; their heavy mountings and thick wooden covers bear witness to the competent craftsmanship of the period.   In these, as in
medieval bindings, there is in general a feeling of strength and so-
lidity.   In France and England, in the Scandinavian countries and

especially in Germany, bindings of this type were general through the 15th century.

The Renaissance was slow in spreading to the countries of northwestern Europe. At the time of Petrarch they were still living in the general spirit of scholasticism and their libraries exhibited this influence. Richard de Bury did, it is true, have some contact with Petrarch and other Italian humanists but he cannot rightly be called a humanist. In French circles we find no bibliophiles in the spirit of the Renaissance until Louis XII, who in 1500 brought back from Padua as war booty the library of the Dukes of Milan, the Sforzas. Francis I imitated the Medici in book collecting and took into his service the Greek scholar Laskaris and the famous philologist Guillaume Budé.

In Germany several great bibliophiles and scholars, such as Baron Albrecht von Eyb and Bishop Nicholas of Cues, were inspired by the interest of the Italian Renaissance in classical antiquity. Under Emperor Maximilian I, Vienna became a focal point for German humanistic studies. The Hungarian king Matthias Corvinus (1458-90) assembled a library that was said to contain 50,000 volumes-- surely an exaggeration. He kept scribes not only at his court in Buda, but also in Florence; he had purchasing agents in the Levant just as did the Medici, and he bought manuscripts from their supplier, Bisticci. It is strange to find in Hungary a person so closely related spiritually to the contemporary Italian book lords. Unfortunately the library of Covinus was largely destroyed when Buda was conquered by the Turks in 1526. Only 125 of his books have come down to our time, and they are preserved as great treasures in various libraries. Special interest attaches to their binding; as shall be noted later, the "Corvinians" have a prominent place in the history of bookbinding.

The Medici naturally had the greatest influence in their own country. In the 15th century one Italian prince after another followed their example on a smaller or larger scale. The Duke of Urbino, Federigo da Montefeltro, provided elaborately equipped quarters for his collection and is said to have kept some twoscore scribes busy, in Urbino and in Florence, under the direction of

Bisticci. The catalog of Federigo's books is still in the Vatican and shows how comprehensive this prominent Renaissance library was.

It is doubtful that these Renaissance book patrons acted entirely from idealistic motives. As in their attitude toward the fine arts, there was certainly a good deal of personal vanity and display of power involved, and in this sense their devotion to literature and books can be said to have had a political basis. But whatever the motives, it was this devotion that prepared the ground in Italy, more than anywhere else, to receive the book in the new form that it would acquire with the introduction of printing.

Chapter 3.   End of the Middle Ages

The art of producing a number of copies of a book by printing was, like the manufacture of paper, first discovered in China.
As early as the second century A.D. impressions are believed to
have been made from pages of text cut in a flat stone, the characters being sunk into it. Later the pages were carved in wood with
the writing standing out in relief. Impressions could then be taken
in large or small number from this wooden slab; the raised text
was coated with coloring matter, a sheet of paper laid over it and
pressed down to transfer the writing to the paper. The oldest
known wood-block printing from China in the form of a book dates
from the year 868 A.D., but the method was in use a good deal
earlier. In Japan, which learned all its bookmaking techniques from
China, wood prints were made as early as the 8th century.

Wood and metal slabs were used for printing in exactly the
same way in Europe, but there is no reason to believe that there
was any connection between European and Chinese wood-block printing (xylographic printing). The oldest known wood prints from Europe were made on cloth, and had nothing to do with books. When
paper came into general use, it was used for xylographic printing.
The ink was made of linseed oil, varnish and lampblack. Pictures of
saints, playing cards, calendars and other single-sheet items, often
with a handwritten legend under the picture, were produced. Some
3,000 of these have been preserved. From single-sheet impressions
it was not far to the book. About 1430 the first xylographic books,
or block books, were produced in Holland and Germany, the better
ones being from Holland. Some of these were made by pressing the
paper against the wooden slab with a hard leather pillow stuffed with
horsehair, though a press was generally used.

Only a very few block books have been preserved--33 different texts, and about 100 copies in all-but they must have been wide-

ly distributed since their contents were usually of a popular nature.
Most of them were in Latin. Their hand-colored illustrations were
the predominant feature, especially in the many small books that the
lower clergy used for instruction and devotional purposes. Among
these were the Biblia Pauperum (poor man's bible) containing ex-
cerpts from the Passion of Christ, the Speculum humanae salvationis (mirror of human salvation), Ars moriendi (the art of dying), etc.
There were also block books of secular content: calendars, planet
books, books of prophecies, etc. The reason that so few block
books have come down to us is that they were worn out by constant
use. The elementary schoolbooks of the Middle Ages, pieces of vellum that contained the alphabet and the most important Christian
prayers, disappeared for the same reason. One of the schoolbooks
found among the block books, the so-called Donet, a Latin grammar,
was originally compiled by the Roman grammarian Aelius Donatus.

Printing with Movable Type in China and Europe
Printing from wooden slabs has continued in China right down
to the present, even though in the 11th century the Chinese began
making movable types from baked clay and later cut them from metal. Each single written character was cut as a separate type and
the pages of the book made up by combining these types; when the
printed impressions had been taken the types could be separated
and then reassembled to form new pages. This method did not attain extensive use in China because of the large number of characters used by the Chinese; an ordinary book required 4-5,000 different types. In Europe, where the alphabet had a relatively small
number of letters, the art of printing with movable type represented
a revolutionary discovery.

The idea of movable type did not come to Europe from China,
nor from Korea, where books printed from movable copper type have
been found dating from early in the 15th century. The European
discovery was made quite independently by Johann Gutenberg of Germany.

28. Page from a block book containing the Bible Pauperum, issued in Bamberg in 1461, with hand-colored illustrations. This Bible is known from many medieval manuscripts; it contains scenes from the life of Christ. Since it was used as an instruction book and was not intended for poor people, its name was misleading.

Gutenberg Invents Typecasting

Unfortunately our sources of information about the life of Gutenberg are very limited. He belonged to the distinguished Gensfleisch family of Mainz, where he was born about the year 1400. His parents lived on one of the family properties called zum Gutenberg, and this name he took for himself. He was presumably trained as a metalworker or goldsmith. During the troubles in the 1420's between the craftsmen and the old bourgeois families he left Mainz and in 1434 was living in Strassburg. Here he went into partnership with three men who advanced him money in return for his teaching them his "arts and skills." Assuming that the reference was to his printing, Gutenberg was already working on his invention about 1438. After one of the partners died owing Gutenberg money, a lawsuit was filed in 1439. In the documents still preserved we find mention of lead, a press and various "forms," and one of the witnesses speaks about "that which belongs to printing." How far Gutenberg developed his invention during the Strassberg period, which lasted at least to 1444, we do not know.

Gutenberg's discovery, like so many others, can be said to have been in the air at the time. Long discussions have been carried on as to whether the invention of typecasting should not instead be credited to a Dutch printer by the name of Laurens Janszoon Coster in Haarlem. There can scarcely be any doubt that Coster knew the art of printing with movable types. A Cologne chronicle of 1499 mentions the Donatus grammars printed in Holland as early examples of book printing but his method of casting types must have been very cumbersome and impractical. Even though Gutenberg may have seen Coster's printing exhibited at the reliquary festival in Aachen in 1440, and thereby been stimulated to work with book printing, he could not have learned anything of significance from Coster's work. It is just as plausible to assume that he was led to the idea of movable types by the stamps or dies used in bookbinding. These could be separated and put together again in different ways--bindings with inscriptions stamped on with separate metal letter-stamps date from the first decades of the 15th century. A Bohemian goldsmith in Avignon, Prokop Valdfoghel, used metal

types in 1444 for some purpose that presumably involved inscriptions, but not for book printing. Gutenberg is credited with being
the father of the art of book printing, because he is the one who
discovered a satisfactory apparatus for casting the types and thereby made the method practical. It is probable that he had collabo-
rators, but what part they had in the discovery we do not know;
hence we must ascribe it to Gutenberg alone.

In 1448 Gutenberg was back in Mainz, where he took out a
loan, presumably to enable him to continue his experiments with
printing. A year or so later he again borrowed money--800 guldens
on two occasions from a wealthy merchant, Johann Fust. This, a
very large sum at that time, was to be used for materials and
equipment presumably needed for printing a large Latin Bible, which
was completed in 1456. Some trouble arose between Gutenberg and
his financier, resulting in a legal process of unknown outcome. We
do know that Gutenberg had to pay back the first loan with interest
and part of his material became the property of Fust. The following years were an unsettled period in Mainz; a struggle took place
between the former archbishop and his successor, Count Adolph of
Nassau, and the town was captured and plundered by the Count's
troops. Whether under these conditions Gutenberg was able to replenish his equipment and resume printing is not known; it is certain that in 1465 he was accepted into Adolph's court and was thus,
among other things, exempt from taxes. Gutenberg died in 1468
and was buried in the Franciscan church of Mainz, which was later
torn down.

We have no printed work that bears the name of Gutenberg,
nor does any of his work bear the date of printing. Only by study-
ing the types in relation to historical and chronological factors is it
possible to assign a number of items to his workshop with some degree of certainty. It was once assumed that the earliest Gutenberg
item was a vellum fragment of a calendar for the year 1448, printed
in 1447, but it has now been established that this calendar actually
was a collection of planetary tables for use in compiling horoscopes,
and must have been printed around the middle of the 1450's. A
sheet printed in the same type as the calendar, and called the

"Weltgericht" because the text deals with the day of judgment, was once considered the oldest extant example of typography, but this theory also has been abandoned. This sheet, found to be a fragment of a German poem about the Sybilline oracles, is preserved in the Gutenberg museum in Mainz. The two items are usually assigned to Gutenberg's workshop, though there are some who believe that they were made in another Mainz printing shop by one of Gutenberg's apprentices. Various Donets, letters of indulgence and other small items, are likewise believed to have been printed there, along with a small pamphlet "Ein Mahnung" (1454) previously attributed to Gutenberg. The large Latin Bible mentioned above is the only work that is ascribed to Gutenberg by general agreement.

Spread of the Art of Printing

When Fust came into possession of part of Gutenberg's equipment he started a printing business in partnership with a former scribe and initial-designer named Peter Schöffer, who undoubtedly had worked for Gutenberg. As early as 1457 Fust and Schöffer were able to issue a large Psalter, which will be discussed later. It was followed by a long series of notable works, among them a magnificent Bible issued in 1462, all of which bear witness to Schöffer's unusual ability as an artist. He was the moving spirit in the undertaking, while Fust mainly provided the money. After Fust's death, Schöffer continued the business alone for many years until his death in 1502 or 1503. Like the other early book printers, Schöffer cast his own types, which surpassed even Gutenberg's in accuracy and appearance.

There were other practitioners of the art of printing in the various towns in southern Germany in the 1460's. One reason for this was the attack on Mainz, during which a large number of the inhabitants were exiled or fled. The journeymen printers also left, Schöffer going to Frankfurt. Thus, destruction of Mainz contributed to the rapid spread of the art. Printing followed the old trade route of the Rhine; Strassburg became one of the chief centers of printing, but Cologne, Augsburg and Nuremberg soon had printing shops as well, in some instances rather large establishments. An unusually

29.   Typecaster pouring lead into the casting matrix.   In the
basket at the left are finished types, which will be worked over with
a file before being used.   Woodcut by Jost Amman in the book
Beschreybung aller Stände (1568), with verses by Hans Sachs.

large enterprise was developed by Anton Koberger in Nuremberg
around 1470.   He is said to have had 100 men and 24 presses at
work.   A generation after the discovery of printing more than a

30. Printing shop of the 17th century (from woodcut by Abraham von Werdt). At the left are the composing tables, at the right,
the type forms and ink balls, and the printing press.

score of German towns had printing shops. The majority were in
western Germany, not only because the home of the art, Mainz, was
in that part of the country, but also because it was here that the
largest trade centers of the time were located. In general the large
commercial centers offered printers the greatest possibilities for
continued activity.

Early typographical workshops had the same general appearance as those of later times, until their character was changed by
the introduction of power machinery. The dominant feature of the
shop was the large oaken presses, fastened to the ceiling as well as
the floor. In these the platen was pressed down on a sheet of paper
laid over the type form; the press was operated by a large wooden
screw and considerable manual force was required to provide suffi-
cient pressure. The platen was considerably smaller than the base
on which the type form itself lay, and as a rule a whole sheet could

not be printed at one time, but had to be divided into two or more folds, which were printed separately and then put together by the binder.

The type was set in the same way that hand-setting is done today. Two leather pillows with handles were used to ink the type; they were similar to those used for block-printing and were called "ink balls." A great deal of practice was required to apply the ink uniformly and to avoid making the impression uneven by drawing out any of the separate pieces of type.

The cutting of the typeface (punch-cutting), particularly its casting, must have been the most difficult operation for Gutenberg and the other early printers. The essential parts of the casting equipment, the matrices in which the type was cast, were made of copper or brass (Fig. 29). With constant use they became worn, so that the types did not remain exactly the same size and consequently were difficult to combine into lines. The types were made of a mixture of lead, antimony and bismuth, the very same mixture that is used today, and it is amazing that Gutenberg himself probably hit upon this substance. It melted so readily that the casting operation could proceed rapidly, and it was hard enough after cooling to withstand the heavy pressure of the press.

In other respects as well Gutenberg mastered typographical technique surprisingly early. Although the Weltgericht still had uneven letters and lines of different length, other contemporary printing showed great precision in the form of the letters, and great uniformity in the spacing between the letters and in the length of lines. Gutenberg gradually developed a very practical system of characters that included the abbreviations and ligatures found in manuscripts, and also a series of letters that did not have small hooks and points. These special letters were used when two letters with hooks in opposing directions came together. One of them was then replaced by the hookless type and the result was that the space between the two letters was no greater than usual. Setting type with such a large number of different characters must have been very taxing, and the casting of the type must have required great care and patience.

31. Ordinary type, type without points, double letters (ligatures) and abbreviation signs (abbreviatures) from Gutenberg's type material. (After Otto Hupp.)

The First Printed Books

Many of the earliest printed books had high esthetic standards; one reason is that they had the manuscript tradition of the Middle Ages behind them. The first printers quite naturally took these manuscripts as their models; the letters were made like those in manuscripts, the general arrangement of the manuscript page was closely followed, and those features that they could not reproduce by printing--the initials and other decorations--were done in the old manner by the hand illuminator with his brushes and paints. To an amazing degree the entire external appearance of the medieval vellum codex was thus transferred to the printed book and the resulting product was just as beautiful as an illuminated manuscript. The Bible printed by Gutenberg in 1456 in two folio volumes, might be mistaken for a manuscript until it is examined closely. This Bible is often called the 42-line Bible because most of the pages have that

number of lines in each column, but it is also known as the Mazarin Bible because the first copy of it was found in the library of the
French cardinal Mazarin. Each page--there are over 1200 in all--
is divided into two columns and the letters are those in the Gothic
style of writing that is found in the magnificent liturgical manuscripts of the late-Gothic period, with their heavy angular shape;
black-letter "text," "missal," and "canon," as the larger forms of
it are called. For headings, initials and borders the printer left
blank spaces where they could be painted in later, in some copies
a few headings are printed in red ink (the red headings were called
rubries from rubrum = red). Forty-six copies of the Gutenberg
Bible are known, twelve of which are on vellum. The entire edition
presumably consisted of about 120 copies. On the rare occasion
when this Bible has come on the market it has brought fantastic
prices. In 1897 at an auction in London a copy brought the equivalent of about $12,000. In 1926 an American purchased the copy of
the Austrian monastery of Melk for $120,000 and presented it to
Yale University, and a few years ago a copy was sold from an English private library to the U.S. for over $150,000. Another famous
early edition of the Bible, the so-called Schellborn Bible from 1459
or 1460, has 36 lines in each column and only thirteen copies of it
are known. It was printed in Bamberg, perhaps by Gutenberg, but
in any case with the same type that he used.

        Even more beautiful than these Bibles, however, is the
Psalter (David's Psalms) referred to above, printed by Fust and
Schöffer on vellum in 1457, in which early printing reached its highest level. It is also the first printed book to contain a notation of
when and by whom it was printed; its closing lines (colophon) can be
translated briefly as follows: "This Psalter has been produced by
the ingenious process of printing and forming letters without any
writing by hand, and was completed with diligence for the glory of
God by Johann Fust, a citizen of Mainz, and Peter Schöffer of Gern-
sheim in the year 1457, the eve of Ascension Day (i.e. Aug. 14)."
There is much to indicate that Gutenberg had started this work and
that it was merely brought to completion in Fust and Schöffer's
workshop.

32.   Page from Gutenberg's 42-line Bible, with hand-painted border and initial.

33. Page from the Catholicon of Johannes Balbus (1460), with red hand-painted initials.

The colophon quoted above makes it clear that everything in
the book was done by printing, including the unusually beautiful initials in red or in red and blue, which seem to have been cut in
metal rather than in wood. The Psalter also carries the first
printer's mark that we know, the coats of arms of the two printers
hanging from a branch (Fig. 45). Later, of course, it became general practice for printers to sign their work with a monogram or an
emblem, some of which were very decorative. Only ten copies are
known today of the Mainz Psalter; these are all printed on vellum,
but they represent variant editions.

34. Woodcut showing Christ before Pilate, from the Speculum humanae salvationis printed about 1472 by Günther Zainer and
also extant in many medieval manuscripts.

Another famous work, considered by many to have been executed by Schöffer in 1460, is the Catholicon of Johannes Balbus, a
sort of encyclopedic lexicon, printed in a peculiar small type. It is
certain that Schöffer was responsible for a later edition of this work,
but whether he also printed the original edition is still moot.

The imitation of manuscripts that was characteristic of the
earliest book printing extended also to the absence of a proper title;

the text began on the very first page with the introductory word incipit, or hic incipit. An isolated exception to this rule is found in
the small work mentioned earlier, Ein Mahnung der Christenheit
wider die Türken printed in 1454 and now extant in only one copy
(Munich Staatsbibliotek); it was issued in facsimile in Copenhagen,
1902. Here the title appears, printed by itself, at the top of the
first page. The first true title page, however, did not occur until
about 1470. Ein Mahnung is in the form of a calendar and contains
exhortations to the Christian countries to resist the Turks, who had
captured Constantinople the year before. Like several other books
printed in German in this initial period, it was a propaganda item
intended for the public at large.

The Earliest Illustrated Books

It was not long before printed books began to desert the
manuscript tradition. For example, they began to have pictures
printed along with the text instead of having them drawn in after the
printing was completed. The block books that continued to be widely distributed during the first decades of printing had illustrations
cut into the wood block along with the text. Quite naturally such illustrations (woodcuts) were quickly transferred to books printed with
movable type, by incorporating the block in which the picture was
cut as part of the page and printing it along with the typeset materials, possibly in a separate printing operation after the text had been
printed. At the beginning, however, these illustrations were simply
outlines to be filled in with color later by the artist (Fig. 36).

The first printer known to have used woodcuts was Albrecht
Pfister of Bamberg, who had presumably once made his living painting pictures of saints, playing cards and similar block prints, and
was consequently quite familiar with illustrations cut in wood. In
1461 he issued a small popular book with many woodcuts, the Edel-
stein of Ulrich Boner, a collection of fables. This book is also of
interest as the oldest book printed in German--only two copies of it
remain. Woodcuts are excellently suited for combining with type
material; the bold black-letter text and the heavy woodcut lines form
a unity of great decorative effect. However, the purpose of the pic-

tures in Pfister's books and in those of his contemporaries was not
decoration; the pictures are to be interpreted as actual visualizations
of the contents of the text for the ordinary reader for whom these
books as well as the block books were intended. This also applies
to the pictures with which the Augsburg printer, Günther Zainer, illustrated the many German devotional and popular books that he issued, and for which there must have been a ready sale. Zainer was
also the first to use woodcut decorative initials on a large scale.

In several of these books from the earliest period of printing
we find the same woodcut used to illustrate widely different subjects;
the same human figure, for instance, is often used to represent a
whole series of different individuals. Perhaps this was done to save
expense; cutting a picture in a block of pear or beech wood was a
task that took time even for an experienced hand. It is more likely, however, that the artist was lacking in imagination. In spite of
all their shortcomings, the woodcuts in Pfister's and other early illustrated books are by no means to be despised from an artistic
standpoint; they are probably of interest today just because of their
original and primitive character. Their connection with the early
saints' pictures and block book illustrations is unmistakable; at the
same time they do carry the seed of the highly developed German
woodcut art of some decades later, whose great names are Dürer
and Holbein, and which branched out in new directions in Italy.

One step along the road from the earliest woodcuts to those
of the Dürer period is represented by the Cologne Bible of 1478,
probably the most famous of the many illustrated Bibles. Its 125
pictures were drawn by an artist of the first rank, whose name is
unknown. In contrast to the books already mentioned, these woodcuts were not merely outline drawings. They made extensive use
of shading to give the figures a three-dimensional appearance, and
the figures also seemed more alive than in earlier pictures. All
the illustrations in the Cologne Bible were used by Anton Koberger
of Nuremberg in 1483 and its wide distribution exerted a strong influence on Bible illustration in later times.

There are several other large illustrated books from the
later decades of the 15th century that represent stages on the road

35.   Woodcut by Erhard Reuwich from Breydenbach's account
of a journey to the Holy Land, 1486.   Bernhard von Breydenbach
and the painter Erhard Reuwich made a pilgrimage together in 1483.

to the great flowering of the woodcut art, such as Bernhard von
Breydenbach's very popular travel description of the Holy Land.   It
was the first book to mention the name of the artist who drew the
pictures (Erhard Reuwich) and these were probably the first pictures
to be drawn from nature and intended to represent the actual features of the various towns and landscapes.   (Fig. 35) There is also the book about medicinal herbs issued by Schöffer, Gart der
Gesundheit (1485), in which the plant drawings are likewise ascribed
to Reuwich, and Hartman Schedel's famous Weltchronik, printed by
Koberger in 1493.   The latter contains approximately 1,800 woodcuts
and is one of the most profusely illustrated books that has ever been
printed; some of the drawings are ascribed to Dürer's teacher Michael Wohlgemuth.   These woodcuts were intended to be painted in
color, and this was done in several copies.   In the Dürer period,
however, this carry-over from the days of the illuminated manuscripts was given up, and black-and-white illustrations became almost universal in books, right up to the advent of hand-colored

Serta etas mũdi

Jacobus iustus mĩnoz apostolus

Jacob⁹ apłs cognomẽto iustus dictus mĩnoz refpe
ctu maioris:nõ quo ad fctitaté: fed ob vocationez
ad aplatũ. Dñi (ex foroze marie matris ei⁹) frater poſt
afcēſione dñi ab apłis hierofolomitane ecclie primus
eps ordinat⁹: Sedit annis. xxx. vſqz ad ſeptimũ annũ
Neronis. Vir certe ab ipſo matris vtero ſanctus:q̃ vi
nũ z ſicerã nõ bibit:nec carnē mãducauit; ferrũ i caput
eius nõ afcēdit:oleo nõ eſt vnct⁹: nec balneo vſus eſt z
veſte linea fapindut⁹ folus ſancta ſanctoz ingrediebat
z ita affidue p ſalute pplî fleris genib⁹ozabat:vt eius
genus camelog moze occalluerũt p hac ſũma iuſticia:
iuſtus appellar⁹. z vt Ignac⁹ tradit facie vita z mõ cõ
verſationis rpo ibu ſimilim⁹ fuit:ac ſi frēs gemelli fuſ
ſent.Hũc itaqz annan⁹põtifex iudeoz:recedẽte feſto ex
iudea ipſi.puicie gubernatoze cõprehēdit. Et rp̃m ne
gare ãceprauit poſuitqz ſup pinaculi tepli z ãgrega
ta multitudine rp̃m verũ dẽi verũ ad iudiciũ viuos
z moztuos pclamauit.rpiani gauiſi.phariſei pturbati
afcēdẽtes eũ de tepli pinna deiecerũt:cõfeſtim in terras
collapſus lapidib⁹obrui ceperit:.put tñ potuit man⁹
ad celũ retẽdit z p pſecutorib⁹ orauit.Quo adhuc ſpi
rãte fullonis fuſte i capite peuſſus expirauit. Sepult⁹
iuxta tẽplũ.huic p⁹reſurrectionē dñs apparuit ei pane
bñdicẽs z frãgens dixit. Sed frater comede pane tuũ
qz a moztuis fili⁹bois reſurrexit:cũ votũ emiſiſſet non
guſtaturꝰ pane niſi cũ pꝛ⁹videt.cũ tante ſctitatis fuiſſe
diē ioſeph⁹qꝑ ob necē ei⁹ ierłyma euẽſa fuit credituſ ſit.

Detrus vir ſanctiſſim⁹ cũ tñ ſibi nois apud oẽs cõparauerat vt plurimũ coleret⁹:hãc ob rē indignat⁹
Nero morte ei⁹qrere cepit:vñ petẽ⁹monẽtib⁹ amicis ad receſſum via appia ab vrbe diſ
cedẽs ad primũ lapide rpo ſit obuia.quẽ adoras rogat dñe quo venis:tus rpo. Romã iterũ crucifigi.ex
tat ſacello eo loco vt vba hic ſunt habita ideo ad vrbe rediit clemẽte cp̃m ſecerat . nõ multo poſt vna cum
paulo tuſſu neronis necaf vltimo ei⁹ anno:diuerſis m̃ cruciand⁹.petꝰ9 cũ cruci affigaf capite in terrã ver
ſo:eleuatiſqz in ſublimepedib⁹ita cũ voluit.Sepult⁹eſt i vaticano nõ lõge a via triũphali:via aurelia ſec⁹
oztos neronis.Sedit aũt annis vigintiquiqz. Paulus vo codē die capite mulctaf⁹:funeraf via hoſtien
ſi añ no poſt morte rpi trigeſimoſeptimo.Eũ aũt ſeparenf abinuicẽ inqt paul⁹ paꝛ teeũ fundamētũ ecclia
rũ z paſtoꝛ oim agnoy rpi. Petrus ridit.Vade in pace p̃dicatoꝛ bonoꝛ: mediatoꝛ z dux ſalutis iuſtozuz
Marcellus z Apuleius frēs diſcipuli cõdieres aromatib⁹ ſepelierũt.Hodie capita aplop̃ petri z pauli au
ro argento ac gẽmis exoꝛnata in ecclia lateranenſi ſancti iobãnis repoſita pplo oſtẽdunt.

Crucifixo Petri apoſtoli   Decapitatio Pauli

36. Page from Hartman Schedel's <u>Weltchronik</u>, printed by
Anton Koberger in 1493.   The woodcuts were colored after printing.

copper engravings.

Development of Printing in Italy

After the capture of Mainz it was not long before printers
appeared in other countries.   Italy, with her rich literary culture,
was quite naturally the country that would attract them, and in 1465
two pupils of Schöffer, Conrad Sweynheim and Arnold Pannartz,
started a printing shop at a monastery in Subiaco near Rome.   They
used a black-letter (gothic) type that later became the pattern for
one of the type fonts cut by John Hornby for the Ashendene Press.
Sweynheim and Pannartz stayed only two years at the Subiaco monastery.   They were encouraged to come to Rome, and there in the
course of the next seven years they issued a long series of books--
36 works and a total of 12,475 volumes, by their own figures--
mainly editions of the Latin classics.   They used a new type, the
roman or antiqua, which unlike the black-letter was patterned on the
humanistic book hand, which went back to the Carolingian minuscule.
Since the Carolingian descended from the Latin cursive, the new
roman type was a "Latin" type, and in many respects was reminiscent of the inscriptions on the old Roman monuments.   It had rounded shapes without breaks or sharp angles, hence was both easier to
cut and easier to read than black-letter.   It was clear and distinctive in style but more severe than black-letter, without the fullness
and the festive air that harmonized so well with heavy woodcuts.

During the next decades many other German printers followed
Sweynheim and Pannartz to Italy and settled there, in Rome (such
as Ulrich Han, who in 1467 printed the first book in Italy with woodcuts) and in other large cities.   The great trade center of Venice
offered the most favorable conditions, and from 1469 on a large
colony of book printers was located there.   Many of them made
names for themselves, such as the brothers Johann and Wendelin of
Speyer, who printed one of the first books in Italian, a volume of
Petrarch's sonnets.   Then there was the French engraver, Nicolaus
Jenson, who had been sent by King Charles VII to Mainz in 1458 to
learn the new art.   He later emigrated to Italy and may have cut
Sweynheim and Pannartz's roman types.   For his own use he cut

nihil iis fegetibus : quæ deiceps in eo loco feminari debent:profuturum
fit. Ac de iis quoq; leguminibus:quæ uellunt:Tremelius obeffe maxie
ait folo uirus ciceris & lini:alterum quia fit falfæ:alterum quia fit fer-
uidæ naturæ. Quod etiam Virgilius fignificat dicendo:
Vrit enim lini campum feges:urit auenæ:
Vrūt lætheo perfufa papauera fomno. Neq; enim dubium quin & iis
feminibus infeftetur ager:ficut & milio & panico : fed omni folo quod
prædictorum leguminū fegetibus fatifcit:una præfens medicina eft:ut
ftercore adiuues:& abfumptas uires hoc uelut pabulo refoueas. Nec tā-
tum propter femina quæ fulcis aratri committuntur:uerum etiā ͵pptet
arbores & uirgulta : quæ maiorem in modum lætantur eiufmodi ali-
mento. Quare fi eft ut uidetur agricolis utiliffimū:diligentius de eo di-
cendum exiftimo:cum prifcis auctoribus quāuis nō omiffa res:leui tamen admodum cura fit prodita.

37.   Nicolaus Jenson's roman type.

38.   Ratdolt initials from the 1480's.   When Ratdolt returned
to Augsburg in 1486 he took part of his material with him.

another roman type, which brought him fame as one of the most outstanding artists of type design that has ever lived; his type has been
imitated time and again, especially by English and American book
artists in recent times.

Jenson worked in Venice, where still another German, Er-
hart Ratdolt from Augsburg, established a printing shop in 1476;
Ratdolt, together with Jenson and the brothers Johann and Wendelin
of Speyer, contributed to giving the city its position of leadership
in the first period of Italian book printing.   Ratdolt's books from
the 1470's introduced Venetian woodcut art, which developed so pro-
lifically in the ensuing decades.   His woodcut borders and initials
are the first in which the Renaissance style is unmistakable; in
them are encountered again the classical motifs of Renaissance manuscripts.   These were not just imitations; great artistry was used
in producing them in their black and white dress, and the result was
just as effective as that attained with color in manuscripts.   Even
after Ratdolt left Italy in 1486 his influence continued to be felt; in
the following years there were more and more books whose opening
page, just as in Ratdolt's books, was entirely surrounded by a wide
Renaissance border of imaginative and varied designs: columns and
vases, acanthus leaves and vine branches, strange mythical animals,
human heads and masks, etc.   In addition there were initials of
great beauty, white on black background, with the decoration enclosed in a square frame of straight lines.   In spite of its excellence,
the decoration never detracted from the text; there was harmony between the two.   Here, then, on the soil of Italian humanism, primarily in Venice, early German woodcut art established a fruitful
contact with the esthetic ideals of the Renaissance.   In the course
of an amazingly short time this resulted in the printing of books so
beautiful that they have scarcely been equalled since.

The significance of Ratdolt's books was primarily in the field
of ornamentation, but the art of illustration also made rapid advances
in this period of Italian printing.   Ratdolt printed several illustrated
books and earned the honor of being the first book printer (when we
disregard the two-colored initials in the Mainz Psalter) to attempt
the difficult feat of printing in more than one color.   A few of his
pictures are printed in four colors, a different cut being used for
each color.   Among the most famous of the early Italian illustrated
books is Niccolo de Malermis' Bible translation of 1490, in which
the numerous small fine-lined woodcuts show the influence of the il-

39. Round-gothic script (rotunda) in an Italian missal from
the end of the 15th century.   This type was developed in Bologna
and spread from there throughout Europe.

lustrations in the Cologne Bible.   This work, together with Ratdolt's
books and the illustrated editions of Dante and Boccaccio, introduced
the great period of Italian book art, the Aldine period.

Development of Printing in Other Countries

The art of printing spread from Germany and Italy in the
years following 1470.   In the Netherlands the first books were presumably printed in Utrecht, but they carry neither date nor printer's
name.   These Dutch books, like the German, were printed in various forms of black-letter type; one of these variants, descended
from Italian manuscript writing (Fig. 39) and common in Italian
printed books, was characterized by its rounded shapes and was
called round-gothic (rotunda).   The best known of the early Belgian
printers was Colard Mansion in Bruges, originally a bookdealer and
scribe, who began to print books in 1475.   He used types cut on the
model of Flemish manuscripts.

Netherlands woodcut art, which developed along with the extensive production of block books in that country, flourished vigorously for a brief period.   An illustrated work of special beauty, Le
Chevalier délibéré, printed in 1486, deals with Charles the Bold and
is assumed to have been printed by Gotfred van Os in Gouda, who
later worked in Copenhagen under the name of Gotfred of Ghemen.

The first English printer, William Caxton, was originally
a merchant.   Since he also had literary interests and was a compe-

tent translator, he decided to try his hand at printing. He had learned the trade in Cologne and in Colard Mansion's shop in Bruges. In 1486 he returned to England, settled in Westminster, and there printed almost a hundred books. Some were his own translations while others were national literary works like Chaucer's Canterbury Tales.

France did not receive the art of book printing until 1470, when two professors in Paris called in three Germans to set up a typographic shop at the Sorbonne and had them print a series of Latin texts for use at the University. Thereafter the new art expanded rapidly in France, and around 1500 Paris had close to seventy printing establishments. Most French printing of the early period was in black-letter type but a few books showed the influence of French manuscripts. This applied, for instance, to the type used by Jean Dupré, whose first book, a missal, was printed in 1481. He was also responsible for the first printed Books of Hours; in their general features these imitated the handwritten ones as much as possible. They were often printed on vellum and supplied with borders and illustrations, which, although printed from wood or metal cuts, kept very close to the illuminated manuscript tradition, and were even painted in colors and gilded. Around the end of the 15th century hundreds of these delightful and popular prayer books were printed; the publisher Antoine Vérard alone issued about 200 editions, including a series of "petites heures" and a series of "grandes heures" or "heures royales," the latter in very elaborate format. From Vérard's establishment also came many illustrated chronicles, tales of knighthood and romances, though to what extent he himself actually engaged in printing is not known. The same can be said of Simon Vostre, who began using metal cuts in his Books of Hours toward the close of the 15th century; in these cuts the background was punched with small dots to give the picture greater body. In the borders around the prayers for the dead he introduced the picture series known as the "Dance of Death." In 1485 these pictures were issued separately by a publisher in Paris with great success.

Only Paris and the large commercial city of Lyons ranked as important printing centers. In Lyons was Johannes Treschel, who

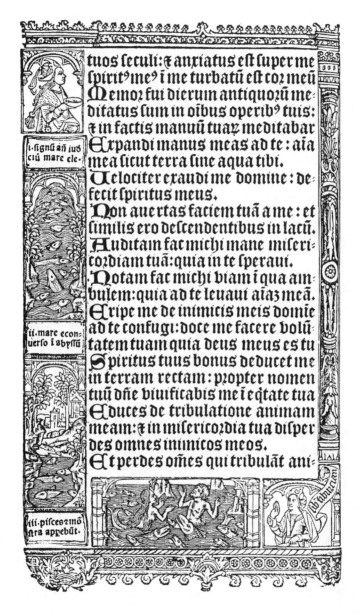

tuos feculi:⁊ anxiatus eſt ſuper me
ſpirit⁹ me⁹ ī me turbatū eſt coz meū
Memoz fui dierum antiquozū me-
ditatus ſum in oibus operib⁹ tuis:
⁊ in factis manuū tuaz meditabar
Expandi manus meas ad te : aia
mea ſicut terra ſine aqua tibi.
Uelociter exaudi me domine : de-
fecit ſpiritus meus.
Don auertas faciem tuā a me : et
ſimilis ero deſcendentibus in lacū.
Auditam fac michi mane miſeri-
cozdiam tuā:quia in te ſperaui.
Dotam fac michi biam ī qua am-
bulem:quia ad te leuaui aiaz meā.
Eripe me de inimicis meis domie
ad te confugi:doce me facere bolū-
tatem tuam quia deus meus es tu
Spiritus tuus bonus deducet me
in terram rectam : pzopter nomen
tuū dñe biuificabis me ī eqtate tua
Educes de tribulatione animam
meam:⁊ in miſericozdia tua diſper
des omnes inimicos meos.
Et perdes omēs qui tribulāt ani-

i.ſignū añ iud
ciū mare cle-

ii.mare econ-
uerſo ī abyſſū

iii.piſceoz mō-
ſtra apzebūt.

40. Page from a Book of Hours (Heures à l'usage de Rome,
1520) issued by Simon Vostre.

had the learned Jodocus Badius Ascenius as his editor; in 1503 the latter established his own printing business in Paris, where he issued some 700 works.

While the Netherlands and France were becoming acquainted with the art of printing it also spread to Spain and finally to North Germany. In this latter region printing found many competent practitioners, some of whom worked in the flourishing Hanseatic city of Lübeck. The first book printer there was Lucas Brandis; several other members of the Brandis family were also active as printers at various times in Lübeck, as well as in Merseburg, Magdeburg and Leipzig. They created a special round-gothic typeface that spread throughout North Germany in several variant forms.

In 1483 Lucas Brandis printed a missal for the diocese of Odense in Denmark; about the same time Our Lady Cathedral in Copenhagen had a missal printed by Schöffer in Mainz. Another Lübeck printer, Johann Snell, became the first book printer in Denmark and in Sweden. In 1482 he was called to Odense by Bishop Karl Ronnov to print a prayer book for the diocese. A printing shop was set up in the St. Hans monastery of the city and he worked there for a year, printing not only the Breviarium Ottoniense ordered by the bishop, but also a small book about the siege of Rhodes by the Turks. In 1483-4 Snell was in Sweden, where he printed a small moralizing book Dialogus Creaturarum (1483) and a missal for the Uppsala diocese (1484). Two years later there was another Lübeck printer in Sweden, Bartholamäus Ghotan, who printed a missal for Strängnäs diocese (1487), and then later, in Lübeck, an illustrated edition of the visions of the holy Birgitta (1492), ordered by Vadstena monastery. His pupil and successor, Johannes Fabri, printed the first book in Swedish in 1495.

In Denmark printing was continued by immigrants after Johann Snell had left. Steffen Arndes came to Slesvig in 1486. He had learned printing in Mainz and had later worked in Italy (Foligno, Perugia), attaining great proficiency in the trade. He printed the great Missale Slesvicense, a beautiful work with its stately missal type, executed in the familiar German liturgical style. His chief work was the Low-German Bible issued in 1944, containing a series

41. Page from the first book printed in Denmark, Breviarium Ottoniense.

Jeg willæ ep leggæ meg nogher i modh
leg effter fith findh hwer leffue lodh
Thi woæ ther mãgæ wthi mit land
fom hwerken fkøttæ gudh elder mand
The fkøttæ or hwerkē loff elder ræth
thi woæ bland folket megit wfeth
Jeg giorde ep repfer boæt wthñ lantz
fpden ieg fik rigz or woæde tyl mantz
Thi fullæ meg tha the ængelfkæ fra
fom hade mpne foælder i dãmark thå
Jeffnt i tpwæ or hũdæedæ aar
fom ieg haffuer hørth or fcriffuet ftaar
Danfkæ gaff ieg foæ low or fedh
at the fkullæ thm mz theres eedh
Om nogher mã fetther paa ãnen fagh
or hã will bliffue foæ hãnn mz magh
Tha fkall hã fweriæ fom faghñ ær ftaaæ
och lowen hũ holdher oædh fraa oædh
The foæ ther hwer en oppaa
ath the willæ hellder i døden gaa
En the willæ mefthe thñ fãme ræth
fom thm gaffs och føæe woæ iæth
Jeg woæ ep kõning wthñ tw aar
leg døde aff foth or ep aff faar

         ¶Sancte Kanud
t   Hz ær hwer mã en hedher fwl ftooæ
      at hã holder faft fpn hedher or ooæ
Och fpnderiig thñ aff all fpn acth
fom fkpcket ær i kõgeligh macth

42.   Page from the first book printed in the Danish language, Den danske Rimkrønike, a history of Denmark in verse, printed in Copenhagen in 1495 by Gotfred of Ghemen. The initial T has not been drawn in, but is indicated by the small printed letter.

of striking woodcuts.

Book printing came to Copenhagen in about 1489, with the arrival of the Dutch printer Gotfried van Os, who called himself Gotfred of Ghemen. He worked in Copenhagen until his death in 1510, printing first a Donet, and later Den danske Rimkronike (1495), the oldest printed book in Danish, besides a great many other popular and devotional books in Danish--all evidencing very good workmanship.

Economic Circumstances of the
Early Book Printers

Many of the early printers were forced to lead a wandering life. Cathedrals and other ecclesiastical units in town that were too small to support a regular book printer would call in a printer for a short time to produce some particular liturgical work, as in the case of Snell and Arndes. An intense competition developed between the printers and the manuscript dealers. The stationers, scribes, illuminators and binders of manuscript books were not ready to give up without a struggle. Aided by the universities, they formed a group that sought to hold the printers down.

Some collectors were actually hostile toward printed books and would neither own them nor allow them in their collections; one of these was Duke Federigo of Urbino. The fact that the first printers sought to imitate manuscripts so closely is explained in part by the higher value attached to manuscripts.

The printed book gained ground with amazing speed. In a library such as that of Corvinus in Hungary manuscripts were presumably in the majority but it did include a considerable number of printed books. The church soon made use of printing; in monasteries printing shops gradually replaced writing rooms. Even Italian humanism, with its great love of manuscripts, soon learned to make use of the new art and to appreciate the advantages it offered.

Along with this rapid development of book printing, came competition within the trade. There were no legal regulations to protect a publisher's right; any book that proved salable could be reprinted by other publishers. The price at which printed books could

sold, from a fifth to an eighth of the price of a corresponding manuscript, had greatly expanded the book market.   It was no accident
that so many of the products of the earliest period were popular
items: chronicles and fables, devotional books, prophecies, etc.,
printed in the national language and supplied with illustrations to appeal to the common people, who up to that time had almost never
bought books.   Nevertheless, this new public was not large enough
or wealthy enough for the flood of printed books that poured forth,
and block books were still an important competitor.   In Italy things
went reasonably well but in other countries most printers did not
have a gold mine in their new trade, and they often had to move
from one town to another.   In the period before the year 1500 it is
estimated that about 30,000 different books were produced by printing.   Even though most of these were probably issued in editions of
only 100 up to perhaps 1,000 copies, the total production was still
quite impressive.

In the beginning the printer usually sold the books he printed.
Before long the so-called colporteurs traveled about from town to
town and offered for sale books that they had bought from the printers, taking advantage of church festivals, trade fairs, markets or
other community events.   Available copies of advertising sheets used
by these dealers date as far back as 1470; the sheets announced
their arrival in the town, listed the books they had for sale, and invited the public to examine the books at some particular inn.   The
only printers who could make a profitable business of their trade
were those who operated on a large scale and could afford to maintain stocks in the larger cities, as Schöffer did in Frankfurt and
Paris.   The market for Latin literature was not, of course, restricted to a single country.

Frankfurt, Cologne and Strassburg became important centers
for the book trade.   Among others, Adolph Rusch was active in the
last-mentioned city; he not only printed books himself but also had
other printers for whom he acted as publisher, paying them double
the number of blank sheets for their products.   The greatest of all
these printer-publishers was Anton Koberger, whose business in
Nuremberg was the most extensive in Germany at that time.   In

Italy the dominant individual at the end of the century was Nicolaus Jenson in Venice. When a particularly large work was to be produced, a printer, a wood-carver and a capitalist would often go into partnership. Among the printers of the early period were several with an extensive literary background, and the larger printing establishments often had scholars attached to them as editors and proofreaders (castigatores) of ancient classical texts.

In the large cities just mentioned and also particularly in Augsburg, Leipzig and Basel there were dealers in the books of various publishers as early as the end of the 15th century. Their business was similar to that of the colporteurs, except that they were permanently located; they could find enough customers within the city. Like the traveling book agents they received a discount from the publishers on large works; otherwise they paid the publisher's full price according to the number of sheets in the book, payment usually being in cash or on six months' credit. There were no fixed retail sale prices; these varied from place to place, being determined by the demand and the dealer's ability as a salesman. In general, however, bookselling was not a lucrative business, and the field was too crowded. Bookbinders also engaged in selling.

The Earliest Printed Books (Incunabula)

The oldest printed books are called incunabula (cradle books; Lat. cunabula = cradle) since they belong to the childhood of the art of printing. The word paleotypes is also used, but it applies to all old printing, while incunabula are only those books printed before the year 1501. In the Scandinavian countries, where printing did not begin until the 1480's, the incunabulum period is extended to 1550. Incunabula can be of interest because of their texts, especially the first printed editions of medieval manuscripts, but their greatest importance is in the study of the early history of book printing. It was not until the 18th century that there was any interest in incunabula as typographic productions, and only in the course of the last three generations has the study of them made significant progress. Detailed analysis of the form and size of the various letters has made it possible to determine the place of origin of many incunabula that do not contain information about when and where they were printed. The early type fonts can be identified by the many small variations that are evident on close examination. In manuscripts it is possible to distinguish the different schools of writing, even when the style is the same; similarly the letters of the earliest printed books show small divergences that make it possible to tell them apart, even though they may represent the same variety of black-letter or roman type. In determining the origin of a printed work there is, however, the difficulty that one printer often took over another's type material or matrices. Hence, for example, Gutenberg can not be credited with all the books printed with his material.

Panel-stamped Bindings

It was not until the introduction of printing that bookbinding developed into a separate trade. During the first century following the invention of printing it was quite common for printers to do their own binding; this was especially true in the larger printing establishments, where the books were often issued in bound form. Usually a specially trained person executed the binding. It is known that Ratdolt, Caxton, Koberger and others had binders working for them, either in or outside their establishments.

Since printing had made books more plentiful and cheaper, binding methods had to keep step; a type of binding had to be found that was cheaper to produce than blind-stamped binding, in which the decoration was made by the separate application of many small stamps. In the last third of the 15th century bindings began to be produced in Holland by engraving the decoration of the entire cover on a metal plate and pressing this down on the book in one operation in a screw press. This was still a blind-stamping or embossing process, the design being cut into the plate just as in the earlier small stamps. The figures represented were saints, angels, birds, flowers, grotesque animals, coats-of-arms, etc. If the binding was too large to be completely covered by the plate, the impression was repeated two or four times and any blank spaces filled in with small stamped borders.

Since these plate-impressed or panel-stamped bindings could be produced more rapidly and cheaply than those made with the small stamps, their use spread rapidly through Holland and the Rhineland. In the rest of Germany, strangely enough, they did not come into use on a large scale until much later; there the custom continued of decorating the central portion of the cover with diagonal lines and small stamped figures. In the border around this central section an inscription was often printed, such as a Biblical quotation or a statement about the binder of the book. Bindings of this type were sometimes made in the monasteries, and some of them were stamped with the name of the monastery or its symbol. As the art of printing developed, bookbinding was no longer an occupation solely for monks or for the bookbinders attached to universities, but became a regular trade. Toward the end of the 15th century in Germany the names of several such independent craftsmen appeared in the decoration of the books they bound. In Lübeck there was Heinrich Coster, whose bindings state "Hainz Coster bant dit," and in Erfurt, Johann Fogel, who is known to have bound two copies of the 42-line Bible.

Panel-stamped bindings were introduced into France and England from Holland by itinerant journeyman bookbinders, many of whom, like the printers, led an unsettled life. The bindings executed for Caxton's establishment still had their decoration made with small stamps, but his followers, especially the printers in Cambridge, used panel-stamping almost exclusively. The process also made progress in England in artistic respects.

Oriental Bookmaking and Its
Influence in Italy

An entirely different and more significant development in contemporary bookbinding took place in Italy, which had active contact with the Orient. At the close of the 15th century, at the very time when book printing was developing and expanding under the influence of the Renaissance, bookbinders came from the Orient to Italy, bringing with them various special techniques and new ideas for decoration.

43. Dutch panel-stamped binding from about 1520. (Royal
Library, Copenhagen.)   The same stamp is repeated four times and
includes the name of the binder, Joris de Gavere.   The middle
space between the panels shows Mary on the dragon between two
chimeras.

The Orient in this case refers only to the Islamic part.
Bookbinding was not used in China and India.   Chinese books, then
as today, received a covering of colored paper or silk, and the narrow palm leaves used for writing in India were gathered between two
decorated endpieces of wood.   But in the Mohammedan world leather

bindings were used as in Europe.

The Persians, in particular, were masters of the art of producing and decorating leather bindings and held a prominent position
in the field of bookmaking. In the time of Tamerlane and his successors calligraphy was practiced with considerable artistry, and in
the 15th century Persian miniature painting flourished. It continued
and was further refined in the two succeeding centuries. Not only
were the illustrations painted but the first page of text was adorned
with rich and colorful designs (ser-i-lauh) consisting of minute stylized flower and leaf ornaments or the arabesques (also called mauresques) so characteristic of Islamic art. In Persian bindings the
back cover was extended to form a flap that could be folded over
half of the front cover and could be decorated along with it. The
ornamentation on the covers usually consisted of an almond-shaped
central design and four corner ornaments--the design principle known
so well from Persian rugs. The center and the corners were filled
with small stylized leaves and flowers, arabesques or entwined
knots, the whole being pressed down into the leather and for the
most part gilded with gold leaf or gold dust. The space between
the pressed ornaments was often decorated with leaf and flower designs in color.

Neither the idea of the flap nor the gilding originated in Islam; they go back to Coptic book binding, and Islamic binding represents a further development of the Coptic pattern. The finest Islamic bindings from the 14-15th centuries showed a highly developed
surface decoration and brilliant technique, and they stood far above
European binding at that time. The art spread from Persia to the
western countries of Islam, including Turkey. In the 15th century
it began to influence the work of Italian bookbinders and turned western binding into entirely new paths. In this connection note should
also be taken of the Moorish bindings that were made in Spain.

The Italian binders learned the art of gold tooling from their
Islamic teachers. Blind-stamping was not immediately given up entirely; gold tooling was at first used sparingly along with blind-
stamped decorations, as in the bindings that belonged to the Hungarian King Corvinus. Some of these must have been made in Buda-

44.   Persian binding from the 16th century.   The decoration on the flap forms a unit with that of the cover, which is partly
covered by the flap.   The binding shown here illustrates the typical
decoration seen also in Persian rugs; this is a luxury binding made
for a valuable manuscript.   Similar decorative patterns are found
on Turkish bindings.   Besides leather bindings the Persians and
Turks also used lacquered paper bindings.   The paper was covered
with chalk and a thin coating of lacquer; water colors were painted
on and then another coating of lacquer applied.

pest in the years 1470-90 by a binder who had become acquainted

with Islamic style from southeastern Europe, for the decoration

shows unmistakable Oriental features.   They are probably the earli-

est bindings in Europe on which gold tooling is found.   But it was

not used exclusively; only the central field and the corner ornaments

were in gold, while the borders along the edges of the covers were

blind-stamped.

These Corvinian bindings were the precursors of Italian Renaissance binding, which was to be the mature fruit of the influence from the Orient. An important contribution to this development was made by the great printer and publisher Aldus Manutius, the most famous of the Venetian printers.

Aldus Manutius Introduces Italic Type

Aldus Manutius, or, as he later called himself, Aldus Pius Manutius, had studied both the Greek and Latin classics and had composed small grammatical textbooks of these languages. He had a full humanistic background when he started his printing and publishing business in Venice around 1490. This purpose, in part, was to issue critical editions of the ancient classical writers, and the first book from his press was a 1495 edition of a standard Greek grammar. Greek books had been printed in Italy, imitating the calligraphy of Greek manuscripts. Aldus introduced a Greek type cut on the pattern of contemporary Greek handwriting with its many abbreviated forms. The first Latin book from Aldus' press was Pietro Bembo's dialog about Aetna (1495), printed in a roman type that became the model for later French types including Garamond's.

At the beginning Aldus gave his books the usual folio or quarto format, but in a Virgil edition of 1501 he broke completely with tradition and started printing the classics in octavo format--almost a pocket format--with an entirely new typeface (Fig. 47) adapted to the reduced size of the page. This type imitated the humanistic cursive handwriting, and like Aldus' roman type it was cut by Francesco Griffo of Bologna. It can best be described as a form of roman type that slopes slightly to the right. Called italic, or cursive, it has continued to the present day, although it is now used mainly for emphasizing individual words or lines. The term "Aldines" refers particularly to the small classical texts printed in italic which Aldus issued over a period of years. Among them were editiones principes, that is, first editions printed directly from hitherto unpublished manuscripts. At first Aldus did the philological work connected with these editions, but as his publishing business grew he had a whole company of scholars--"Aldi Neacademia" it was called--in

45. Three famous printers' marks: Fust and Schöffer, Aldus Manutius and Christophe Plantin.

ALDVS PIVS MANVTIVS.

46. Aldus Manutius, born 1449, died 1515. From a 16th-century engraving. His printer's mark is shown in Fig. 45. Aldus was the first publisher to issue a catalog giving the prices of his books.

his shop and in his home.

The popularity of Aldines, with their handsome printer's mark, a dolphin twined about an anchor (Fig. 45), became so great that they were soon imitated. In Lyons, in particular, a large number of counterfeit Aldines were produced; they were more or less successful copies, even including the printer's mark. Aldines were used a great deal by students; so many copies were worn out that some editions are now very great rarities. Their fame was not due only to their format and the new italic type, or to their good paper

IVNII IVVENALIS AQVINA
TIS SATYRA PRIMA.

EMPER EGO AVDITOR
tantum?nunquám ne reponem
S   V exatus toties raua theseide
Codri?
I mpune ergo mihireatauerit ille
togatus?
H ic elegos?impune diem confumpferit ingens
T elephus?aut fummi plena iam margine libri
S criptus,et in tergo nec dum finitus,Oreftes?
N ota magis nulli domus est sua,quam mihi lucus
M artis,et æoliis uicinum rupibus antrum
V ulcani. Quid agant uenti,quas torqueat umbras
A eacus,unde alius furtuæ deuehat aurum
P elliculæ,quantas iaculetur Monychus ornos,
F rontonis platani,conuulsáq; marmora clamant
S emper,et assiduo ruptæ lectore columnæ.
E xpectes eadem a summo, minimóq; poeta.
E t nos ergo manum ferulæ subduximus,et nos
C onsilium dedimus Syllæ,priuatus ut altum
D ormiret.ftulta eft clementia,cum tot ubique
V atibus ocurras,perituræ parare chartæ.
C ur tamen hoc libeat potius decurrere campo,
P er quem magnus equos Auruncæ flexit alumnus,
S i uacat,et placidi rationem admittitis,edam.
C um tener uxorem ducat fpado,Meuia thufcum
F igat aprum,et nuda teneat uenabula mamma,
P atricios omnes opibus cum prouocat unus,
A ii

47. Page from Aldus' edition of Virgil, 1501, printed in
italic type. Space has been left for painting in the initial S.

and excellent workmanship, but also to the care that was taken to
provide a correct version of the text. The edition of Aristotle's
works that Aldus published in five folio volumes in 1495-98 was the
first complete edition in Greek.

48.   Venetian initials in the Aldine style.

49.   Headpiece from Aldus' edition of Aristotle, 1497.

The italic typeface was not Aldus' only contribution to book printing. His time is referred to as the Aldine period because he was particularly successful in giving a classical character to the initials, borders and friezes with which he, always in judicious moderation, decorated his books. While Ratdolt's ornaments were mainly executed in
white on a black background, those in Aldus' books were all line drawing without any filling-in of the background, giving a facile and bright
appearance equally well suited to italic type or Greek letters. Every
one of Aldus' friezes and initials is a small masterpiece, whether it is
made up entirely of entwined plants or grotesque masks and other
classical features or whether it shows Oriental influence in its interlaced bands and ribbons. Aldus reached his high point in 1499 when
he issued the allegorical romance of Francesco Colonna, entitled
Hypnerotomachia Poliphili, which depicted, in dream visions, the
realm of classical art. The book contains some 70 illustrations,
mostly line drawings, done in true classical style but with their own
special character. However graceful and poetic these pictures and
the accompanying friezes and vignettes, it is the balance between

them and the text that places this book so high; many persons consider it the most perfect book that has ever come off a printing press.

Aldus' establishment also included a bindery and the Aldine bindings, which in large part were done in "maroquin" or morocco leather (goatskin) from North Africa, were among the first to show definite traces of the influence of Islamic bookbinding. Their wide distribution aided in spreading the knowledge of gold tooling. At first Aldus used only blind-stamping, but later on he added gilded arabesques or flowing lines around the central panel where the title of the book was stamped in gilded roman letters, always showing a fine sense of moderation.

Aldine bindings showed Oriental influence in one respect; instead of the usual wooden core for the covers of the binding Aldus followed the Oriental practice of using cardboard, which was much lighter and more practical, particularly for small formats. Wooden boards did not disappear from bookbinding until the 18th century; as late as the 16th century there were many bindings in which the wooden boards were only partly covered with leather, presumably to save material. Gradually cardboard came more and more into use. Often spoiled sheets, pages from discarded books and pieces of old vellum manuscripts, were pasted together and used as boards; fragments of otherwise unknown texts have sometimes been found inside the covers of old books.

Grolier and His Contemporaries

Of greater importance, however, than Aldus' trade bindings were the luxury bindings that he had made for rich book collectors who were not content with ordinary books but required special copies printed on vellum or large paper, and finely bound. The most famous of these collectors was Jean Grolier, who was born in Lyons in 1479. Between 1510 and 1537 he was in Italy most of the time as a French legate; thereafter he became government treasurer and lived in Paris until his death in 1565.

Aldus, who had dealings with Grolier from 1512 on, presumably had considerable influence on the execution of the highly treas-

Hora quale animale che per la dolce efca,lo occulto dolo non perpen
de,poftponendo el naturale bifogno,retro ad quella inhumana nota fen
cia mora cum uehementia feftinante la uia,io andai. Alla quale quando
eſſere uenuto ragioneuolmente arbitraua,in altra parte la udiua, Oue &
quando a quello loco properante era giunto,altronde apparea eſſere affir
mata. Et cuſi como gli lochi mutaua,ſimilmente piu ſuaue & deleɛteuo-
le uoce mutaua cum cœleſti concenti . Dunque per queſta inane fatica,
& tanto cum moleſta fete corfo hauendo,me debilitai tanto, che apena
poteua io el laſſo corpo fuſtentare. Et gli affannati fpiriti habili non eſſen
do el corpo grauemente affaticato hogi mai foftenire,ſi per el tranſaɛto pa
uore, ſi per la urgente fete, quale per el longo peruagabondo indagare,
& etiam per le graue anxietate, & per la calda hora, difeſo, & reliɛto
dalle proprie uirtute, altro unquantulo deſiderando ne appetendo, fe
non ad le debilitate membra quieto ripofo. Mirabondo dell'accidente
cafo,ſtupido della melliflua uoce,& molto piu per ritrouarme in regio-
ne incognita & inculta, ma aſſai amœno paeſe. Oltra de queſto,forte
me doleua, che el liquente fonte laboriofamente trouato,& cum tanto
folerte inquiſito fuſſe ſublato & perdito da gliochii mei. Per le quale tu-
te cofe,io ſtetti cum lanimo intricato de ambiguitate, & molto trapen-
fofo. Finalmente per tanta laſſitudine correpto,tutto el corpo frigeſcen-

     50. Page from the Hypherotomachia Poliphili of Francesco
Colonna, 1499.

ured Grolier bindings, which were the culmination of Italian Renaissance binding. The entire cover of the book was filled with geometric figures or other designs made by a band or ribbon of two
lines enclosing a central space that contained the title of the book
on the front cover and Grolier's motto on the back. At the bottom
of the front cover there was also the inscription "Jo. Grolierii et

amicorum, " declaring that the book belonged to Grolier and his
friends.   In some of the later bindings the entwining ribbon or strap-
work that formed the basis of the decoration was often emphasized
by being lacquered in color or stained black; the designs it formed
were more arabesque and included branch and leaf ornaments. (Fig.
53). On a number of bindings the leaves and arabesques were done
with hatched or shaded stamps (fers azurês).   The spine of the
book, which earlier had been left bare, was also decorated in some
Grolier bindings; the inner faces of the covers were covered with
vellum and there were several extra pages at the front and back,
some of vellum.   Extraordinary imagination, always with artistic
restraint, was exhibited in the variations of the designs.   Only a
few of the bindings were made at the Aldine press or at other places
in Italy; the majority, including the most artistic, were certainly
made in Paris by binders who had learned the trade in Italy. Grolier's library was sold and widely scattered in the 17th century; only
some 400 Grolier bindings are known today.   These extraordinarily
beautiful calfskin and morocco bindings with their characteristic decoration and inscription are highly prized by collectors.

Some similarity to Grolier's bindings is seen in certain bindings executed for his younger contemporary, Thomas Mahieu (Maiolu), who was secretary to Catherine de Medici in 1549-60. A special feature of his bindings was the braided work, made up of rolled
leaves.   Mahieu also used an inscription on his bindings stating that
the books belonged to him and his friends, as did Grolier.   These
two men were the first real bibliophiles in the modern sense, being
possessed of a passion for beautiful books in beautiful bindings.

Another collector, often named along with Grolier and Mahieu,
was Demetrio Canevari, a physician to the Pope. Certain morocco
bindings of the Aldine type made in Rome in the 1540's have been
wrongly ascribed to Canevari.   The centers of the front covers were
embellished with an oval relief showing Apollo driving his chariot
against a mountain, a design that resembled the earlier cameos (Fig.
54).   It is now established that these cameo bindings belonged to the
Farnese family and were probably made for Cardinal Alessandro
Farnese (later Pope Paul III).   Together with other contemporary

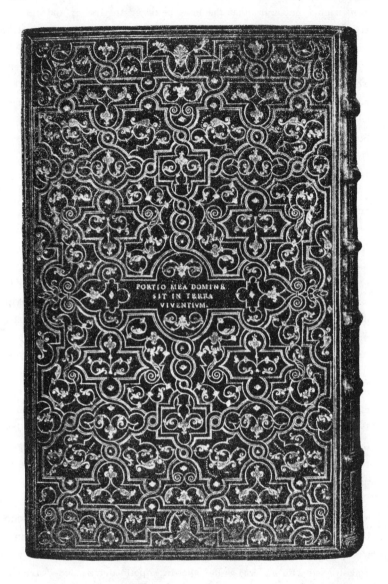

51. Grolier binding (National Library, Vienna) with his motto in the center. This binding is from Grolier's later years; it is in red morocco and the decoration is suggestive of the later fanfare style. A more typical Grolier binding is seen in Fig. 53.

cameo bindings they form a special group within Italian Renaissance binding.   Like several other types of binding in particular demand by present-day collectors, the Farnese bindings have been subject to a number of disappointing imitations.

Aldus died in 1515; his press was continued, but it no longer played any major role. His work was imitated in many respects by another family of printers, the Giunta (Junta), whose members were active up into the 17th century in Italy, Spain and France.   From the establishment of Filippo Giunta in Florence came numerous small editions of the classics printed in italic, and Aldus' publisher bindings were also imitated here, perhaps by the same craftsmen that had worked for Aldus.   The Giunta's trade bindings can be seen on many books in libraries throughout Europe today, indicating the wide distribution they had in their time.   Florence had also developed a flourishing woodcut art that could compete with the Venetian in artistic value; of special fame were the dramatic illustrations for various writings of Savanarola.   Venice, however, continued to maintain its position of leadership in book printing; one of its prominent printers in the second half of the 16th century was Gabriel de Ferrari, who issued about 850 books, many with beautiful woodcut illustrations, ornaments and initials, the latter often containing scenes from classical mythology.

German Woodcut Illustrations

The golden age of woodcut illustration in southern Germany came while Italian bookmaking was celebrating the great triumphs of the Venetian and Florentian printers of the first two decades of the 16th century.   It was in Germany that woodcuts had first been used for illustration, and the development that began in the last years of the incunabula period was introduced by such works as Breydenbach's pilgrim book and Schedel's Weltchronik.   In 1498 Albrecht Dürer's Apocalypse appeared in Nuremberg.   Its fifteen large woodcuts represent one of the epoch-making works of graphic art, for in them the brilliant artistic effect is attained by the interplay of light and shadow alone.   In these woodcuts, and in other series in which Dürer depicted the life and suffering of the Virgin Mary, his deep

52.   Binding made for Thomas Mahieu.   Formerly owned by
Robert Hoe and sold for $3,200 at the auction of his books in 1912.

religious feeling found its full artistic expression.

The course of events in Germany paralleled that in Italy.

53. Binding in yellow calfskin   54. Italian cameo binding from
made for Jean Grolier in the first   about 1550.
half of the 16th century.

Within a surprisingly short span of years the woodcut art developed
to full maturity, then it became an item of fashion, and finally it
declined.   This art, which set its mark on several thousand German
books, was centered in Strassburg first, where some of the great
botanical works (Kräuterbücher) were produced, then in Augsburg
and Basel.   The last of these had early attained fame as the literary
center of German Switzerland and was the place where one of the
most popular books of the time was issued in 1494: Sebastian
Brant's satire Narrenschiff, with its brilliant woodcuts (among them
the famous "book fool" which some have considered the youthful
work of Dürer).   Presumably because of the great church meetings that were held there in 1431-49, Basel was one of the towns
through which the Germanic world first came into contact with
the Italian Renaissance. During the great woodcut period Basel
became the principal seat of German humanism.   There Erasmus
of Rotterdam issued his famous editions of the classics and of the
church fathers.   These outshone even the Aldines in philological

scholarship. Basel was the home of one of the greatest artists in
this field, Hans Holbein the younger. He worked with a first rate
wood-carver, Hans Lützelburger, and with an outstanding printer,
Johan Froben (Frobenius), in whose house Erasmus lived for several years as an active adviser and helper, and where he also issued
the New Testament in Greek (1516).

Together these men were able to create works that attained fame
throughout Europe. Froben was responsible for the typography. He
had a large stock of roman and italic type fonts and used italic not
only for small octavo editions, but for marginal notes in quartos
and folios. Holbein and Lützelburger contributed the handsome title
borders and initials cut in metal plates. In these, a host of small
happy children tumble around in a framework of antique columns
and arches or other Renaissance ornaments. Holbein's illustrations
for the Old Testament, which first appeared in 1538 in a book issued in Lyons, and his depiction of the old Dance of Death motif,
also first issued in Lyons in 1538, were among his most outstanding works. He used a clear and simple woodcut line which was
suitable for either roman or italic type. It produced a pleasing
harmony between the text page and the illustrations, just as in the
Hypnerotomachia, however different the style of these books in other
respects.

The Emperor Maximilian's Books

Augsburg became the second main seat of German Renaissance bookmaking. Its active trade with Venice had been stimulated
by the Renaissance movement south of the Alps. Through the initiative of Emperor Maximilian I this movement soon set its mark on
the books produced in Augsburg and brought new life to an art hitherto dominated by the gothic style. Eager to glorify his own regime
and to strengthen his people's national consciousness, Maximilian
had a number of historical works undertaken. Best known is Teuerdank (Fig. 56), which recounts in allegorical form the emperor's
adventures on his courtship journey to Burgundy. The fame of this
work is due to its illustrations and to the charming lines of its type,
in which the scrolls and flourishes used in the handwriting of the im-

55. Woodcut by Hans Holbein the younger, showing Erasmus of Rotterdam with his hand on a bust of Hermes--a symbol of his literary work. This woodcut, extant in only a few copies, was probably intended for an edition of Erasmus' works, but was never used. (Copper-engraving Collection, Copenhagen.)

110

 Nach inhalt gesprochner vrteyl
Nam der nachrichter an das sayl
Furwittig den vast armen Man
Furt in hinaus für das thor / an
Die stat / daran man die armen lewt
Vmb Ir missetat richte noch hewt
Als Furwittig kein rettung sach
Fieng Er an vnnd offenlich sprach   N iiii

56. Page from <u>Teuerdank</u>, 1517. The type is a forerunner
of fraktur type.

perial documents are transferred to print. This "Teuerdank type" is a sort of forerunner of the so-called fraktur (Latin _fractum_ = broken, bent), a typeface that appeared in 1524 and is recognizable by its "elephant's trunks," scrolls added to the capital letters. Fraktur type was originally made by the Nuremberg type cutter Hieronymus Andreä and from his and other fraktur types developed the form that came into general use in Germany and the countries under her influence during the following centuries and that has continued down to the present day. In Denmark its use was not given up entirely until the last generation. Fraktur type was thus an offshoot of the black-letter or gothic types of the incunabula period and later superseded these.

Another somewhat earlier offshoot was the so-called Schwabacher type (the origin of the name is uncertain) which also came from Nuremberg. In it the sharp features of black-letter type were more or less rounded off, so that it constituted a German variant of the Italian rounded-gothic type; its lines were too heavy for ordinary use, though in the Reformation period it was used extensively throughout all Germany (Fig. 58).

Teuerdank was published for the first time in 1517, printed by the imperial court printer, Hans Schönsperger. Like the other works planned by the Emperor Maximilian but only partly completed, it is famous for its large illustrations, which almost make it a picture book with supplemental text rather than an illustrated text. Albrecht Dürer, Lucas Cranach the elder, Hans Burgkmair, Daniel Hopfer and many other excellent artists worked for Maximilian. Dürer illustrated a magnificent prayer book for the Knights of St. George, which was to have been used as propaganda for the Crusades. Because of the Emperor's early death it was never finished.

Just as the Grolier bindings and the other luxury bindings were of great significance in the history of art but did not reach beyond the circle of the wealthy, so the woodcut masterpieces, although produced in large numbers, represented only individual high points rising above the ordinary level of book production.

Also of high quality were many of the missals, choir books, breviaries, psalters and other large liturgical works produced by the

Dem Durchleuchtigen Hochge=
bornen Fürsten vnd Herrn / Herrn Ferdinan=
den / Ertzhertzogen zu Osterreich / Hertzogen zu Bur=
gundi / rc. Graffen zu Tyrol / rc. Meinem gne=
digen Fürsten vnd Herrn.

Vrchleuchtiger hoch
geborner Fürst / Gnediger Herr /
Euwer Fürstlichen Durchleuchtig=
keyt seyen meine vnterthenige gehor=
same dienst jeder zeyt zuvor / Gnedi=
ger Herr. Der Großmechtig Keyser
Heinrich / dieses Namens der Erste / zugenannt der Vog=
ler / seliger vñ hochlöblicher gedechtnuß / nach dem er mehr

57. Fraktur type as used by Sigismund Feuerabend in
Frankfort, 1566.

Silla der römisch rattherr hat nach vil tatte in dem Jugurthinischē krieg
geübet die ere vnd glori eins keysers von dem römischen rat erlangt. ð
dañ wider Mithridatem geschickt in Achaia vnd asia obsiget. diser was auß
dem alten vnd hohberümbten geslecht der Scipioner geporn vñ all sein tag
von iugent auff in vbung schentlicher lesterlicher henndel gestanden. bis er
vnder Mario wider Jugurtham zu dem rentmaister ambt geordnet wardt
in demselben ambt verwädelt er sein leben gantz. dañ er hat Jngurtham gefet
tent. Mitridatem geschwaigt. die bettrübnus des gesellischen kriegs nyderge
drugckt. die herrschung Cinne zerbrochen vnd Marium in das ellend gezwü
gen. Er was in kriechyscher vnd lateinischer schrift gar wol erfarñ. gesprech.
paldfahig. geschickt. eregirig. milt vnnd großmüetig. also das man zweyfeln
mocht ob er stercker oder glückfaliger wer. Als er nw zu einem dictator vnnd

58. Schwabacher type as used by Anton Koberger in Nuremberg, 1493.

Church in large numbers. In the period 1457-1525 Germany alone
printed between 550 and 600 liturgical works. A variety of large
and small typefaces were used to indicate the various divisions of
the liturgical text and there was a continual interchange of red and
black ink, giving these folios a very decorative appearance. Many
large presses made a specialty of liturgical books; Mainz, Leipzig,
Speier, Cologne, Magdeburg, Basel, Geneva, Paris, Lyons and Venice were the seats of the greatest activity in this field. Outstanding
artists contributed to these books. The same is true to some extent of the small French livres d'heures, as well as the corresponding German devotional books--Seelengärtlein (Garden of the Soul),
and the so-called Heiltumsbücher, guides for the towns to which pil-
grims traveled. Lucas Cranach worked on one of the most successful of the latter. Many of these small devotional books showed indi-
cations of the tendency to overcrowding that later in the century
brought on the decline of the woodcut art in Italy, France and Germany.

Books of the Reformation Period

The great revolutionary developments that followed 1517, when
Luther began his fight against the Church of Rome, left deep traces
on the history of the book. It has been said, with some justification, that the invention of printing was the basis of the rapid triumph of the Reformation.

Printing was one of the most effective weapons of the new
movement but there was usually no thought of putting more work on
the physical features of the book than was absolutely necessary; this
was ephemeral literature and had to be sold cheaply in order to ful-
fill its mission. Poor quality paper was used; Schwabacher and
fraktur type, in anything but flawless form, took the place of the
older black-letter type; the same worn-out woodcuts were used in
one publication after another; the workmanship became more and more
routine so that the products acquired an almost factory-like appearance. This was generally true of the literary production of the
Reformation. On the other hand, the Reformation brought with it
a hitherto unknown democratization of the book, the effect of

which can scarcely be overestimated. Our present efforts at popular enlightenment can be said to have originated in the interest
that Lutheranism showed in the spiritual life of the ordinary
man.

Now North Germany came to the forefront. Wittenberg, with
its newly founded university, suddenly became an important center
of the book world. Here a great deal of Luther's enormous production of sermons and devotional and polemic writings was printed,
especially at the press of Melchior Lotter the younger. Lotter also printed the famous first edition of Luther's translation of the New
Testament (September and December 1522). The first complete
Bible translation, beautifully illustrated, was printed in 1534 by another Wittenberg printer, Hans Lufft. Two of Lucas Cranach's
sons made the borders and initials for many of the Luther items.
In spite of Luther's protests many of his works, including the
Bibles, were reprinted on a large scale, even by respectable printers, in towns such as Basel, Augsburg, Nuremberg and Strassburg.

Business boomed for the itinerant booksellers. In addition
to the Bibles that they sold from their booths, they now could offer
hymn books in German. Luther's catechism was a particularly popular item and one of Luther's pamphlets sold 4,000 copies in five
days. More than 100 editions of the New Testament were issued between 1519-34, selling a total of about 20,000 copies. The whole of
Germany, both town and country, was overrun by book agents selling the numerous pamphlets issued by both Lutherans and Catholics.

The regular book dealers, many of whom were both publishers and booksellers, also handled a good deal of the new literature,
particularly the larger works. Twice a year, in the spring and in
the fall, they met at the fair in Frankfurt and traded books among
themselves sheet for sheet. Greater and more varied activity developed here than ever before, and the book trade of Germany as
well as of other countries was represented. Later, however, the
fair in Leipzig took precedence over the Frankfurt fair and Leipzig
continued until recently to be the center of the German book trade.
The first catalogs of the books on sale at the fair were printed in
1564; from these fair catalogs developed the excellent semi-annual

German trade catalogs of later times.

Destruction of Monastery Libraries

Although the Reformation gave rise to flourishing literary activity, it also became the occasion for the destruction of many books
already in existence. In its fight against the Church of Rome it
turned against Catholic literature, and many old monastery manuscripts and incunabula suffered a sad fate. During the peasant up-
risings in Germany in 1524-25 German monastic libraries suffered
very great losses, just as French monastic libraries did later, during the Huguenot wars.

Nevertheless, it is unjust to ascribe to the followers of the
Reformation the chief blame for the fact that so little of the great
book treasures of the Middle Ages has been preserved. A great
deal had been destroyed earlier by the many fires that ravaged
churches and monasteries and by the monks' own carelessness. A
great deal has also been destroyed by fire and wars in more recent
times.

After the first excitement of the Reformation, the Lutheran
church was not without appreciation of the value of medieval manuscripts. In Denmark, for example, an order issued at the church
conference in Odense in 1577 said, "The old books of the church,
missals, graduals, hymn books and Bibles, whether on vellum or
paper, must not be thrown away or used as binding for other books. "
Luther himself, in a letter to the leaders of the German states in
1524, specified that neither money nor effort was to be spared to
establish "gute Libareyen odder Bücherheuser, " especially in the
larger towns. The result of this was the establishment of many new
"Stadtbibliotheken" and church and school libraries. Luther's friend,
the Wittenberg pastor Johann Bugenhagen, was especially zealous in
carrying out this order. To a large extent these libraries were
based on existing collections from the Catholic period.

Few of these new institutions were important in comparison
with the great monastery libraries. The influence of the Reformation on the history of libraries was indirect. When the governments
began to confiscate church and monastery property the book collec-

tions came into the possession of the state, and often the old books
received no gentle treatment.   The situation was at its worst in
England, since secularization came very soon after the triumph of
the Reformation and the destructive urge was still at its height.   In
the first two or three decades following secession from the Church
of Rome, the larger part of the 1,000 or so monastery and church
libraries throughout the land were secularized, and in many instances the books fared badly.   It might have been expected that the
well-known English attachment to everything old and honorable would
have made itself felt, but this occurred in only a very limited degree.   Henry VIII's librarian, John Leland, made a trip around the
country in 1536-42 and was able to save some of the most valuable
book treasures from destruction.   On the other hand, the famous
library in Oxford, which went back to the 14th century, was plundered in 1550 by Edward VI's men, who burned some of the books
and sold others.   Six years later the empty shelves were also sold.
Not until half a century thereafter, in 1602, was the library reestablished, through the efforts of one of Queen Elizabeth's statesmen, Thomas Bodley.   Named in his honor, the Bodleian Library
has become the second largest library in England (Fig. 114).

      In Denmark the situation was somewhat better.   King Chris-
tian III commissioned a German teacher to visit churches and monasteries to collect books for the Library of the University of Copenhagen.   A large number of books was collected in this manner.   In
adding to its collection--50 rix-dollars were available annually for
book purchases--the library followed the procedure recommended by
Luther: first the missing works of the church fathers were acquired, then Latin and Greek authors, and finally books on law,
medicine and natural science.   A similar development took place in
Luther's own country, where both the existing and the newly established university libraries, such as those at Marburg, Königsberg,
and Jena, acquired many books from the monasteries.

      Later in the century the University of Copenhagen Library
received additions from the old monastery and church collections and
the royal historiographers also obtained some source material from
them.   What was left after that was usually destroyed.   Local offi-

cials or their scribes, both in Denmark and in Norway, had no respect for the order from the Odense conference.   They cut up great
numbers of the old vellum manuscripts and used them as covers for
their accounts and tax lists, or cut them into strips to strengthen
the backs of bindings.   Pages of old Saxo Grammaticus manuscripts,
for instance, have been found used as covers on Kronborg Castle's
court rolls for 1627-28.   The custom of using vellum as covers for
books or as inlays for bindings was so general that by the middle
of the 17th century there was very little of it left.

In Italy, France, Austria and South Germany, old Catholic
libraries, after a brief priod of disorder, continued to exist as before and new collections were also established, especially where the
Jesuits were in control.   It was not until the 18th and 19th centuries that the civil governments took over the medieval book collections.

Book Printing and Binding in Denmark
During the Reformation

Just as the Protestant movement excluded from its church
services the brilliant colors and the beautiful music of the Catholic
church, so it also pushed artistic decoration of books into the background in favor of the text itself.   Protestant liturgical books did
not measure up to those of the previous period.   If, for instance,
a book like the oldest complete Danish Bible translation, Christian
III's Bible, which was issued in Copenhagen in 1550 in 3,000 copies,
is placed alongside the great German works of the Dürer period, it
will not appear to advantage, although its woodcuts have many good
points.   This Bible is typical of its time.   With respect to book
printing Denmark was at that time only a province of North Germany,
and Christian III's Bible was printed by a German printer, Ludwig
Dietz, who had been called to Denmark for that purpose.   It was
simply a copy of a Low-German Bible that Dietz had made earlier;
its many woodcuts were also made by a German artist.

Many book printers were drawn into the conflicts of the Reformation period and had to take sides.   Paul Raeff, the first Danish-born printer; worked in the service of the Catholics and printed

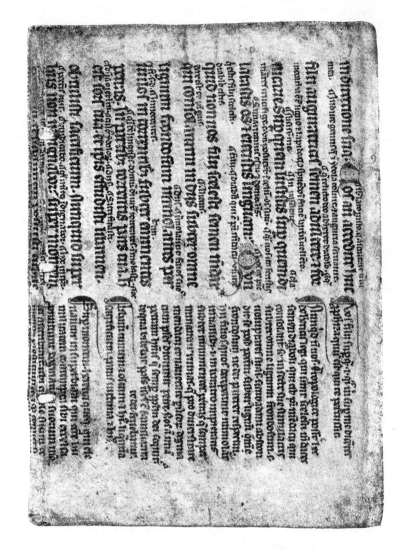

59. Binding for a 15th-century book made from a parchment manuscript sheet. (Royal Library, Copenhagen.)

such things as Poul Helgesen's writings. An immigrant German, Hans Vingaard, issued a number of Protestant pamphlets from his press in Viborg and later in Copenhagen worked for Peder Palladius.

Malmö was one of the chief printing centers of the Danish Reformation. Here the earliest preserved Danish editions of Luther's Catechism were issued. Christiern Pederson, who had returned after
many years abroad, bringing with him a large stock of type and a
Dutch typographer, worked in Malmö from 1533 to 1535. In 1514
he had had the first edition of Saxo's great Denmark Chronicle
printed by the famous printer Ascenius in Paris. This imposing
work, which is not excessively rare, has title borders in Renaissance style and its initials carry Pedersen's signature. In his Malmö editions he also used Renaissance ornaments and he was the
first to use italic type in Denmark. Roman type appeared for the
first time in 1538 in the work of a Roskilde printer, Hans Barth,
in a Latin work by Melanchthon.

     Denmark was also subsidiary to Germany in matters of bind-
ing. The names of a number of Swedish bookbinders of the 16th
century are known but very little is known about Danish bookbinding
of this period. One Danish binder was Niels Poulsen, who became
court binder in 1559 at an annual salary of 100 Danish marks; the
initials of a few others are known from their bindings. It can safe-
ly be assumed that a large number of Danish bindings were made in
German shops or by Germans who had learned their trade there.
When Christian III had his great Bible translation bound for use in
churches, he called in both a French and a German binder.

Roller-stamped Bindings

     In Germany panel-stamped bindings had gradually been adopted
and were the prevailing type throughout the 16th century, even though
decoration was not entirely stamped from plates. As early as 1469
a new tool, the roller or roulette, had appeared in German binderies. The design was engraved on the edge of a narrow wheel,
and as this was pushed over the moistened leather under heavy pressure a continuous frame or border was produced. This instrument
saved much effort and time for the binder. Its use spread rapidly
and has continued down to the present. The designs engraved on the
roulettes were small religious pictures (figures of Christ or biblical
scenes), allegorical representations of the Christian virtues, or por-

60. Binding made for Tycho Brahe. His portrait is plate-
stamped in gold; the decoration is blind-stamped with roulettes.
(Röhsska Museum, Gothenburg.)

traits of princes and rulers. No attention was paid to the fact that
on the horizontal parts of the border the figures were lying down.
Rollers often were used for the central field also, though here panel-
stamping predominated. At the time of the Reformation, pictures of
Luther and Melanchthon, either busts or full figures, often were
used on front and back covers respectively. There are some bindings for which Lucas Cranach the younger drew portraits of these
two principle personages of the Reformation. Portraits of princes
and other nobles or of classical authors were also common. Many
of these binding portraits indicate that they were made in a country
where the art of wood and metal carving had reached a high stage
of development.

The binding most frequently encountered in Germany and the
Scandinavian countries during the century of the Reformation and
long afterwards was stereotyped in appearance. It was made of
calfskin, parchment or bleached pigskin. Two or three rolled borders within one another enclosed a relatively small panel-stamped
central field. This was often divided horizontally, so that the owner's initials were in the upper part and the year of binding below,
while the center section was taken up by a picture or by the owner's
coat of arms--the whole being blind-stamped. There was no decoration on the spine, but the heavy cording of vellum or hemp bulged
out under the leather and divided the spine into several sections.

The smooth spines that later became common appeared on a
few 16th-century bindings. In these the cording was set down into
slots cut across the backs of the pages. After the middle of the
century gold stamping became more and more common in this type
of binding. Some of the best gold-tooled bindings were those made
for Count Otto Heinrich for his library in Heidelberg. The arabesques and interlaced ribbons known from Italian bindings began ap-
pearing more and more frequently.

Jakob Krause Bindings
Italian influence is rarely found in German bindings except
in Saxony. Together with the Palatinate, Saxony became a center
for German bookbinding and the Electors of Saxony, like the Count

Palatine, had many gold-tooled bindings of the type described above.
Under the Elector August, a connoisseur of art and books who ruled
1553-86, the development took a definite oriental-Italian turn. Together with his Danish-born queen, Anna, the daughter of Christian
III, he collected a large library. The bindings were made by Jakob
Krause between 1566 and 1585, and after 1574 also by Caspar Meuser, both outstanding men in their craft. Krause had been appren-
ticed at Augsburg to Antoni Ludwig, who had originally worked as a
bookbinder in Venice, so that many of the Elector's bindings exhibited the characteristics of Venetian Renaissance binding--paper
inlay, gold tooling, the standard oriental ornamental designs, the
arabesques and intertwined bands of the Grolier style, spine decoration, etc. Krause mastered all this and was able to combine the
decorative elements in a multitude of different ways. Some covers
were filled with vines or leaves and flowers in the French style.
The designs were gilded, sometimes tooled and painted. Even though
the Krause bindings were mainly imitations and were not always free
of overcrowding, they exhibited brilliant technical execution. A number of Krause bindings are still preserved, but the greatest collection of them, comprising over 800 items, was largely destroyed
when the Sächsische Landesbibliothek was demolished during the second World War.

The gem bindings of the Middle Ages experienced a sort of
revival in the 16th century in Germany. Twenty silver bindings
from the collection of Duke Albrecht of Prussia are especially famous; they were made by a silversmith in Königsberg, and are now
one of the principal treasures of the University library.

French Renaissance Bookmaking

The Grolier style of binding played a significant role at only
one place in Germany, but in France it was adopted widely. With
the return of Grolier to his native land in 1537 the influence of the
Italian Renaissance began to assert itself in French binderies, as
shown by the bindings made in Lyons and by bindings made for King
Francis I. Francis I was the first to introduce compulsory deposit
of books. In 1537 he ordered all French presses to deliver a copy

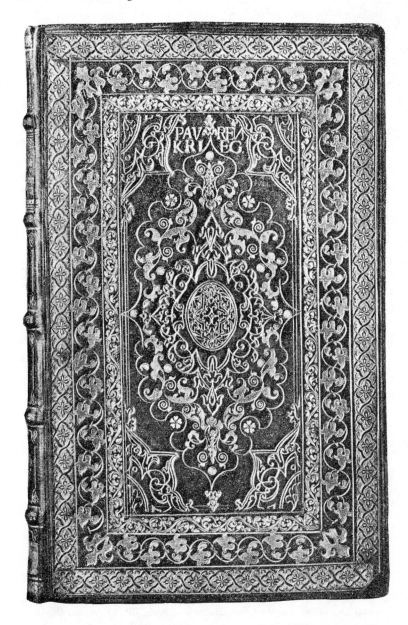

61.   Binding by Jakob Krause in brown calfskin with gold
tooling.   (Landesbibliothek, Dresden.)

of everything they printed to the royal library. Several of his bindings, which were usually in black calfskin, have typical Grolier ornaments. In the central panel on the cover there were the French
coat-of-arms and the king's own seal, a salamander in flames.
Others of Francis I's bindings were decorated with rows of fleurs-
de-lis alternating with his initial, F; these fleur-de-lis bindings were
a very popular style of French book binding for a long time.

When Geoffroy Tory became the first "royal printer" in Paris,
in 1530, the gothic style was still dominant in French books though
Italian influence had begun to make itself felt and the roman type had
found its way into quite a few French books. It was used, for instance, by Jodocus Badius Ascenius, who printed numerous works
of Erasmus and other great humanists of the period. However,
when Tory in the years following 1520 turned from scholarship to
art and developed his remarkable talents as a designer and stamp-
cutter, roman type and Renaissance book decoration experienced their
flowering in France. Outstanding among Tory's work is a series
of Books of Hours which he decorated with illustrations and single-
lined borders that harmonized well with the roman type of the text.
The most famous of his works is Champfleury, issued in 1529--a book
that concerns itself with the question of orthography and the esthet-
ics of typography. In designing his type Tory drew the letters
within a square that was divided into smaller squares. Among those
who followed him were Simon de Colines, who published small editions of the classics patterned after those of Aldus and printed in
three italic typefaces cut by himself, and Robert Granjon, who was
active in Lyons from 1557 on as a printer and as a type cutter.
Granjon supplied large quantities of type to famous European presses.
He created his "civilité" type from an expanded italic. This type
gained wide acceptance and Granjon's composite flower and leaf ornaments also became standard equipment in printing shops.

The most famous of the Renaissance presses that broke with
the gothic tradition was that of the Étienne family in Paris, whose
most prominent member was Robert Étienne (Robertus Stephanus).
Like Aldus, Froben, Tory and several other great printers he was
a scholar; in 1532 he compiled and issued a great Latin lexicon.

Like Tory he was appointed royal printer by Francis I. He was in
continuous struggle with the theologians of the University of Paris,
who attacked him because of his sympathy for the reform movement,
which he exhibited in his editions of the Bible. Finally, in spite of
the royal protection, he was forced to leave the country. Étienne
also used Hebrew and Greek characters; the latter were cut by one
of Tory's pupils, Claude Garamond (Garamont). Garamond also cut
a roman type in several variations, somewhat like that of Nicolaus
Jenson but with a lighter and finer line; it has become recognized
as one of the best proportioned types ever created. Modern Garamond typefaces made for linotype use have gained acceptance in several countries. Robert Étienne's son, Henri, continued to operate
the family press and was also in contact with the great Augsburg
merchant family Fugger, several members of whom were book collectors on a scale uncommon in middle class circles in Germany at
that time. Johann Jakob Fugger had some of his bindings made in
Paris and some by Antoni Ludwig in Augsburg.

On certain fine bindings made for Étienne, Grolier ornaments
occur again, and the same is true of several bindings made for
Henry II, who was an even greater friend and protector of books
than his predecessor, Francis I. Henry II's reign (1547-59) came
when Italy had already begun to recede into the background with respect to bookmaking. Signs of degeneration were also beginning to
appear in contemporary French book illustration, mainly in some of
the small Books of Hours issued as luxury items.

It was at this same time that fine bookbinding in France
reached its height. The bindings that Henry II had made for himself, for his queen, Catherine of Medici, and for his mistress, Diana of Poitiers, were imitated by other book collectors at the court
and by the nobility. They were, at least in technical respects,
among the best that have ever been produced in France. With their
characteristic monograms, an H intertwined with a C or a D, and
often with halfmoons and the bow-and-arrow symbol of Diana, god-
dess of the hunt, they show that French book binders had not only
adopted the spirit of the Grolier style but had learned to manifest
it in an independent manner.

62.   Final page of Geoffroy Tory's Champfleury (Paris, 1529) with his mark and a decorative border.   Tory's mark (a broken vase, pot cassé) is an imitation of a woodcut in Hypnerotomachia Poliphili.

miſerables condition-ſ d'adminiſtre, e regie ſes citez e
prouinces, eſquelles diligence eſt pleine dc rancune, negligen-
ce & blaſme e meſprie : eſquelles ſeureité eſt dangereuſe, libe-
raſité non aggreable, ſe parlee plaiy d'embucghes, flaterie per-
nicieuſe, ſe front familiere à toue, l'eſprit de pluſieure plaiy d'in-
dignatioy, courrouy ſecrette, et flatterie ouuerte : toute ſeſ-
quelles choſe attendent ſes pretture ſenante y poſſeſſioy de
ſeure dignitez, elle ſeruent à cuy quand iſe ſom, preſene, et ſe
delaiſſent ſore quiſ s'iy ſom.

63. Robert Granjon's "Caractères de civilité," designed
from an expanded gothic-type and used by Plantin and others.

Olympius Iupiter: eius autem quod in Pythiis fit certaminis, Apollo. Prin-
cipium igitur huiuſmodi orationis, quæcumq; fuerit, laus dei nobis fit, tam-
quam vultus ſeu perſona quædam ſplendida, in ſermonis initio poſita atque
conſtituta. Laudandi autem exordium, ab iis quæ deo inſunt, eique attri-
buuntur, prout res copiam ſuppeditent, ſumes. Si quidem Iupiter fuerit, ad-
ducendum erit, deorum regem, rerumque omnium opificem eſſe : Si vero
Apollo, muſices inuétorem exſtitiſſe, & eundem eſſe cum ſole: Solem autem
omnium omnibus bonorum auctorem. Præterea ſi Hercules erit, Iouis eſſe
filium: & ea quæ mortalium vitæ præbuit, cónumerabis. Et locus ferme có-
plebitur ex ijs quæ quilibet aut inuenerit, aut hominibus tradiderit. Verum
hæc breuibus narrabis; ne præcedens oratio ſequenti maior euadere videa-
tur. Deinceps vrbis laudes, in qua publicus conuentus celebratur, vel a ſitu,

64. Garamond's roman, designed from Nicolaus Jenson's
15th-century type, which was also the model for Aldus' and many
other roman types.

Fine bookbinding flourished under both Charles IX and Henry
III. Henry III, in particular, was passionately fond of fine bindings
and had as his royal binder (relieur du Roy) Nicolas Eve, who was
also engaged in bookselling and publishing in Paris. In some of
Eve's bindings the entire cover is filled with the French fleurs-de-
lis, but he was especially known for his "fanfare" style, in which

65.   Binding made for Henry II and Diana of Poitiers.
(Royal Library, Copenhagen.)

66.   Fanfare binding with J. A. de Thou's coat-of-arms in the
center, from about 1575.   Some fanfare bindings have the spirals
set even more closely together, almost completely covering the surface.

the greater part of the cover is closely filled with spiraling flower plants, palms and laurel branches. Decoration of this type could only develop in a country where the art of gold tooling had been completely mastered, for the golden threads that covered the sides and back of the binding in graceful swirls were made with a great many small stamps put together with unusual craftsmanship. The name fanfare was probably not used until the 19th century, when Nodier had one of his books, Les fanfares, bound in a similar style.

The style continued in use even after the deaths of Henry III and Nicolas Eve and there are many examples of it in the great collections of the French nobility. One is the collection of the statesman and historian, Jacques Auguste de Thou, whose father had been Grolier's friend and whose library numbered some 8,000 printed volumes and about 1,000 manuscripts. De Thou's books are easy to recognize because the bindings carry his coat-of-arms with the three wasps and the monogram IADT. His books were sold by one of his descendants in 1788.

French trade bindings and other ordinary bindings of the 16th century were very little influenced by the fine bindings described above. They were made of calf or pigskin or vellum, and their designs were either blind or gilded panel-stampings or were made up of blind designs with roller stamps.

English Roller-stamped and
Embroidered Bindings

Use of rollers became even more general in England than in France as the artisans in Cambridge gradually began using them in preference to other stamps. In fact, many of their bindings were made entirely with rollers, the central field being filled with rolled borders. The English designs were quite different from those used in Germany; they included dancing figures and strange animal forms, or S-shaped flower branches and leaves. Along toward the middle of the century, however, the Italian Renaissance binding styles and gold tooling came to England. The English court and nobles were interested in books, although not to the same extent or in such an elaborate style as among the French nobility. Both Henry VII and

Henry VIII, as well as Edward VI and Queen Elizabeth, collected
books and had them bound in fine bindings in the French or Italian
manner.   Henry VIII and Edward VI's bookbinders were French and
successfully imitated the Aldine and Grolier styles.   One of the
many collectors among the nobility, Thomas Wotton, has been called
"the English Grolier" because he imitated the great French book collector even to the extent of having his bindings inscribed "Thomas
Wottoni et amicorun. " Queen Elizabeth was very fond of velvet and
silk bindings on which the decoration was embroidered in gold or
silver thread or colored silk thread and sometimes with pearls--a
style of binding that was used by the English royal house all through
the 16th and 17th centuries.   But like the earlier gem bindings these
textile bindings were atypical of the bookbinding art.

Plantin. The Final Flowering
of German Woodcut Art

        The great Belgian bookmaker Christopher Plantin was born
in France and was originally a bookbinder.   But it was as printer
and publisher that he made his name one of the greatest in the history of typography.   His shop was in the flourishing city of Antwerp,
where over half of all the presses of the Netherlands were located
in the first half of the 16th century.   He issued over 1,600 works,
some of them quite large, in the course of the forty years or so
before his death in 1589.   His stock of type was so extensive that
he was able to print books in all languages then known in Europe;
his Polyglot Bible in eight volumes gave the text in four different
languages (Fig. 68).   Few printer-publishers have had as a wide a
market as he; his publications were sold in Germany and Scandinavia,
in France, Spain and England, and he had branches in Leyden and
Paris.   He printed scientific works on philology, law, mathematics,
etc., as well as classical authors, French literature, theological
works and a series of large liturgical works.   His mark was a hand
with a pair of dividers and his motto was "labore et constantia"
(Fig. 45).

        Plantin's broad and heavy roman type, cut by Granjon and
other French artisans, was scarcely inferior to Etienne's and his

italic almost surpassed that of Aldus. Like his predecessors, he
had scholars in his service and his son-in-law, Frans Raphelengius,
who inherited the press in Antwerp, was a learned man. Two other
sons-in-law took over branches; a son of one of these, Balthasar
Moretus, later became known for his collaboration with Rubens.
Plantin's great business brought together a whole colony of printers,
typecasters, punch-cutters, illustrators and bookbinders. Their activity continued until 1876, when the Belgian government purchased
the beautiful ancestral house in Antwerp which had been the headquarters of the establishment and made it into a museum (Musée
Plantin-Moretus). The old workrooms are still preserved as an
instructive presentation of early typographic methods and working
conditions. Unfortunately the museum was damaged in the bombard-
ments of World War II.

        Plantin used woodcuts generously.   Since the art of wood
carving was on the decline, he also made considerable use of the
new process of copperplate engraving. Around the middle of the
16th century wood carving experienced a revival in Germany. The
great publisher Sigismund Feuerabend in Frankfort brought together
a group of artists who collaborated on a number of large Bibles and
editions of the classics. The best known of this group are Hans Se-
bald Beham, Jost Amman (Amann), Virgil Solis and Tobias Stimmer. An especially popular work was the woodcut book prepared
by Jost Amman in 1568 and entitled Beschreybung aller Stande auff
Erden.   The illustrations in this book have been reproduced again
and again as the most accurate representations of the crafts and
workshops of the past; among them are some of the earliest pictures
of a typecasting shop (Fig. 29), a printing press, a bookbindery and
a papermaking plant. Tobias Stimmer collaborated on some of the
large portrait works so highly prized in those days (Icones or Effi-
gies).

        While the familiar classical designs, acanthus leaves, vine
branches, columns, playful cupids, etc., had been almost completely dominant in high-Renaissance book decoration, arabesque ornaments came more and more into use at the middle of the 16th century, for vignettes and headpieces in French books, and then spread

67. Christophe Plantin.   Painting by Rubens, after Plantin's
death in 1589.

to other countries.   At the same time more and more frequent use
was made of the cartouche for title and picture borders; it was
favored in all types of decorative art, even into the 17th century.

Interp. ex Græc. lxx. CAP. 1.   ΗΣΑΙΑΣ. μεθηρμηνευμθνεις των ὁ.

ESAIAS. CAPVT I.   ΗΣΑΙΑΣ. κεφ. α'.

1S1O quâ vidit Esaias filius Amos, quam vidit contra Judæam & contra Jerusalem in regno Oziæ, et Joatham, Achaz et Ezechiæ, qui regnauerunt in Judæa.

² Audi cælum, et auribus percipe terra, quia Dominus locutus est : Filios genui & exaltaui; ipsi autem me spreuerunt. ³ Cognouit bos possessorē, & asinus præsepe domini sui, Israel autem me non cognouit, & populus me non intellexit.

⁴ Væ gens peccatrix, populo plene peccati, semen nequam, filij iniqui dereliquistis Dominū, & ad iracundiam concitastis sanctum Israel : alienati sunt in retro.

⁵ Quid vltrà percutiemini addentes iniquitatem? Omne caput in laborem, & omne cor in tristitiam. ⁶ A pedibus vsque ad caput non est in eo sanitas: vulnus, liuor, plaga tumens; non est mali gina imponere, neque oleum neque alligaturas. ⁷ Terra vestra deserta, ciuitates vestræ succensæ igni: regionem vestram coram vobis alieni deuorant eam: & desolata est subuersa à populis alienis.

⁸ Derelinquetur filia Sion sicut tentorium in vinea, et sicut pomorum custodia in cucumerario, sicut ciuitas obsessa. ⁹ Et nisi Dominus Sabaoth reliquisset nobis semen, quasi Sodoma vtique facti fuissemus, & quasi Gomorra vti, assimilati essemus. ¹⁰ Audite verbum Domini principes Sodomorum, attendite legē Dei nostri populus Gomorræ. ¹¹ Quid mihi multitudo victimarum vestrarum, dicit Dominus? plenus sum holocaustis arietum, et adipem agnorum, & sanguinem taurorum & hircorum non volo.

¹² Neque veneritis apparere mihi. quis enim quæsiuit hæc de manibus vestris? calcare atrium meum. ¹³ Non apponetis, si obtuleritis siligimem, vanum: incensum abominatio mihi est. Neomenias vestras & sabbata, & diem magnum non feram : ieiunium & orium.

Ρασις ἣν εἶδεν ἡσαίας υἱὸς ἀμός, ἣν εἶδον κζ τ ἰουδαίας, καὶ κζ ἱερουσαλὴμ ἐν βασιλεία Ὀζίε καὶ ἰωάθαμ καὶ ἀχαζ & ἐζεκίε, οἱ ἐβασίλευσαν τῆς ἰουδαίας.

ἄκουε οὐρανὲ καὶ ἐνωτίζου γῆ, ὅτι κύριος ἐλάλησεν. υἱὲς ἐγέννησα καὶ ὕψωσα, αὐτοὶ δέ με ἠθέτησαν. ἔγνω βοῦς τὸν κτησάμενον, καὶ ὄνΘ τὴν φάτνην ξ κυρίου αὐτῶ, ἰσραὴλ δέ με οὐκ ἔγνω, καὶ ὁ λαὸς με ὃ συνῆκεν. οὐαὶ ἔθνΘ ἁμαρτωλόν, λαὸς πλήρης ἁμαρτιῶν, σπέρμα πονηρὸν, υἱοὶ ἄνομοι ἐγκατελίπετε τὸν κύριον, καὶ παρωργίσατε τὸν ἅγιον ξ ἰσραήλ, ἀπηλλοτριώθηςαν εἰς τὰ ὀπίσω.

τί ἔτι πληγῆτε προστιθέντες ἀνομίαν; πᾶσα κεφαλὴ εἰς πόνον, καὶ πᾶσα καρδία εἰς λύπην. ἀπὸ ποδῶν ἕως κεφαλῆς οὐκ ἔστιν ἐν αὐτῷ ὁλοκληρία, τραῦμα μώλωψ πληγὴ φλεγμαίνουσα, οὐκ ἔστι μάλαγμα ἐπιθεῖναι οὔτε ἔλαιον οὔτε καταδέσμους.

ἡ γῆ ὑμῶν ἔρημος, αἱ πόλεις ὑμῶν πυρίκαυσι, τὴν χώραν ὑμῶν ἐνώπιον ὑμῶν ἀλλότριοι κατεσθίωσιν αὐτὴν, καὶ ἠρήμωται κατεστραμμένη ὑπὸ λαῶν ἀλλοτρίων.

ἐγκαταλειφθήσεται ἡ θυγάτηρ σιὼν ὡς σκηνὴ ἐν ἀμπελῶνι, καὶ ὡς ὀπωροφυλάκιον ἐν σικυηράτῳ, ὡς πόλις πολιορκουμένη. καὶ εἰ μὴ κύριΘ σαβαὼθ ἐγκατέλιπεν ἡμῖν σπέρμα, ὡς σόδομα ἂν ἐγενήθημεν, καὶ ὡς γόμορρα ἂν ὡμοιώθημεν.

ἀκούσατε λόγον κυρίου ἄρχοντες σοδόμων, προσέχετε νόμον θεοῦ ὑμῶν λαὸς γομόρρας. τί μοι πλῆθΘ τῶν θυσιῶν ὑμῶν, λέγει κύριΘ; πλήρης εἰμὶ ὁλοκαυτωμάτων κριῶν, καὶ στέαρ ἀρνῶν, & αἷμα ταύρων & τράγων ὃ βούλομαι.

οὐδ' ἂν ἔρχησθε ὀφθῆναί μοι· τίς γὰρ ἐξεζήτησε ταῦτα ἐκ τῶν χειρῶν ὑμῶν, πατεῖν τὴν αὐλήν μου;

οὐ προσθήσεσθε. ἐὰν φέρητε σεμίδαλιν, μάταιον· θυμίαμα βδέλυγμά μοι ἐστι· τὰς νεμηνίας ὑμῶν καὶ τὰ σάββατα & ἡμέραν μεγάλην οὐκ ἀνέξομαι. νηστείαν καὶ ἀργίαν.

INTERPRETATIO LATINA TRANSLATIONIS CHALDAICAE IN ESAIAM.
Ex Complutensi Bibliotheca, ad Hebraicam & Chaldaicam vtritatem à B. Aria Montano correcta.

PROPHETIA Esaiæ filij Amos, quam prophetauit super viros Iuda, & habitatores Ierusalē in diebus Oziæ, Iotham, Achaz, Ezechiæ, regum domus Iuda. ² Audite cæli, qui commoti estis, quando dedi legem meam populo meo; & auscultatera, quæ contremuisti à facie Verbi mei, quoniā Dñs locutus est. Populus meus domus Israel, quos vocaui filios, & dilexi eos, & honorificaui eos, & ipsi rebellauerunt in verbum meum. ³ Cognouit bos emptorem suum, & asinus præsepe domini sui, Israel autem non didicit vt sciret timorem mei: populus meus non intellexit vt conuerteretur ad timorem mei. ⁴ Væ eis qui vocati sunt populus sanctus, & peccauerunt; congregatio electa, & multiplicauerunt delicta. cognominati sunt timorem electum, & malè egerunt, & dicti sunt filij dilecti, & corruperunt vias suas, dereliquerunt cultum Domini, detestati sunt timorem Sancti Israel, & propter opera eorum praua auersi sunt, & facti sunt retrorsum. ⁵ Non animaduerterunt, dicentes: Propter quid percussi sumus? adhuc addunt peccare, nec dicunt : Quare omne caput languidū, & omne cor mœrens? ⁶ A reliquo populo vsque ad principes, non est in eis qui perfectus sit in timore mei: omnes sunt cōtumaces, & rebelles; coinquinati sunt in peccatis suis, sicut plaga vlcerosa, nō dimittunt superbias suas, nec desiderant agere pœnitentiam. neque sunt in eis iustitiæ quibus protegantur. ⁷ Terra vestra deserta, ciuitates vestræ succensæ igni: terrā vestram coram vobis populi possident eam, & propter peccata vestra deserta est terra, & translata est ad alienos. ⁸ Et relinquetur cœtus Sion, sicut vmbraculū in vinea, postquam vindemiarunt eam; sicut tugurium manens in cucumerario postquam legerunt cucumeres ab eo; sicut ciuitas quæ obsidetur. ⁹ Nisi superexcedens bonitate Domini exercituum reliquisset nobis redemptionem in miserationibus suis; peccata sunt in nobis propter quæ quasi viri Sodomæ perissemus, & quasi habitatores Gomorræ consumpti essemus. ¹⁰ Suscipite verbum Domini principes, quorū operā sunt mala, sicut principum Sodomæ; auscultate legem Dei nostri populi quorum opera similia sunt populo Gomorræ. ¹¹ Non est benè placitum coram me in multitudine victimarum vestrarum, dicit Dominus; satiatus sum abundantia holocaustorum arietum, & adipe pinguium, & sanguine taurorum, & agnorum, & hircorum: quia in eis nō est beneplacitum coram me. ¹² Cùm veniitis vt appareatis in conspectu meo, quis quæsiuit hoc de manibus vestris, vt veniatis ad conculcandā atria mea? ¹³ Non addatis vltrā offerre oblationem ex rapina; sacrificium abominabile est coram me, & neomeniæ & sabbatha cœtus congregationis vestræ, quoniam non relinquitis peccata vestra, vt exaudiatur oratio vestra in tempore congregationis vestræ.

A ⁵

68. Page from Plantin's Polyglot Bible, printed 1569-72 for Philip II of Spain. The earliest polyglot Bible was issued in Spain 1502-17.

Introduction of Copper Engraving

By the middle of the 16th century in Denmark the Renaissance style, which had been introduced by Christiern Pedersen, had begun to set its mark on book printing. Scholarship and literature flourished; while there are only 226 Danish books preserved from the period 1482-1550, there are some 1400 from 1550-1600. Fortunately Denmark had a competent person to direct the development of bookmaking--Lorenz (Lauritz) Benedicht, presumably German-born, who worked in Copenhagen from about 1560 to 1601. He was the first in Denmark to use fraktur as his main type, but what gave his books their special character and distinction was the excellent proportioning of the text page and the ornamentation. Benedicht was also a wood-carver, and his title borders, initials and illustrations rank with the best German work of the time. Among his famous printed products were Hans Thomeson's Hymnal (1569) and Nils Jesperson's Gradual (1573), which introduced the printing of music into Denmark (Fig. 69), and the book he printed in 1578 in a single copy for King Frederick II, a work on warfare with numerous large hand-colored woodcuts. Frederick II's Bible, which appeared in 1589, was not printed by Benedicht but by Mads Vingaard. Benedicht is known to have printed some 350 different works in all, but over 100 of them have disappeared. Presumably his production was even greater; it extended from ephemeral pamphlets to large scientific works, the latter including Tycho Brahe's book about the new star (1573).

Later Tycho Brahe set up his own printing press and bindery on the island of Hven and also had his own paper mill. Most of his works bear the imprint "Uraniburgum." Even when he lived as an exile in Wandsbeck in Holstein at the home of the learned humanist Henrik Rantzan, himself an ardent book collector, Tycho Brahe had his press with him. Most of his products were printed in large varieties of roman and italic, which gave them a stately appearance. Those of his bindings that are preserved are in keeping with this style. They are usually of vellum or satin and have his picture stamped in gold on the front cover and his coat-of-arms on the back (Fig. 60).

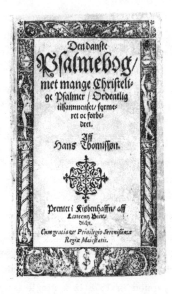

69. Title page and text page from Hans Thomeson's hymnal
of 1569, printed by Lorenz Benedicht. The title page has woodcut
borders and the text includes musical notation, the first ever printed
in Denmark.

One of Tycho Brahe's books printed in Holstein was the monumental Astronomiae instauratae mechanica, now quite scarce, with
both woodcuts and copper engravings.

Toward the end of the 16th century the art of wood carving
declined steadily as excessive use led to factory-like methods of
production. Most of the designs had become stereotyped, whether
cast in metal or cut in wood, and the late Renaissance taste for
luxuriance in a high degree led to profusion and overcrowding at the
expense of artistic balance.

Decline was apparent in typography as well. The flourishing
scholarly literature of the 16th century made great demands on the
printer in the way of complicated typesetting, elaborate dedications,
involved musical notation, etc. With no models to follow, the printer was tempted into stylized overextension. Unfortunately, typecasting had become a separate trade as early as 1530, as the result of

a number of workers' disputes, and the intimate relationship between printing and type production was gradually lost.

Chapter 4. The 17th Century

Ascendancy of Copperplate Engraving

The first book in which copperplate engravings were used
was issued in Florence in 1477. During the next hundred years copper engravings were used only occasionally and in several instances
books that had originally had copper engravings were reissued with
woodcuts. Copper engravings met with resistance at first from
printers because unlike woodcuts they could not be printed in one
operation with the text. In a woodcut the block is carved so that
the outlines of the drawing stand out in relief and these raised portions take the ink and make the impression. This is called relief
or letterpress printing. In a copper engraving, the lines of the
drawing are traced on the copperplate and cut down into it; these
depressions are then filled with ink for printing, i.e. intaglio printing. In theory, copper engravings are not suited for use in books,
and it is difficult to understand why for some two hundred years
they were the dominant method for printing book illustrations.

In cases where illustrations or plates are printed separately
and then bound in with the book, copperplate engraving has a natural place, and it was in this form that it was used at the beginning.
The engraved frontispiece was introduced and inserted before the
regular letterpress title page. The frontispiece contained the title
of the book set against a background of allegorical figures or imaginative representations of the contents of the book or it might contain a portrait of the author. Engraved plates were extensively used
in the large illustrated works that were becoming more and more
fashionable. They were also used in scientific works where the illustrations were of special importance, as in books on geography,
natural history, history of art and archeology. Large books containing reproductions of paintings or illustrations of architecture and
sculpture or of archeological finds were produced in large numbers

160

at the end of the 16th century and all through the 17th century, and
production of travel accounts and topographic works with maps and
drawings of landscapes, cities and buildings was also extensive.
Some famous examples are Theodor de Bry's voluminous work on
India (1590-1625); Georg Braun's Theatrum urbium (1572), a description of certain towns; Martin Zeiller's enormous geographical work
with over 200 maps and views; a large collection of illustrations
issued in periodical form under the title of Theatrum Europaeum
and describing contemporary historical events; the archeological
work of the papal antiquarian Pietro Santo Bartoli on the ancient
monuments of Rome; and Pietro Aguila's reproductions of famous
contemporary paintings.

Copperplate printing was especially suited for the reproduction of paintings, since it could imitate the fine shades of color and
the general artistic effect.   Hence its greatest advance came in this
period when the art of painting was developing so rapidly.   The copperplate engraver, however, made less of an independent artistic
contribution than did the wood-carver.   In the large works just mentioned it was a question of representing an original as accurately as
possible, whether by transferring the colors of a painting to black-
and-white form, or by presenting a picture of a building, a work of
sculpture, an animal or a plant.   In the fields of archeology, art history and natural history, copper engraving was an invaluable aid for
accurate representation until the 19th century, when photographic
methods came into use and made possible even greater accuracy.
The better copperplate engravings showed artistic ability as well as
good craftsmanship; the Swiss engraver Matthäus Merian, for instance, who collaborated with his sons and his daughter, Maria Sibylla, on some of the works mentioned above, attained considerable
fame as an artist.

Baroque Style in Book Arts

The baroque style next became dominant in the field of bookmaking.   The insatiable desire for grandiose effects found expression in large folio formats and large typefaces, but it was manifested especially in a overwhelming profusion on the frontispiece with

which ordinary and otherwise unillustrated books were provided. In
a travel account the frontispiece would often represent a foreign
scene with all sorts of exotic humans and animals scattered about;
in archeological works the frontispieces were filled with classical
figures in deep meditation among picturesque ruins, etc.; and everywhere there were allegorical figures symbolizing Wisdom, Love,
Justice, the State, Religion, etc. Many, perhaps most, of these
frontispiece title pages, on which there was scarcely room enough
for the title itself, cannot be compared with the better productions
of 16th-century bookmaking, but there were a few that were far
above the general level. That was especially true of the frontispieces sketched by Rubens in the years that he worked with the Galle
family of copper engravers for Balthasar Moretus of the Plantin establishment. Rubens' and his pupils' engravings still showed a predilection for allegorical figures, but the artist's genius asserted itself. In spite of their profusion and other faults, these engravings
showed an artistic restraint that was uncommon in the book decoration of the time. In many instances Rubens made only a rough outline for the design (Rubens invenit), while someone else completed
the drawing (delineavit) and a third engraved it in copper (sculpsit).

Plantin's printing business in Antwerp came to have great
significance for the application of copper engraving to book illustration. Even after his death, and all through the 17th century, Belgium and, especially, Holland took the lead in most aspects of book
production in Europe. This was due partly to the powerful political
position that the Netherlands had attained, and partly to a liberal
form of government that left the artist free of the strict censorship
that prevailed in absolute states. In addition the Netherlands also
held a position of leadership in the scientific and scholarly world.
Students came from all countries to the famous University of Leyden.

The Elzevirs. The Blaeu Family

Toward the close of the 16th century a bookbinder and col-
porteur named Lodewijk Elzevir (Elsevier) was appointed at the University of Leyden. He obtained permission to sell books to the stu-

dents and gradually worked up a book business of considerable size.
His field of activity extended beyond the borders of Holland and he
maintained a stock of books in Frankfurt and throughout Southern
Germany.   Lodewijk Elzevir sired a great family of printers and publishers, who established themselves in several towns in Holland during the 17th century and made the name Elzevir famous throughout
Europe. Most outstanding were Lodewijk's son Bonaventura and his
grandsons, Isaac, Lodewijk the younger, and Abraham. Their period of activity, 1625-64, was the great period of the Elzevirs. A
multitude of duodecimo editions were distributed from the Elzevirs'
press. At a time when large folios were in vogue these small
books were quite unusual and, like the Aldines, more democratic.
They rapidly became popular because of their practical format and
low price; the editions of Caesar, Pliny, Terence and Virgil were
in particular demand. While they could not compare with the Aldines in philological accuracy, the general effect of their clear roman type was impressive. The type was cut by Christofel van Dyck
on the model of Garamond's type, and it was also used in England
after Bishop John Fell introduced it at the Oxford University Press
in 1670.

Besides these editions of the classics the Elzevirs published
many other books; in 1626 they were granted a license to issue a
series of statistical and topographical descriptions of various countries, the so-called "Republics," which enjoyed considerable success.
Many of the greatest literary figures of the time belonged to the
Elzevir circle: Descartes, Molière, Calvin, Bacon, Hobbes, Gal-
ileo, and especially the great Dutch jurist Hugo Grotius, whose
famous work on the freedom of the seas was issued in 1609 by the
older Lodewijk. Other well-known Elzevir books are an edition of
St. Augustine dated 1675, an edition of Corneille's translation of
Thomas à Kempis' Imitation of Christ (1652), a folio edition of Roman Law (1663) and editions of Molière, Corneille, Pascal and other
great French writers. The total of Elzevir editions and authentic
Elzevir imprints--like the Aldines, they had many imitators--
amounts to around 2,200, besides some 3,000 university publica-

FRANCISCI HARÆI
ANNALES
DVCVM SEV PRINCIPVM
BRABANTIÆ
TOTIVSQ. BELGII.

TOMI TRES:
Quorum Primo folius BRABANTIÆ.
Secundo BELGII vniti PRINCIPVM
res geftæ;Tertio BELGICI TVMVLTVS.
vfque ad INDVCIAS anno M. DC. IX.
pactas, enarrantur.

Cum DVCVM feu PRINCIPVM Imaginibus,
et breui rerum per omnem EVROPAM
illuftrum narratione.

ANTVERPIÆ,
EX OFFICINA PLANTINIANA
Apud Balthafarem Moretum
et Viduam Ioannis Moreti
et Io. Meurfium.
M. DC. XXIII.

70.   Copper-engraved title page of a book published by Balthasar Moretus in 1623; drawn by Rubens.

tions. In the 18th and especially the 19th century Elzevir publications were greatly sought after by book collectors, and that has persisted, mainly in wealthy American collectors. Great value has
been attached to copies that have been trimmed as little as possible,
and a special Elzevir scale has been adopted for measuring the
width of the margins. Well-preserved Elzevir books from the family's best period have risen to fantastic prices even when they are
not rare. One example is the little French book on pastry making,
Le pastissier francois. The Elzevirs reprinted this book in 1655
from the French original and in one of their catalogs they listed it
at a price of slightly over half a gulden. The book became scarce,
and in the latter half of the 19th century good copies brought as
high as 10, 000 francs. One of the largest and finest Elzevir collections is the Berghman collection in the Royal Library at Stockholm.

Part of the Elzevirs' stock of type was taken over in the
18th century by another famous printing dynasty, the Enschedé family in Haarlem, whose firm was founded in 1703 by Izaak Enschedé.
It is still in existence and possesses a greater variety of typefaces
from different periods than any other European press; it also acquired the type of the famous Berlin printer J. F. Unger.

As booksellers the Elzevirs outdistanced their competition;
no others had their widespread trade connections. The younger
Lodewijk even came to Copenhagen on one of his trips and founded
a branch at Børsen, which was later also used by another Dutch
printer, Johannes Jansonius, the greatest reprint publisher of the
17th century. Through his and the Elzevirs' reprints of French
works, contemporary French literature was given a wider distribution than it would otherwise have had. All of England's book connections with the continent at that time went through Holland and
here again the Elzevirs were in the lead.

Like other large publishers, they issued many of their books
in bound form. The Magnus family of bookbinders worked for them,
imitating the French bindings of the time. This family also found
employment at several other Dutch printing establishments, particularly in the Blaeu firm, which was active from 1618 to 1672 and attained renown for its large atlases.

P. VIRGILII MARONIS

B V C O L I C A.

TITYRVS, ECLOGA I.

ARGVMENTVM.

Virgilius fub perfona Tityri paftoru , quo arietem
majorem , aut hircum fignificari ajunt , ut evi-
dentius fortunam fuam,beneficiaque Cæfaru ex-
plicaret, ex adverfo Melibæum,id eft,qui curam
agit boum , introducit , à patria , adempto agre,
pulfum.

MELIBOEVS, TITYRVS.

M. Ityre, tu patulæ recubans fub tegmi-
ne fagi,
Silveftrem tenui Mufam meditaris
avena

Nos patriæ fineis , & dulcia linquimus arva,
Nos patriam fugimus : tu Tityre lentus in umbra
Formofam refonare doces Amaryllida filvas.
T. O Melibœe, deus nobis hæc otia fecit.
Namque erit ille mihi femper deus. illius aram
Sæpe tener noftris ab ovilibus imbuet agnus.
Ille meas errare boves, ut cernis, & ipfum
Ludere quæ vellem calamo permifit agrefti.
M. Non equidem invideo : miror magis: undique
totis
Vfque adeo turbatur agris. en ipfe capellas
Protenus æger ago: hanc etiam vix Tityre duco.
Heic inter denfas corulos modo namq; gemellos,
Spem

71. Page from an Elzevir edition of Virgil in duodecimo.
In the octavo format the sheet is folded three times, while in the
duodecimo it is folded to make 12 sheets or 24 pages. Duodecimo
is abbreviated "12mo."

Cartography had reached a high stage of development among
the seafaring Dutch. The founder of the Blaeu firm, Willem Janszoon Blaeu, had become acquainted with Tycho Brahe on a trip to
Denmark and had acquired a basic knowledge of astronomy and cartography. As "globen- en kaartenmaker" in Amsterdam, he issued
several large editions of marine charts that surpassed all earlier
ones in accuracy and attractiveness. His main work was the Novus
Atlas, but the family attained its greatest fame from the work by
the founder's son Johann entitled Atlas major, which was first pub-

lished in 1662 in 11 folio volumes. Here the art of copper engraving came into its own, not only in the hand-colored maps but in the
titles and ornaments. In spite of its size and cost the Atlas major
was very much in demand. It is said that the Archduchess of Tus-
cany paid 30,000 guldens for a particularly beautiful copy, and the
work is still valued highly today.

The financing of this, and of many of the other monumental
literary enterprises of that time, seems miraculous. Part of the
answer undoubtedly lay in the low-paid labor that was available.
But in many instances financial support must have come from patrons among royalty and the nobility, in return for dedications and
eulogies in prose and verse at the beginning of the printed work.
Without this support these large scholarly works would have had just
as little chance of publication as they would have today without grants
from the government or from private foundations.

The First Book Auctions

The early years of the 17th century marked the beginning of
a new form of book trade--selling books at auction to the highest
bidder. The first book auctions were held in Leyden. The initiative was presumably taken by the elder Lodewijk Elzevir, and it
soon became apparent that this procedure had advantages for both
the buyer and the seller. The seller obtained maximum financial
return and the buyer was offered collections that did not have the
miscellaneous composition of the ordinary bookseller's stock. Quite
early, however, there were complaints that bookdealers used the
auctions to get rid of the less desirable books in their stock by mix-
ing them with those to be put up at auction. Printed catalogs were
sent out in advance, usually listing the books by size: octavos,
quartos and folios.

The Dutch book auctions soon attracted attention in other countries and acquired increasing international significance. An English
clergyman, Joseph Hill, who had spent some time in Holland, introduced the custom into London in 1676, when he proposed that the library of a deceased parson be sold at auction. A spirit of excitement pervaded the book auctions; when important rarities were put

under the hammer, episodes of a truly dramatic nature often occurred. The practice of holding book auctions spread in France and
Germany during the second half of the 17th century even though German dealers tried to fight it. The first book auction in Denmark
was held in Copenhagen in the 1650's (the oldest preserved auction
catalog is dated 1654).

French Book Collectors

Holland assumed a leading role in the European book world
of the 17th century. France--despite her brilliant literary produc-
tion--had to take a secondary position, and French literature was
largely disseminated through books reprinted in Holland. In the
field of book collecting, however, the French were in the front rank;
French bibliophiles had continued the Grolier tradition and preserved
the luxury aspects that distinguished it throughout Europe. The
more the power of the French royal house increased, the greater
and more luxurious was the book display at court. The king, the
other royal book collectors, the noble lords and ladies--all took part
in the competition for fine books that was under way in the reign of
Louis XIV and gathered momentum under his successors, Louis XV
and XVI. It would be a considerable exaggeration, however, to ascribe any abiding interest in literature to these kings and nobles.

Of course, there were some educated and well-read men who
collected books for other reasons than to satisfy their vanity. There
was, for instance, the learned Nicolas Claude de Peiresc, whose
special interest was in Coptic manuscripts and in printed books with
marginal notations by the previous owners. True interest in books
must also be ascribed to the great statesmen Richelieu, Mazarin and
Colbert. Richelieu's literary interests were evidenced by his establishment of a royal press in the Louvre, an institution that later had
great influence on typography in France. Colbert made a considerable contribution to Louis XIV's library, which grew to 40,000 volumes and 10,000 manuscripts. Mazarin's special passion for books
dated back to his early youth.

Richelieu and Mazarin received considerable assistance from
their librarian, Gabriel Naudé, who is known through a book that he

issued in 1627 entitled <u>Advis pour dresser une bibliothèque</u>. This
can be called the earliest guide to library work. Naudé showed
great energy and financial acumen in searching the stocks of dealers
throughout Europe; he gradually built up the Mazarin library to
45,000 volumes.

It was Cardinal Mazarin's ambition to be France's Asinius
Pollio. In 1643 he opened his collections to scientists and literary
scholars for six hours each day (Naudé's book had emphasized the
importance of making libraries accessible to everyone). A few
years later, Mazarin was banished and during the wars of the
Fronde his magnificent library was scattered.

Naudé, sorrowed by this misfortune, answered a call to
Sweden as librarian to Queen Christina. When Mazarin was returned to power and began again to collect books he summoned his
old librarian, but Naudé died on the journey. The second Bibliothèque Mazarine was opened to the public in 1691. It is still one of
the most important libraries in the Department of the Seine.

The St. Victor library of the Augustinian order was made accessible to scholars in the middle of the century. The old and
wealthy Benedictine monastery, Saint-Germain-des-Prés, only re-
luctantly opened its doors and the Abbey of Sainte-Geneviève did not
make its library public until the 18th century. The latter was the
only library that survived the ravages of the Revolution, and it still
holds a prominent place among the public libraries of France.

Library Architecture

The outer form of libraries had been changing gradually. Until the end of the 16th century the medieval custom of keeping the
books on desks had persisted. Later library quarters took the form
of a large room or hall with the books arranged on shelves along the
walls; often these shelves extended up to the ceiling, so that a gallery had to be installed to reach them. This type of library construction found its first full realization in the magnificent building
erected in the latter half of the 16th century for the Escorial Library in Madrid. It soon became the prevailing style, not to be
superseded by more practical forms until the middle of the 19th

Die Kaiserliche Bibliothek in Rariuteen Lander.

72. Interior of hall in the Imperial Library in Vienna in the
17th century. The Emperor is paying a visit to the library. (From
Edward Brown, Account of some travels, 1685.)

century. In these large library halls the architect gave free play
to his imagination, and there was often great artistic merit in the
domes, columns, friezes and ceiling decorations. The architectural
splendor of the structure almost overshadowed the books, but in this
baroque period, it was intended that a library should have the appearance of a museum. This effect was further emphasized by placing globes of the heavens and the earth in the center of the hall,
and all sorts of art objects on pedestals round about. One reason
for this was that many of the great book collectors were also collectors of art; the French minister, Pierre Séguier, had collected
over 20,000 volumes, but in the library rooms of his palace the
display of porcelain almost outshone the books. Another magnificent
library hall was the famous domed room built in the 18th century
for the Court Library in Vienna.

Bookbinding

The architectural magnificence of the 17th century was reflected in elegant bookbinding; nevertheless, as in earlier periods,
most books were in ordinary bindings. We still have many French
calf and sheepskin bindings of that period, marbled to give a tor-
toise-shell appearance or simply stained black, with no decoration
except on the spine. A still more Spartan effect is presented by
the English bindings in brown sheepskin, whose plain appearance is
further emphasized by the fact that the insides of the covers do not
even have paper pasted over their gray cardboard. The ordinary
Dutch "horn bindings" were made of hard white vellum polished
smooth, with very little decoration; the title was written in India ink
at the top of the spine. On Italian and Spanish vellum bindings, the
title was stamped down along the spine, and there was no cardboard
insert in the covers, which were soft and flexible like the small
suede leather bindings of today.

The wealthy collectors were not satisfied with the plainer
types of binding, and the art of fine bookbinding continued to be cultivated, in France in particular, as in the time of Francis I and
Henry II. At the beginning of the 17th century the fanfare style with
its conventional laurel branches was still dominant, but in the later
years of Louis XIII's reign a new style of decoration appeared.
Stamps with dotted lines (fer pointillés) began to be used; the fine
curved or spiral lines were broken up into a series of small dots
and arranged to form a web or network over the entire cover or
around the central panel containing the owner's coat-of-arms.
Strangely enough, there were faint traces of baroque ornaments.
The dotted stamps were also used on the backs of books and even on
the insides of the covers, which in fine bindings were often covered
with leather or silk. The endpapers, which had usually been of
plain white paper, were often marbled, as were the edges of the
book.

The originator of the dotted-line (or pinhead) style is considered to be Le Gascon, about whom very little is known. It is
not even certain that Le Gascon was his real name or merely an
appellation to indicate his home district. Some have tried, without

73.   The great hall in the Imperial Library (now the Austrian National Library) in Vienna, built by J. B. Fischer von Erlach
and completed in 1726.

justification, to identify him with another bookbinder, Florimond
Badier, who made bindings in the same style and put his signature
on them.   Le Gascon or his pupils worked for the great collectors
of the time, Mazarin, Seguier and Nicolas de Peiresc, and his style
was imitated throughout France as well as in neighboring countries.
Dotted lines were easier to execute than solid lines, so that the introduction of the Gascon style meant some simplification.   A further
simplification occurred when the bookbinder Macé Ruette introduced
the practice of replacing the numerous small stamps with larger
stamps that combined the dotted ornaments into larger units placed
inside and around a line border.   In the latter half of the century
many of these larger stamps were made in the shape of a crescent
or rocker with the ends turned back, or they were kidney-shaped;

74. Red morocco binding in the Gascon style, from the beginning of the 17th century.

these variations of the Gascon style achieved wide distribution.

In Holland the Gascon style was imitated by the Magnus family. They used dotted stamps on Elzevir trade bindings. In England a special variation of the Gascon style was used by Charles
II's court binder, Samuel Mearne, who combined the dotted stamps
with solid crescents, conventional tulips, carnations and other flowers. On some of his bindings of the all-over type the crescent
stamps are predominant, but he also made the so-called cottage
bindings, in which the top and bottom lines of the central panel gave
the appearance of an English cottage.

An entirely different kind of binding was made for Louis XIV
and his court by Antoine Ruette. It had practically no decoration,
and the effect was produced by the dark-colored leather alone. This
ascetic look was in strong contrast to the elaborate style of the time.

75.   Binding by Florimond Badier (his name is seen at
lower left), decorated in the pointillé style.

76. Binding by Samuel Maerne in the "all-over" style with crescent designs stamped in the borders surrounding the three central panels.

77. English binding in the Harleian style, 1702. (British Museum.)

At the beginning of the 18th century it was called Jansenist binding, after the religious sect. The books of some other French bibliophiles also showed a minimum of decoration, limited to a border along the edge, a few corner ornaments, a coat-of-arms or a monogram in the center, with additional decoration only on the spine. By way of compensation, however, only the highest quality of goatskin was used; it may be that appreciation of the beauty of the material itself caused a reaction against excessive gold tooling.

The original Gascon stamps were gradually supplemented by new variants (including the so-called Duseuil stamps) that were marketed by die-cutters along with patterns and designs drawn for the bookbinder to follow. Stamps in the form of rosettes on fans (fers à l'évantail) were especially in demand in Italy, where the bindings generally featured large heraldic designs. They were also accepted in Germany, but only the Heidelberg binders, who had maintained the tradition from the days of Otto Heinrich, succeeded in bringing their work up to the level of the French model.

The Thirty Years' War

In Germany the period following the 1620's was mostly one of stagnation or decline. The Thirty Years' War destroyed the power of the country both politically and economically, and this was followed by a long cultural decline. This situation gave the bookmakers and booksellers of Holland their opportunity. The products of 17th-century Germany in the field of illustrative art were mainly an echo of Dutch or French copperplate engraving. The level of European typography in the 17th century was generally below that of the preceding centuries, but German book printing was the worst of all. Large numbers of books were issued in Germany but their typographical appearance was usually quite inferior. Any advance in the printing arts was prevented by the rigid guild regulations that continued in force right down to the beginning of the 19th century. The German book trade also suffered greatly from the practice of unrestricted reprinting, which made publishers' rights illusory. Efforts to control the practice were ineffective, since the regulations could not be enforced in a country so divided as Germany.   Danish printers also suffered.   Not only was Danish literature reprinted within Denmark, but the printers of North Germany, especially those of Lübeck, also copied Danish editions and many books of that time that bear a Copenhagen imprint were actually printed in Germany. The Germans continued the bookbinding tradition of the 16th century but fine craftsmanship, except for the Heidelberg bindings in the new French styles, became rare.

The ravages of the religious wars had an even more repressive effect on German libraries.   The oldest of the German university libraries and one of the most outstanding of the time, Heidelberg's Bibliotheca Palatina, was presented to the Pope by Emperor Maximilian of Bavaria, when the town was captured by Tilly's troops in 1623.   The books were incorporated into the Vatican Library. The Protestants had their revenge later when Gustavus Adolphus organized Protestant resistance.   As he repelled the Catholics' advances

he confiscated all libraries in his path, especially those in the Jesu-
it colleges, and the countries into which he carried his campaigns
saw one library after another pass to Sweden as spoils of war. The
University of Uppsala had been founded in 1620 and to it Gustavus
Adolphus presented many of the collections that he took from Riga
and Prussia and South Germany.

Thus was introduced a period of greatness in the history of
Swedish libraries that continued long after the death of Gustavus
Adolphus. The Swedish nobles who acted as officers in the army or
held administrative positions during the war took full advantage of
their success in battle. Since ancient times it had been the practice
for victorious troops to carry off books and libraries, but not until
World War II was this done again with such thoroughness as during
the period of Sweden's greatness. Moreover, what the Swedes acquired they did not give up, although in later wars book collections
acquired in this way were usually returned after the conclusion of a
peace treaty.

During the latter part of the Thirty Years' War the monastery libraries of Bohemia and Moravia suffered especially. When
the Swedes stormed Prague in 1648 they took rich booty in books,
including the magnificent collection of the Bohemian kings at Hrad-
schin, which contained what is probably the largest extant vellum
manuscript, the Devil's Bible. Along with the rest of the Bohemian
royal library it was brought to Stockholm and incorporated into
Queen Christina's library. A large part of this she took with her
when she left Sweden--most of the manuscripts, for instance, are
now in the Vatican. The part that remained still forms the main
body of the Royal Library in Stockholm, supplemented by the booty
taken during Charles Gustavus' (Charles X) wars in Poland and Denmark. Many libraries of the Swedish nobility were also stocked by
these expeditions. Several of the great statesmen, Axel and Erik
Oxenstierna, Schering Rosenhane, Claes Rålamb, and the king's
brother-in-law and chancellor, Magnus Gabriel de la Gardie, were
educated men with literary interests. De la Gardie made considerable book acquisitions in Denmark. He purchased the collection of
the royal historiographer, Prof. Stephan Hansen Stephanius, which

contained important source material for Danish history, and a famous manuscript of the Younger Edda. As war spoil he took Gunde Rosenkrantz' library, which included a part of Anders Sørensen Vedel's collection. Under Charles XI, De la Gardie's possessions, like those of the other nobility, were taken over by the crown after his death. They were presented to the historical archives and to the University Library at Uppsala, which thereby came into possession of the Gothic Bible of Bishop Ulfilas (Codex argenteus); it had been taken from Prague and purchased by De la Gardie.

While the collections of De la Gardie, including the Danish portions, are still preserved, another large Danish private library that came into the possession of the Swedes did not fare so well. The high court judge at Ringsted monastery, Jørgen Seefeldt, possessed over 25,000 volumes, including Old Norse-Icelandic manuscripts and many rare printed books; this entire collection was given to Corfitz Ulfeld to take to Malmø. Later however, both these and Ulfeld's own books were confiscated by the Swedish government and incorporated into the Royal Library at Stockholm. When the greater part of the library went up in flames in the palace fire of 1697, Seefeldt's collection was destroyed. A very small part of this collection had come into the possession of the Swedish envoy, Peter Julius Coyet. When his possessions were taken over by Danish soldiers in 1710, these books were brought back to Seefeldt's homeland.

Jørgen Seefeldt was by far the greatest collector in Denmark in the 17th century, but several others deserve to be mentioned. The well-known author of the great topographical work Resens Danske Atlas, Professor Peter Hansen Resen, collected a library strong in Scandinavian literature and jurisprudence, and in 1675 he presented it to the University Library in Copenhagen. The University Library had grown through numerous gifts: King Christian IV had given it the bulk of the royal family's books in 1605, and the royal historians had bequeathed their books, including numerous medieval manuscripts and other source material on the history of Denmark and Norway. But its growth had been irregular, and Resen's collection filled important gaps, especially in Scandinavian literature.

An even more distinctly national collector was Anne Gjøe.

She willed her books to a relative, Karen Brahe, who presented the
library to the aristocratic nunnery that she founded in Odense. Here
the collection gradually deteriorated and it was not till the beginning
of the 19th century that it was rescued from oblivion. It is now in
the regional archives at Odense and represents the only independent
collection that has been preserved from 17th-century Denmark. It
contains several Danish books that are extant in no other copies,
and among the manuscripts there is a famous one of folk songs,
known as 'Karen Brahe's folio.''

The Age of the Polyhistors

In the Scandinavian countries at that time there was scarcely
anyone to equal Resen and the two noble Danish ladies in their appreciation of Danish national literature. Book collections in Denmark as well as elsewhere in Europe usually were cosmopolitan.
Scholarly literature was mostly written in Latin and in the field of
general literature Danish collectors were mainly concerned with the
popular French, Italian and Spanish authors of the time, and to some
extent also Dutch, German and English writers. Their collections
covered a wide range of subjects. It was the age of the polyhistors,
when knowledge had a universal basis and specialization was still unknown. Scholars were familiar with practically all fields of knowl-
edge--professors lectured now in one field and now in another, having presumably mastered them equally well. The encyclopedic character of this age, and of the 18th century as well, showed in the libraries of the period.

The Origin of National Libraries

The collection of Archduke Cosimo III of Florence, whose librarian was Antonio Maggliabecchi, developed into the present Italian
National Library. Several other national libraries of the present day
had their origin in libraries of the aristocracy of the 17th century, or
were considerably increased in size at that period. Even in war-
ravaged Germany there were examples of this. In 1659 the Elector
Palatine, Frederick William, signed a document in his camp at Viborg making the palace library in Berlin accessible to the 'public''

(to be taken in much more limited sense than today)and thereby laid
the foundation for the later Prussian Staats-bibliothek. In the early
years of the century Duke August of Braunschweig-Lüneburg started
assembling one of the largest libraries in Europe. The catalog of
his library required almost 4,000 pages. The library later came
under the zealous care of the great polyhistor and philosopher Leib-
nitz. Now known as the Wolfenbüttel Library it is still a gem
among Germany's libraries.

Danish Bookbinding and Printing

Frederik III called in binders from France, thereby introducing the new French Gascon style of dotted-line decorations to Denmark. In general, however, Danish bookbinding continued to follow
Germany's lead, and it was not until toward the end of the 17th century that the dotted spirals, fans and crescents of the new style became common.

By the middle of the century bookbinders in Copenhagen had
become so numerous that the need for a trade organization was felt.
In 1646 a bookbinders association was formed under the leadership
of Jørgen Holst, bookbinder to the University and former bookdealer
and author. This association developed many peculiar trade practices, some of which are still found in trade unions of today, and
which can in part be traced back to the ceremonies of the medieval
guilds. The binders' association opposed those who established
themselves as master bookbinders without proper training.

The journeymen who traveled from Denmark through Germany
had to be well versed in their craft in order to take their place
among foreign workers. Printers did not have a separate organization but more or less followed German trade practices, including the
"Artickeln und Satzungen" that had been laid down by various German
authorities in 1573. King Frederik III outlawed these, but they continued in use till around 1800.

Two of the greatest Danish printers of the first half of the
17th century were Henrich Waldkirch and Melchior Martzan. Like
many of their predecessors they were German-born, and like many
of their German colleagues they were also bookdealers, doing busi-

ness in one of the chapels of Our Lady's Cathedral in Copenhagen.
German influence was reflected clearly in their work, as it was in
that of many other Danish printers, by the growing excess of ornamentation, often composed of very tasteless rosettes and headpieces;
the old woodcut material from the 16th century was still being used,
no matter how worn. Even after copper engraving began to be used,
as in the folio Bible that Martzan printed for Christian IV in 1633,
the old material still was not discarded; in the same book a peculiar
mixture of old and new could be found: woodcut Reniassance ornaments along with copperplate frontispieces in baroque style.

The oldest work with copper-engraved illustrations produced
in Denmark is one on fencing written by Christian IV's Italian fencing master and printed by Waldkirch in 1606. It is almost the only
Danish work in reasonably pure baroque style that remains from the
17th century. The plates were made by a Dutch engraver--most engravings in Danish books of the period were made by Dutch or German artisans. Possibly the first Danish-born engraver who can be
compared with foreign engravers was Albert Haelweg; his work included the charming frontispiece to Simon Paulli's Flora Danica
(1648), the portrait of Arild Huitfeldt in the folio edition of the latter's History of Denmark (1652), and the portrait of Birgitte Thott
in her translation of Seneca issued in Sorø in 1658.

Danish books entirely in the baroque style did not appear until
the final decades of the 17th century. An example of this was Hol-
ger Jacobaeus' large folio work of 1696 on the royal art gallery,
Museum regium. Its headpieces, initials and vignettes, as well as
the plates, were printed from copper engravings.

The economy of the country did not permit the indulgence in
luxury that might otherwise have been quite natural with the establishment of the absolute monarchy. The printers suffered from the
reprinting practices mentioned earlier and from strict political censorship. Under such conditions most printers produced small popular works, devotional literature, funeral sermons, etc. The 'newspaper privilege" was much sought after--it was granted for the first
time to the printer Martzan and the bookdealer Joachim Moltke, and
gave them the right to issue the small sheets (Relationer) containing

accounts in German and Danish of important happenings abroad.
Those printers who were fortunate enough to obtain this privilege or
the sole license to print school textbooks and almanacs, or who became royal printers or printers to the University, could count on a
good income. That was true of men like Henrik Gøde and Johan
Philip Bockenhoffer. Most of the other printers, like the majority
of the bookbinders, made only a modest living. This stagnation of
Danish book printing lasted far into the 18th century, a time which
was a great period in the history of the book in other countries.

Chapter 5.   The 18th Century

Rococo Vignette Art

The heavy baroque style that dominated art and bookmaking
in the early days of Louis XV's reign, did not suit the way of life
and the philosophy of the upper classes in the 18th century.   The
undercurrent of social forces that culminated in the Revolution at the
end of the century was still quite weak and did not show on the surface; everything seemed calm and quiet, with the Court setting the
tone and the common people dazzled by the splendor.   For the upper
classes life was a continuous chain of amusements and festivities.
In literature, pastoral poetry was one of the most popular forms; in
art, love was the constantly recurring theme; and even in political
life the tender passion made its influence felt through the intrigues
of the royal mistresses.

This philosophy of life found artistic expression in the rococo
style, whose light, festive and elegant tone replaced the heavy
and grandiose.   In books, large folios were more and more superseded by smaller formats, and copperplate engraving was used more
extensively for decorative purposes.   Books were not only provided
with illustrations as such, but small vignettes were scattered liberal-
ly throughout the pages in the form of headpieces (fleurons, en-tetes)
at the beginning of each chapter and tailpieces (culs de lampe) at the
end.   Flying cupids encircled by rose garlands were frequently used
for these vignettes (the word means literally vine branch), and rococo ornaments with their C- and S- shaped lines were prominent features of the surrounding borders.   Rococo ornamentation thus freed
itself from the rigid symmetry that had previously prevailed; its
characteristic designs--shells, palm branches, bouquets and festoons
of flowers and fruit--were arranged in a more or less informal
fashion.

A group of French artists and painters soon perfected the

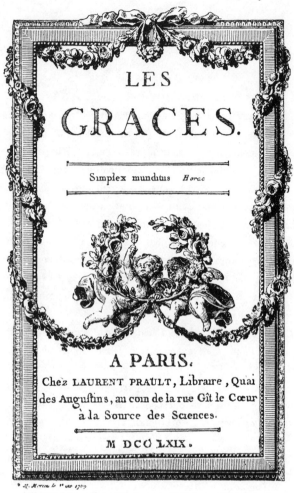

78.   Typical rococo title page from 1769, drawn by Moreau le jeune.

rococo style in books and the Flemish, Swiss, German and English artists, who worked in great numbers in Paris, adopted the French style completely.   In graceful lines so well suited to the nature of copper engraving, these artists created pictures that accurately expressed the gay and refined taste of the time; some of the most

79. Vignette by Charles Eisen in Claude Joseph Dorat's Les
baisers. The Hague, 1770.

characteristic of these are found in the vignette books. However,
as in many Renaissance books, there often was a lack of balance;
the illustrations stood out at the expense of the text, since nearly all
the attention was devoted to the illustrations and the decoration.
There were also many books consisting entirely of pictures--books of
architectural drawings, furniture and ornamental designs, archeological, botanical and zoological works, picture books of travels in foreign countries, etc. For these the larger formats were still used.
Most of the typical rococo books, however, were in octavo or duodecimo format.

One of the earliest examples of this new type of book was the
edition of Daphnis and Chloë by the Greek writer Longus that was issued in Paris in 1718, illustrated with copperplate engravings from
paintings by Duke Philip of Orléans. The real flowering of vignette
art, however, began in 1734 with an edition of Molière containing
over 200 vignettes by the famous painter Boucher. He succeeded in
producing a greater three-dimensional effect than should have been
thought possible in such small pictures. This effect was also
achieved by other artists who devoted themselves to book illustra-

Sophie remettex vous;

80. Copper-engraving drawn by Moreau le jeune for J. J.
Rousseau, Oeuvres, vol. 4, 1784.

tion: Cochin le jeune, Choffard, Eisen, Marillier, and above all
Gravelot and the younger Moreau.   Charles Nicolas Cochin le jeune
introduced the copper-engraved title page with the title set in ex-

tended type and in a grayish color. He was a brilliant artist and
showed great decorative talent in his numerous vignettes.   Pierre
Philippe Choffard was responsible for a large number of vignette
headpieces and tailpieces, as seen in the edition of La Fontaine's
fables issued in 1762. The other illustrations in this book were by
Charles Eisen, a Flemish artist who attained great fame for his
skill in composition. Eisen was particularly successful in illustrating books with amorous themes, such as Montesquieu's Le temple de
Gnide (1772) or the sentimental verses, Les baisers (1770), of the
mediocre poet Dorat (Fig. 79), to which his slightly affected style
was so well suited. Pierre Clément Marillier was known for his
more than 200 clever vignettes for Dorat's fables (1775); Hubert
Francois Gravelot used a more rigid but also more forceful style in
illustrating works like Marmontel's moralizing tales (1765) and Voltaire's edition of Corneille (1764). He was an outstanding artist and
engraver, especially skilled in depicting the manners and modes of
the aristocracy.

The most highly gifted of all, however, was Jean Michel
Moreau (Moreau le jeune). He placed great emphasis on making his
drawings from life and nature, hence there was a great freshness
about them. In contrast, many of the others had a slight air of
pruriency, however great the artistry. Authors like Boccaccio and
Aretino might easily tempt the artist to overstep the bounds of good
taste, but that occurred even in editions of Horace and Ovid. Moreau's pictures had none of this boudoir atmosphere; their natural
charm diffused what might otherwise seem too bold and made it
pleasing. Moreau was a worshipper of nature and no one could give
better visual expression to the spirit of Rousseau than he did in the
edition of 1782-90. His major works were in the 24 large pages
that he executed for Monument du costume (1775-83), a book of illustrations representing the daily life of the upper classes. The pictures became famous for their almost impressionistic composition
and their daring treatment of light and shadow. Another of Moreau's
masterpieces was the illustrations for the Kehl edition of Voltaire's
works (1784-89).

One characteristic of all the artists mentioned was a lack of

interest in their characters--the faces depicted were usually devoid
of expression. The emphasis was on physical form, setting and
costumes.

A few of the vignette books were executed entirely by copperplate engraving, even the text being drawn by hand and engraved, but
in the majority the text was printed by letterpress. The types that
were used were descendent from Garamond's roman types, but mod-
ernized in form. At the royal press in the Louvre, where several
of the best vignette books were produced, much use was made of a
typeface designed by Philippe Grandjean and called "roman du roi,"
the king's roman type; it can be recognized by the fact that the letter l has a small protuberance at the left. It was an imposing typeface, but could not measure up to Garamond's. Somewhat nearer to
Garamond's, though still not up to its level, was a roman typeface
designed by Pierre Simon Fournier. At the middle of the century
he was Europe's most famous typecaster, and his composite ornamental designs enjoyed tremendous popularity. Another typeface of
the rococo period was one with very narrow letters, called "poét-
ique" because of its special suitability for printing poetry.

French Bibliophiles

Along with the new developments in book arts during the rococo period in France there was a flowering of bibliophilism. It had
been fashionable for the upper classes to collect books before, but
the practice came into much greater vogue and appeared in more refined form during the reigns of Louis XV and Louis XVI. This interest in book collecting caused the great demand for vignette books.
Without it these expensive works would certainly never have found
so ready a sale, nor would so many artists and copperplate engravers have been able to make a livelihood at their trade.

The wealthy French collectors also prized the literature of
the preceding century: "les grands écrivains," the monumental works
on art and natural history, travel accounts and atlases, the great
editions of the Greek and Latin classics. One much sought-after
item was the edition in 64 volumes of a series of classical authors
that Louis XIV had commissioned (1674-1730) for the use of the Dau-

phin and in which all objectionable passages were deleted.

This large group of book collectors provided support for the numerous book auctions that were held in Paris during that period and the prices of desirable items rose. It was also a good time for outdoor booksellers who had established themselves on Pont Neuf and along the banks of the Seine--scarce and beautiful books might be found in their stalls along with a great deal of trash. The government did not look favorably on these outsiders because they were suspected of selling works that had been prohibited by the ecclesiastical and political censors. The regular bookdealers, who had long been well organized in France, also sought to have them suppressed. But these "bouquinists," as they were called from the Dutch word boekin (little book), continued their business.

The greatest, at least quantitatively, among the many French collectors of the 18th century was Duke Louis de la Vallière, who started his collecting in 1738 at the great auction of the library of Count Karl Heinrich von Hoym, the Saxon ambassador to Paris. The Duke acquired so many unusual books in expensive bindings at this and at subsequent auctions that on three occasions he held auctions to dispose of the duplicates. Among the unusual items in his collection was the only extant copy of an illustrated work entitled Tableaux des moeurs du temps. La Vallière's collection became known and when it was sold in 1784, following his death, it brought book collectors to Paris from all corners of Europe. The auction lasted 181 days and the sales amounted to about 465,000 francs.

A part of La Vallière's collection not included in the auction was sold privately to the Marquis of Paulmy, whose books were later taken over by Charles X to form the basis for one of the public libraries of Paris, the Arsenal Library. Among the institutions that acquired books at the La Vallière auction was the French royal library, Bibliothèque du Roi. The royal library included a collection of copperplate engravings and of coins and was widely recognized as the largest and wealthiest book treasury of the civilized world. Since Paris had the most and best libraries in 18th-century Europe, and many of these libraries were made more or less accessible to the public, scholars from all over came to Paris to work.

Lace Patterns in Bookbinding

In the time of Louis XV the royal household and several of
the bibliophiles among the nobility employed the bookbinder Antoine
Michel Padeloup. Some of the bindings made for Louis XV's queen,
Maria Leszcinska, and for his mistress, Madame de Pompadour,
are signed by Padeloup, as are also some bindings from Count von
Hoym's collection. For the king, he bound in uniform red morocco
a great many of the works printed at the royal press recounting and
extolling the festivities of the royal house. Like another famous
binder of that time, Le Monnier, Padeloup used a technique that later
became very popular: mosaic work in leather, using differently colored pieces to form a tapestry-like pattern. He was the originator
of the lacework pattern (fers à la dentelle) or at least brought it to
a high stage of development. Lace was widely used in the costumes
of the period and it was natural to transfer its patterns to binding
designs. Lacework bindings soon became prominent in the French
collector's rococo bookcase. As a rule, the decoration consisted of
a wide laced edge with projections extending in toward the middle of
the cover, where space was left for the owner's mark, or super ex
libris. This type of decoration was used in many variations on a
great number of bindings. The spine of the book was also decorated,
often with a conventional flower in each of the panels and small ornaments in the corners of each panel. The designs were gilded but not
often tooled, as on 17th-century bindings. The lace pattern was
treated with special grace and virtuosity on the bindings made by
Jacques Antoine Derome and his son Nicolas Denis Derome (Fig.
81); some of these had the special feature of a small bird with out-
spread wings set in the corners of the decoration. Two other famous names of this period were those of the binders to the Duke of
Orléans, Du Seuil and Pierre Paul Dubuisson.

An air of elegance pervaded these French rococo bindings, an
effect further increased by the red leather, but they exhibited only
faint traces of the characteristic rococo ornamentation. The true C-
and S- shaped rococo lines appear only in rare instances on 18th-
century bindings; most of the bindings with rococo ornaments belong
to the later neo-rococo period. The characteristic rococo features

81.   Binding in red morocco with lacework designs by Nicolas
Denis Derome.   Five of Derome's characteristic bird figures are
seen here.

did occur frequently in the ex libris that collectors had made for
their books to indicate ownership.   This custom appeared in the 15th

and 16th centuries, the ownership marks of that time being printed from woodcuts, but in the 17th and 18th centuries the use of ex libris spread with the increasing fashion of book collecting, and they were printed from copper engravings.

The ex libris was a label of varying size pasted on the inner side of the cover, stating the owner of the book by initials, by full name, or by his coat-of-arms framed in a cartouche. Heraldic emblems were quite common, even when the ex libris was in the form of a small picture. These pictures might be symbolic, they might represent the interior of the owner's own library, or might be small landscape vignettes. A charming example of the latter is an ex libris made by one of the best Danish artists in this field, O.H. Delode, showing a young man reading a book at the foot of a tree; it bears no name, but the initial letters of its motto, "Fallitur hora legendo" (reading passes the time), are assumed to stand for Friderici Hornii liber, referring to the lawyer Frederik Horn (Fig. 82). Many other ex libris contained the owner's motto. Most of the great French illustrators of the rococo period designed ex libris, and many of these were small masterpieces.

These bookplates were so named because they often contained the words ex libris (or ex museo or ex bibliotheca) before the name of the owner. At the beginning of the 19th century the ex libris art showed signs of decadence, but at the middle of the century it blossomed anew; currently it is regaining popularity among book collectors.

English Book Collectors

The English noblemen who gathered at the court of George I were strongly influenced by French fashions. There were many bibliophiles among the English nobility and, as in France, private collecting was influential in the development of public libraries.

The national library of Britain came into being in 1753 when Parliament decided to purchase the collection of books and manuscripts that had been left by Hans Sloane. Two other important manuscript collections were added to this, those of Bruce Cotton and Edward Harley, and thus the foundation was laid for the world-famous

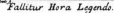

82. Left, ex libris of Frederik Horn with landscape; right,
ex libris of Laurids de Thurah with heraldic design.

British Museum. A few years later George II presented the Museum with the library of the royal house, and along with it the right
to receive deposit copies of all books issued in England. The new
institution was opened to the public in 1859 with a staff of 48 members, half of whom were appointed by the government.

Harley, Earl of Oxford, had inherited an outstanding collection of books and manuscripts from his father, Robert Harley. He
increased it to such an extent that at his death it numbered 7,600
manuscripts, 40,000 letters and documents and 50,000 printed books,
besides 400,000 pamphlets and smaller items--a worthy counterpart
to the La Vallière collection in France. Harley's collection included
a considerable number of books printed by William Caxton and his
immediate successors, and it gave evidence of an interest in incunabula that was by no means common at that time. The bishop of Ely,
John Moore, whose books had been purchased by George I in 1715
and donated to the University Library of Cambridge, had also paid
special attention to these early English black-letter books, but it was
not until the final decades of the 18th century that collectors of incunabula began to increase in number. English collectors have maintained a leading position in this field down to the present.

The bindings that were made for Harley resulted in a "Harleian style," which featured a small central field surrounded by a
very wide border and a peculiar combination of lace designs and
realistic flowers. These bindings (Fig. 77) became the pattern for

the bookbinding of that time, but today the style seems severe and
heavy.

Books in Germany

Although French bibliophilism was the model, book collecting
in England was no servile imitation. The same held true in Germany. Voltaire's friend Frederick the Great was a zealous admirer
of French culture and philosophy. He was an enthusiastic reader
and an extensive writer. The 25-volume edition of his works published in 1787-89 was one of the most impressive typographical productions of 18th-century Germany. Frederick the Great had large
collections of books at Sans-Souci and in Potsdam, and he even carried a library with him on his military campaigns. The French ra-
tionalists and French literature in general were his favorite reading,
and he preferred octavo and duodecimo formats to such an extent
that he actually avoided quartos and folios. He shared the French
preference for red morocco bindings with gold tooling.

Contrary to what might be expected it was mainly in northern
Germany that French influence made itself felt. It apparently reached
there in part by way of England. It was felt also in Saxony, which
since the days of the Elector August had never entirely lost its connections with the French tradition. Dresden was the home of many
large private libraries in the 18th century, and here, as in Paris,
it was considered fashionable to collect books. Count Heinrich von
Brühl's collection of 62,000 volumes finally landed in the library of
the Saxon court (the present Landesbibliothek).

The library of Göttingen University became the model for all
of Europe. At Göttingen a serious effort was made to build up the
book collection and to make it useful and accessible to scholars. Under the direction of Christian Gottlieb Heyne, the library followed a
development that did not become effective elsewhere until the 19th
century, and Göttingen became the first research library in Europe
in the modern sense.

In 1769 the Göttingen library received a valuable addition in
the books of Johann Fredrich von Uffenbach, which he had for the
most part collected on a long book-buying journey with his brother

Zacharias Conrad, who was even more enthusiastic about books. These two had provided themselves with a complete list of the books they wanted to acquire and had then traveled through Germany, Holland and England, filling their diaries with a wealth of bibliographical information. The greatest number of book acquisitions were made in Holland, whose copious stock supplied English, German and Scandinavian collectors.

Books and literature were more of a middle-class phenomenon in Germany than in England and France; interest in reading had spread to larger and larger segments of the population. In the Age of Enlightenment, cultural and general educational literature made hitherto unheard of advances. The ideas of the Enlightenment, which spread from England to Frence and then developed into the general European intellectual movement of rationalism, also became important for the evolution of science. The modern research library, of which Göttingen was the first example, can rightly be called one of the fruits of the Enlightenment. There was, however, a background of organization of scientific activity in the larger countries going back to the 17th century. It was then that the first scientific academies were founded and the first scientific journals made their appearance --Journal des savants in Paris, Philosophical Transactions in London, both still alive today, and Acta eruditorum in Leipzig. Large encyclopedic works presenting the knowledge of all time in convenient form were prepared by the scholars of the 18th century--Diderot, d'Alembert and their circle compiled the famous French Encyklopaedi, and in Germany Zedler issued his Universal-Lexikon in 64 heavy volumes, a work that is still of value. Gradually an increasing volume of critical and literary journals appeared, and almanacs and pocket books became very popular. These started in France around the middle of the 18th century and benefited from the current vignette art, especially the theater almanacs, fashion almanacs and those devoted to amorous subjects. Some attention also began to be paid to children's literature, and Campe's adaptation of Defoe's Robinson Crusoe is one of the best children's books ever written.

Pocket editions of literary works and calendars were especially popular in Germany, where they were provided with copper-en-

graved vignettes in which German artists imitated the French masters. Only Daniel Chodowiecki made an independent approach, adopting German middle-class or petty-bourgeois features in his work.
This made Chodowiecki the most nationalistic of the German vignette
artists and made his small-scale representations of daily life very
popular among the common people. A book that was already popular, Gellert's collection of fables, was made even more popular by
Chodowiecki's work, and his charming vignettes for Goethe's writings
also became famous, especially those for Hermann und Dorthea
which appeared in a ladies' almanac for 1799.

The growing interest in reading opened up new possibilities
for the book trade and, with Leipzig as a center, it began to develop rapidly. The old method of book exchange, which consisted in
trading sheet for sheet or book for book, was disappearing. The
publisher-dealers had separated themselves more and more from the
miscellaneous booksellers and their business had taken on a more
stable character with the adoption of a definite price schedule. The
other booksellers received so little discount that they often had to
exceed the established sale price. The fight against the abuses of
reprinting was waged with increasing vigor in Germany, but for a
long time in vain. Not until toward the end of the century was protection obtained for the rights of authors and publishers; this had
been provided in England by the Copyright Act of 1709.

As the dissemination of literature increased, multiple printings of the same book became common, and a method was sought
for keeping the type matter in a form from which duplicate printings
could be made as desired. A Scotch goldsmith, William Ged, was
the first to experiment with stereotyping; he made his experiments
in the 1720's but they were not very successful. Stereotyping did
not come into practical use until the process had been improved at
the beginning of the 19th century by Charles, 3rd Earl of Stanhope,
who printed stereotyped Bibles at the Cambridge University Press.
In 1800 Lord Stanhope built the first iron press, to replace the
wooden presses that had been in use ever since Gutenberg's time.

Bookmaking in Denmark

In Denmark the development of bookmaking followed that in
Germany in many respects.   Printing was done in a mixture of
styles and was generally poor.   German fraktur type in more or
less crude variations constituted the bulk of a Danish printer's type
stock, with old worn-out woodcuts used for illustrations and decoration.   In the more elaborate books German baroque style was dominant, especially in the many funeral sermons for noblemen, which
had grown to folio size.   Around the middle of the century the rococo style began to make its appearance, at first only in the form
of scattered vignettes in otherwise baroque books.

French style gradually found its way into Danish books, as
indicated by two of the most imposing books ever printed in Denmark.   One contained Fr. L. Norden's account in French of his
travels to Egypt and Nubia, with some 150 copper-engraved plates
and many headpieces and vignettes (Fig. 85).   Two vignette artists,
Marcus Tuscher and Peter Cramer, worked on this publication,
which was printed at one of Copenhagen's largest and best presses,
Vajsenhuset.   The second book was the unfinished treatise on shells
by the German engraver Frantz Michael Regenfuss.   The first volume, which appeared in 1758, was printed by Höpffner's stepson,
Andreas Hartvig Godiche.   Many well-made and artistically produced
books came from the Godiche press, including Pontoppidan's Danish
Atlas and the first volumes of Langebek's great collection of medieval sources for Danish history, Scriptores rerum Danicarum.   Several of the later volumes of this work were printed by Nicolaus
Møller, who became printer at the royal court in 1765 and was considered the best of his time.

Some publishing work of high artistic quality was undertaken
by a group under the leadership of Bolle Luxdorph.   At his estate
in Naerum high public officials like Suhm, Langebek, Henrik Hielmstierne and others, including Luxdorph's librarian, Lavrids Skov,
came together to talk about books.   French typography and vignette
art were the models they followed.   The most famous work that this
group generated was entirely French in character: Holberg's Peder
Paars, printed in quarto by Godiche, with engravings from drawings

83. Copper-engraved frontispiece by Daniel Chodowiecki for
Goethe's Works, vol. 1, Leipzig, 1787.

by the sculptor Wiedewelt.

In the field of bookbinding, French influence in Denmark went
back to the 17th century, but later there was a gradual increase in
English influence.   The Gascon-style stamps were taken over from
France, great preference being shown for a stylized flower with its
lines broken up into small dots.   The crescent-shaped tool so extensively used by the English was widely adopted in various varia-

Cap. I.
Handler om Kiøbenhavn i Almindelighed.

Mit Forsæt er ey, at anføre noget i denne Beskrivelse om Kiøbenhavns gamle og første Oprindelse, hvorledes den, siden den blev udvalt til Kongernes ordentlige Boe-Sæde, og derudover, og formedelst dens ypperlige Beliggenhed til Handel, med adskillige fortdeelagtige Friheder af een og anden Konge er bleven beskienket, Tid efter anden har tiltaget i Storelse, Magt, Anseelse og Hertighed, indtil den har naaet den Fuldkommenhed, hvorudi den i disse vore Tider viser sig; thi sligt er saavel i den Danske Vitruvio nogenledes forklaret, som ved adskillige berømmelige Mænds Pen, baade gamle og nyere, noye og omstændelig beskrevet.

Jeg

Chap. I.
Traité de la Ville de Copenhague en général.

Ce n'est pas mon dessein, de m'étendre en la description de Copenhague sur son ancienne & premiere origine, ni d'etaler, de quelle façon elle s'est agrandie de tems en tems, après qu'elle fut choisié pour la demeure, ou Residence ordinaire des Rois, & que par cette raison, & à cause de sa situation excellente pour le negoce, elle fut gratifiée par differens Rois de plusieurs privileges avantageux, & de quelle maniere elle s'est augmentée depuis, en grandeur, en puissance, en splendeur & en majesté, jusqu'à ce qu'elle soit parvenue à la perfection, où elle se présente de nos jours; tout cela étant en quelque façon expliqué dans le Vitruve Danois, & traité amplement & circonstantiellement par plusieurs celebres Savans, tant anciens que modernes,

Je

Cap. I.
Handelt von Copenhagen überhaupt.

Mein Vorsatz ist gar nicht, in dieser Beschreibung von dem alten und ersten Ursprunge der Stadt Copenhagen etwas anzuführen, wie selbige, seitdem sie zur ordentlichen Residenz der Könige ausersehen, und dahero, und wegen ihrer vortrefflichen Lage zum Handel, von einem und dem andern Könige mit verschiedenen vortheilhaften Freyheiten beschenket worden, von Zeit zu Zeit an Grösse, Macht, Ansehen und Herrlichkeit zugenommen, bis sie endlich zu der Vollkommenheit gelanget, darinnen sie sich zu unsern Zeiten zeiget; denn solches ist sowohl in dem Dänischen Vitruvio einigermassen erkläret, als durch verschiedener Leute Federn genau und umständlich beschrieben.

Ich

84. Page from Laurids de Thurah's Hafnia hodierna (1748), a description of Copenhagen with 110 copper engravings. Thurah also published two volumes of The Danish Vitruvius, an important resource for the history of Danish architecture.

tions. English patterns also may have been responsible for the evolution of the so-called "mirror bindings," which became the outstanding feature of bookbinding in Denmark in the 18th century. The
English used the principle of a central panel devoid of decoration,
surrounded by a gilded border--Danish bookbinders developed this
idea in an original manner. It has also been called "Holberg binding" because it began to flourish in the 1720's, the time of Holberg's
comedies. Danish mirror bindings were made in calf or sheepskin.
The dark rectangular panel in the middle of the cover--the "mirror"
--was surrounded by a frame of lighter-colored leather, and outside
this the leather was again darker. The mirror panel and the light-
colored frame were set off by blind-stamped borders made with
roller stamps and consisting of small flowered designs; both borders,
or sometimes only the outer one, continued out to the corners of
the cover, where they ended in somewhat larger ornaments. Along
the outer edge of the binding there was usually a fine gold line. In
contrast to this modest decoration on the covers, there was a profusion of gilded decoration in the small panels on the spine; the top
panel often contained the owner's mark, or super ex libris, which
in other bindings was usually on the sides. (Fig. 86).

    In the second half of the century mirror bindings became
more and more common in Denmark, and blind-stamping of the borders was partly replaced by gold tooling. Rococo patterns appeared
both in the borders and on the spine of the book, and the mirror
panel was accentuated by dark spots applied with a sponge or
sprinkled on with a brush. The designs were rarely gilded, but
were usually colored red or bluish green, sometimes marbled or
speckled; the end papers were also colored or marbled in striking
patterns--stripes, spirals, etc. The bookbinders of that time--men
like Andreas Lyman and his sons, Johann Boppenhausen and his sons,
and the court binder G.J. Liebe--showed great imagination in their
adaptations; among the thousands of mirror bindings preserved in
Danish libraries there are few exactly alike.

Swedish and Norwegian Collectors
    In Sweden as elsewhere the 18th century was a great period

PRÉFACE.

es Egyptiens ſe vantent d'être un des Peuples les plus anciens de l'Univers. Peu de Nations en effet pourroient leur diſputer cette prérogative. Leurs prétenſions à cet egard ſe fondent ſur une multitude de Monumens marqués au coin de l'antiquité la plus reculée; titres d'autant plus reſpeƈtables, que les Auteurs de tous les ſiècles en ont parlé avec admiration.

Un Pays rendu fameux par tant de merveilles de l'Antiquité n'a pu que s'attirer l'attention des Curieux & dévenir

a   nir

85. First page of the preface to F. L. Norden's Voyage d'Égypte et de Nubie. Vignette drawn by J. M. Preisler and engraved by I. Haas in 1755.

86. Mirror binding in calfskin. The "mirror" is the dark
marbled central panel; surrounding it is a gold-tooled frame and
outside this a lighter area surrounded by a blind-stamped line. The
spine is heavily decorated with gold stamping.

for bibliophiles. Gustav III probably went farthest of all the princes
of Europe in copying the court life of his French counterpart. The
tone for the many Swedish castle and manor libraries that grew up
in the second half of the century was set by Carl Gustaf Tessin. He
had an extensive knowledge of books and was a bibliophile and art

collector after the French pattern. First-rate bookbinders, with
Kristoffer Schneidler in the lead, raised their craft out of stagnation and created bindings that clearly showed French influence. One
collector, to whom we owe much for the preservation of early Swedish literature, was the learned court councilor, Carl Gustaf Warm-
holtz. His own library provided the source material for his famous
work on Swedish history.

Norway had no class of landowners that could follow in the
steps of the Danish and Swedish nobility, but the country did not lack
important book collectors. Gerhard Schøning's books in large part
came from the poet Benjamin Dass. At Schøning's death they became part of the library of the Norwegian Academy of Sciences in
Trondheim. There was also Bishop B. Deichman, whose library was
sold in Copenhagen in 1732, and his son Carl Deichman, whose collection formed the basis of the present municipal library of Oslo,
the Deichmanske Library. Several members of the Anker family,
especially Carsten Anker of Eidsvold, also built up valuable book
collections.

Neo-classicism in Book Arts

By the time the rococo style gained acceptance in Scandinavia
it was losing ground in its homeland. During the reign of Louis XVI
artists began turning away from it, and the ensuing reaction could
scarcely have been stronger. The gay and festive rococo lines were
replaced by an imitation of the firm lines of classical antiquity; in-
formality gave way to order. The excavations at Pompeii and Herculaneum had revived interest in Roman art and motifs from the
wall-paintings of the excavated cities came into fashion in both Italy
and France. Meander borders, acanthus leaves, laurel festoons,
vases and candelabra were repeated over and over again as decorative elements. Classical antiquity was again enthroned as it had
been in the Renaissance, though some of the rococo spirit was retained. Symmetry and the straight line again came into prominence,
though not in the heavy and rigid form of the baroque style; natural-
ness and elegance were still the artist's guiding stars. Vignette art
was also affected by this change in taste; several of the great illus-

87.   Four great Danish book collectors.   Upper left, P. F. Suhm; upper right, Otto Thott; lower left, B. W. Luxdorph; lower right, Henrik Hielmstierne.

trators of the rococo period, including Marillier, Cochin and Morea'
le jeune, came under its influence when they visited Italy. In Denmark neo-classicism showed in illustrations by the artist Nic. Ab-
ildgaard for the famous edition of <u>Nils Klim</u> in 1789, and were engraved in copper by Johan Frederik Clemens. Most of the other copper engravers who worked in Denmark in the 18th century were
merely competent craftsmen, but Clemens was a true artist. He
was eventually appointed professor at the National Art Academy.

The roman types that came into being in this period tended
to reproduce the dignity and regularity of the classical style, to
such a degree that even the best of them had a certain air of inflex-
ibility and dullness. In Paris the famous Didot family of printers
created some of the most popular typefaces of the time. One of the
greatest members of this family was François Ambroise Didot, who
not only attained fame for a roman type that gave the effect of having been engraved in copper, but became even more famous through
his introduction of a new system of measuring type. In Didot's system type fonts were classified according to "points," of which there
were 2,660 to a meter; this French system gradually superseded
the German system. The Didot press was taken over in 1789 by
François' son Pierre, who was responsible for a number of the most
successful neo-classical roman types, used in his great folio editions of Virgil and Horace and his illustrated edition of Racine. A
brother of Pierre, the scholarly Firmin Didot, became known for
his small and inexpensive but beautifully stereotyped editions of the
classics. These became as important as those issued by the Elzevirs in the 17th century.

At the time of the elder Didots there was a printer in Italy,
Giambattista Bodoni, working for the Duke of Parma; he cut a roman type in no less than 143 different forms and sizes, and, at the
behest of the Pope, printed the Lord's Prayer in 155 languages. Bodoni's types attained wide fame and were adopted by various European printers. Like other types of this period they are very regular, but one of their characteristics is the strongly emphasized contrast between light and heavy lines in the individual letters.

Neither Didot's nor Bodoni's types, however, have been of

dono puro di Dio e felicità di natu-
ra, benchè spesso provenga da lunga
esercitazione e abitudine, che le più
difficili cose agevola a segno che in
fine senza più pur pensarvi riescono
ottimamente fatte. Che però la gra-

88. Bodoni's roman type, from the preface to his Manuale tipografico (Parma, 1818).

ODE I.

AD VENEREM.

Intermissa, Venus, diu
Rursus bella moves. Parce, precor, precor!
    Non sum qualis eram bonæ
    Sub regno Cinaræ. Desine, dulcium
        Mater sæva Cupidinum,
Circa lustra decem flectere mollibus
    Iam durum imperiis. Abi
Quo blandæ iuvenum te revocant preces.

89. Firmin Didot's roman type from the beginning of the 19th century. As in Bodoni's types the difference between the light and heavy lines is quite pronounced. Bodoni's and Didot's types are both typical of the Empire style.

ME. Hac te nos fragili donabimus ante cicuta.
Hæc nos, Formofum Corydon ardebat Alexin :
Hæc eadem docuit, Cujum pecus? an Melibœi?
MO. At tu fume pedum, quod, me quum fæpe rogaret,
Non tulit Antigenes, (et erat tum dignus amari)
Formofum paribus nodis atque ære, Menalca.

90. Baskerville's roman, from his edition of Virgil (Birmingham, 1757).

lasting significance. Much greater vitality was found in some of
the types of the English printer John Baskerville. Even in his own
time Baskerville's types were very successful, although they met
with some criticism. They show some connection with the French
''roman du roi'' type mentioned earlier, but they had many calligraphic features--very likely because Baskerville had been a teacher of
handwriting.

Superior to all these was a type attributed to one of Baskerville's predecessors, William Caslon. Like Baskerville's, Caslon's
type was a transitional form between the Renaissance type of Aldus
and Garamond and the new roman of Didot and Bodoni. Caslon designed his type on the basis of the Dutch types that had been widely
used in England since the time of the Elzevirs--it was a roman type,
vigorous and free of all artificial stiffness. It did not immediately
attain the success that it deserved. Since its revival in 1844 it has
maintained a strong position, and alongside Nicolaus Jenson's, Garamond's and Baskerville's, Caslon's roman (Fig. 91) is the one in
widest use today. England has thus, with the more recent aid of
American type designers, set her mark on the development of roman type. The many private presses in England have been a significant factor in this development. One of the first of these was
established by the great collector of books and art, Horace Walpole,
for printing his own as well as other writings.

Baskerville's type was purchased by a French author and
printer, Pierre Augustin de Beaumarchais, who had formed a society

Quoufque tandem abutere,
Catilina, patientia noftra? qu
Quoufque tandem abutere, Ca-
tilina, patientia noftra? quam-

91. Caslon's roman and italic, from his book of type
samples (1763), the first such book issued in England.

to publish a monumental edition of Voltaire. When this undertaking
was opposed by the church the society moved its press to the small
town of Kehl near Strassburg, where it issued the famous 70-volume
edition of the works of Voltaire in 1785 as well as an edition of
Rousseau.

Roman typefaces had never really been accepted in Germany
except for use in scientific works. Almost down to the present the
principal type has been the black-letter fraktur. At one time there
was a strong movement in favor of roman type, but the famous
Leipzig printer, J. G. Immanuel Breitkopf, the founder of the music
publishing house, came out very forcibly in favor of preserving fraktur as the national typeface of Germany, and his position prevailed.
But the movement did have its effect on the development of fraktur
type. The type introduced by Johan F. Unger (Fig. 92), with broad
and somewhat rounded shapes, was an attempt to creat something
between roman and fraktur. It was a product of neo-classicism;
Unger worked with Didot and sought to introduce the latter's type into Germany, and hence has been called 'the German Didot."

The new trend in art appeared in bookbinding as well. Even
some bindings of the 1770's used straight lines, meander borders,
acanthus leaves and the other classical elements, and decoration was
confined to a narrow border while the rest of the cover was plain.
Even the super ex libris in the middle of the cover gradually disappeared. A special touch was given to this style by the English bookbinder Roger Payne, a peculiar individual who usually worked without assistants. In spite of the many expensive bindings that he com-

Nachricht des Verlegers.

Mein erster Versuch neuer deutscher Druckschrift, den ich in der Oster= messe 1793 bekannt machte, fand Bei= fall, wurde aber auch hie und da geta= delt. Männer ohne Vorurtheil gegen Neuerungen, und denen guter Geschmack wohl schwerlich abgesprochen werden kann, munterten mich zu fernerer Ver= vollkommnung auf, und nun wartete ich nur noch die öffentlichen Urtheile darüber ab. Diese sind jezt wohl größtentheils erschienen, und lauten dafür und dawider. Einer findet die neuen Lettern den schon vorhanden gewesenen ähnlich, mit welchen die groß= octav Bibel in Halle gedruckt ist. Ich verglich sie, und fand, so wie mehrere Personen, nicht die geringste Ähnlich=

92. J. F. Unger's type of 1794, a fraktur type brought closer to the roman form by rounding off the letters somewhat.

pleted and the detailed bills that he rendered his customers he re- mained poor throughout his lifetime. His masterpieces, for which he usually used olive-colored or blue long-grained morocco or Rus- sia leather, were decorated with neo-classical or oriental patterns. On some of his bindings the decoration was limited to a narrow bor- der of fine lines or small ornaments along the edges with a small rosette in each corner; these simple bindings were among his best.

The Effect of the French Revolution
Gradually the neo-classical style in book decoration followed

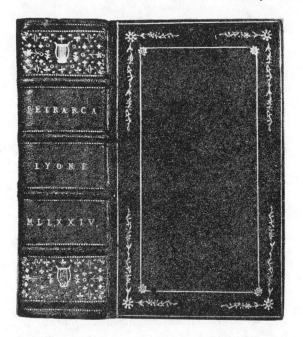

93.   Binding by Roger Payne in olive-colored morocco. (Royal Library, Copenhagen.)

classical forms more closely.   The elegance that had characterized it at first, when there was still interplay between it and the rococo style, disappeared, leaving only a simplicity of the sort found in some of the neo-classical roman typefaces.   The cause of this lay in the violent reaction of the French Revolution to the refinement of the 18th century.   The stern Roman spirit was exalted, in place of the effeminacy of the earlier generation, and all aspects of Roman republican civilization were slavishly imitated.   Profuse illustrations disappeared from books, leaving only the typography and a few vignettes of a symbolic nature to produce an esthetic effect.   The bindings were dominated by warlike emblems from Roman times along with the ornaments mentioned earlier; even a master craftsman like Derome from the high period of laced patterns, submitted to the demands of the new movement.   In Denmark the development was the same though slower, and in Sweden there were first-rate binders working along the same lines.

The Revolution sounded the fateful hour not only for French bookmaking but also for French book collecting. In November of 1789 all church and monastery libraries were declared property of the state and in 1792 the book collections of the emigrés were confiscated. The various governments that followed one another in rapid succession in those years had great plans--libraries were to become public in the full sense of the word. But the times were not favorable for realization of these plans, and the unsettled conditions were responsible for the destruction of many of the eight million or so books that are said to have been transferred from private to public ownership. Just how many were destroyed is impossible to say. During the first period of the Revolution the libraries of the church and the aristocracy were plundered with a fanaticism reminiscent of the destruction of Catholic libraries during the Reformation. The books that escaped destruction were brought to the "literary depots" that had been established at various places throughout the country. In Paris alone there were nine of these. Here all sorts of books and manuscripts were thrown together in enormous piles. From these depots the books were sent to the various libraries that were already public to some extent: the Arsenal library, the Bibliothèque Mazarine, and others, but above all to the Royal Library, which was now named Bibliothèque Nationale. No less than 300,000 volumes and numerous manuscripts, including 9,000 from the famous monastery of St. Germain-des-Prés, were added to the national library, and the French library system was centralized as never before. It was a gigantic task to bring order into these heaps of books and fit them into the existing framework; it took the Bibliothèque Nationale some hundred years to assimilate and catalog the accessions of the Revolutionary period.

Books that were not destroyed or added to the public collections were put on the auction block by the government. The auctions were held under very unfavorable circumstances, as the demand was much less than the supply. Often real rarities had to be sold at ridiculously low prices. For a relatively small sum a bookdealer of that time could acquire a stock that he might dispose of later,

when times were quieter and prices better, at a profit of several
hundred percent.   The stalls of the bouquinists along the Seine
bulged with books confiscated from the libraries of the nobility.

Chapter 6.   The 19th Century and the Beginning
of the 20th Century

The disruptive effect of the French Revolution in the world of
books extended to Germany and, during the Napoleonic Wars, to
large parts of the rest of Europe. Napoleon was a book collector,
and like Frederick the Great he carried a small library with him on
his campaigns. It was his desire that his nation hold not only political but also cultural leadership in Europe. During 1802-05 he had
the former Benedictine monk, Jean Baptiste Maugérard, travel
through the Rhine country buying up for trifling sums thousands of
valuable medieval manuscripts and rare printed books from the many
monastery libraries in that region. In most other instances, however, no attempt was made to disguise this form of looting. In con-
formance with the traditions of the Thirty Years' War Napoleon himself sent large numbers of books from conquered countries to Paris
as war booty. They became part of the French national library.
Trained agents accompanied the victorious French troops with lists
of books that the library wanted and their work was done thoroughly.
The Royal Library at Brussels, the Escorial Library in Madrid, the
Vatican Library, the Court Library in Vienna, the Wolfenbüttel Library, and many others had parts of their collections taken away by
French soldiers. In Vienna, however, the most valuable books had
been sent down the Danube to Hungary, where they were kept hidden
for eight years until the danger was past. After the fall of Napoleon
in 1815 a considerable part of his library loot had to be returned in
accordance with the terms of the Peace of Vienna. As a result the
libraries mentioned have books bearing the stamp of Napoleon or of
the Bibliotheque Imperiale (as the Bibliothèque Nationale was called
in his time) as evidence of their excursion to Paris.

While Napoleon never managed to extend his empire to England, his wars had considerable influence on books and libraries in

the island kingdom. The blockade of the continent meant that no
books could be brought in from Holland or the other countries that
supplied English collectors, and that resulted in a tremendous rise
in the price of books in England. Whenever the library of an English collector was put up at auction by one of the great auction firms,
such as Leigh & Sotheby, G. & W. Nicol, King, Evans, etc., the
competition for rare items was intense. In 1812 at the auction of
the books left by the Duke of Roxburghe, the Marquis of Blanford,
after an exciting battle with Lord Spencer, took home a 1471 edition
of Boccaccio for 2,260 pounds sterling. Seven years thereafter,
however, Lord Spencer was able to acquire the same book for some
900 pounds at the auction of the Marquis' estate. In the ensuing
decades book prices dropped even lower.

England could boast an imposing array of collectors in the
19th century. Sir Thomas Phillips, in the course of his travels on
the continent, collected about 60,000 manuscripts and became the
greatest private manuscript collector the world has ever known. The
position that Lord Spencer held in the field of printed books was held
by Phillips in the field of manuscripts; his famous collection was
broken up later at prolonged auction sales. Many such large auctions were held in 19th-century England; in the history of bibliophilism, what is gathered by one generation is split up by a later generation. The largest sum realized at any English book auction in the
first part of the century was the 50,000 pounds sterling taken in at
the sale of Richard Heber's books in 1834-36. In his insatiable
mania for books Heber had collected libraries in several cities
throughout Europe. A similar sum was realized in 1881-83 at the
sale of the famous Sunderland collection, founded by Charles, Earl
of Sunderland, toward the end of the 17th century. At this sale one
of the largest buyers was German-born Bernard Quaritch, who in
the latter decades of the 19th century, became the "Napoleon of the
antiquarian book trade," and controlled the European book market in
this field for many years.

Many other large and valuable collections were scattered by
auction. However, Lord Spencer's collection, which had reached
40,000 volumes, was purchased in 1892 by the widow of the wealthy

Manchester manufacturer John Rylands. She had already made her
husband's library public, and by the purchase of Spencer's books
and later the manuscripts and fine bindings of the Earl of Crawford,
the John Rylands Library was expanded to become one of England's
wealthiest book museums.

Lord Spencer's bookbinder was Roger Payne and his librarian
was a village curate by the name of Thomas Frognall Dibdin. Dibdin left handsomely printed accounts of Althorp Castle, where
Spencer's books were housed, and also of his own travels in
Spencer's service. These, like his book on bibliomania, are a
hodge-podge of more or less reliable bibliographical and historical
information, written in a rather affected style and interlarded with
"learned" footnotes. Dibdin was probably guilty of vanity and snob-
bishness, but he must be given credit for an almost religious devotion to old and rare books. He was instrumental in forming the
Roxburghe Club. It was founded in 1812, on the occasion of the
famous Roxburghe auction, and was the first of many English book
clubs.

Steel Engravings.   Revival
of Woodcuts.   Lithography

Several of Dibdin's works have illustrations made by steel engraving, a process that came into wide use in the first half of the
19th century alongside copper engraving. A copper engraving is
quite soft and will wear rapidly when a large number of impressions
must be taken. The harder steel engraving overcame this difficulty,
but the general technique used was the same in both instances. Steel
engravings, however, have a certain sleek and unnatural quality
about them that tends to destroy their artistic effect. They were
used quite extensively in England but the results attained were seldom of any great significance. When a process was developed later
for coating copper engravings with an electrolytic deposit of steel to
give them a hard surface, the day of steel engravings was practically over.

At about the time when steel engravings made their appearance in English books, the poet William Blake was experimenting

with a process by which copperplates were used for relief printing.
By this ingenious method he printed his own works in a style that
closely resembled that of the illuminated manuscripts of the Middle
Ages; each page, including text, headpieces and borders, was drawn
by hand and then colored by hand in the manner of the old illuminators. Blake's method did not find any imitators, so that in this respect, as in his literary style, he stood alone.

More far-reaching in its effect was the work that Thomas Bewick began in Newcastle at the end of the 18th century. He revived
the use of woodcuts for book illustration after the art had been dor-
mant for some two hundred years. Bewick and his many pupils and
followers developed new woodcut techniques. In the old woodcuts the
black lines had been the most outstanding feature; Bewick made the
white line the dominant element in the picture, accentuated by a
background in which the varying density of the lines created the effect of light and shadow. The effectiveness of these shaded woodcuts was also due to the fact that they were cut in very hard box-
wood and the carving was not done with a knife as formerly, but
with a burin like that used by engravers.

Bewick was an excellent draughtsman, especially skilled in
animal subjects. His major works were two large books on mam-
mals and birds, with copious illustrations distinguished not only by
an accurate representation of each animal's outward appearance but
also by a definite feeling for its individuality. Bewick's art reached
its highest point in the numerous small vignettes with which he decorated his books, and in which, often with true Dickensian humor, he
depicted life in the country as lived by men as well as animals.

The woodcut art of the Bewick school was not only influential
in England but was brought to the Continent and also to America by
English xylographers. In France J. B. Papillon had done considerable work with woodcuts toward the close of the 18th century, but it
was not until the advent of English influence around 1830 that French
woodcut art reached a high level in the work of artists like the great
satirist Honoré Daumier, the brothers Alfred and Tony Johannot, and
that masterful portrayer of the elegant life of Paris, Paul Gavarni.
Later in the century Gustave Doré, whose enormous production ex-

94.   Vignette by Thomas Bewick in his <u>History of the British Birds</u>, 1797-1804.

95.   Woodcut by Adolf von Menzel in Franz Kugler's book on Frederick the Great, 1840.

tended from Rabelais to the Bible, from Dante to Edgar Allan Poe, was equally great in depicting mob scenes and individual human features.   With Doré the 19th-century flowering of woodcut art in France came to an end.

Woodcut illustration had been kept alive more in Germany than anywhere else but it was not until the end of the 18th century that the art again came into prominence.   Moritz von Schwind achieved great popularity with his fairy tale illustrations, and so did the amiable Ludwig Richter with his many charming scenes from folk life and fairy tales, which showed kinship with the bourgeois spirit of Chodowiecki's copper engravings. At this time Alfred Rethel became famous for his stirring Dance of Death pictures drawn in Dürer's style. Later, so did Adolf von Menzel, for his illustrations glorifying the military exploits of Frederick the Great.

All these artists belonged to the so-called Romantic period that succeeded the neo-classical and showed its enthusiasm for the Middle Ages in various forms of expression. In Germany, Romanticism was mixed with nationalistic and religious factors, while in France the movement was of a worldly nature. French illustrative art of this period strove for lively representation and picturesque effect.

In 1796-98 Alois Senefelder, experimenting with the printing of his own works, discovered printing from stone blocks, or lithography. He used a mixture of wax, soap and lampblack to write the text on a piece of polished limestone and then poured acid and a thin gum solution over the surface. When printing ink was applied to the stone it adhered only to the written lines and not to the rest of the surface. This method of printing was neither intaglio printing, as from copper engravings, nor relief printing, as from woodcuts, but plano or flat printing. The parts that were to make the impression were on the same level as the rest of the surface. Although this new method meant that the writing or drawing had to be done on stone rather than on paper and had to be done in reverse as if reflected in a mirror, the process soon came into wide use, especially for the printing of single sheets and for illustrations. By using several stones it was relatively easy to print colored maps and plates. When photographic methods became available for transferring the drawing to the stone the lithographic process was simplified, and then the stone was superseded by modern photographic etching in metal. In the half-tone engraving process the picture is photographed through a cross-ruled glass plate or screen that breaks it up into a series of dots that are dense in the dark portions and less so in the lighter portions. In this manner the shading of the picture can be reproduced with considerable accuracy.

Historical Trends in Book Collecting

When French bibliophiles were able to resume their activities after the upheavals of the Revolution and the Napoleonic Wars, their guiding star was the Manuel du libraire by Jacques Charles Brunet. This great bibliographical work appeared first in 1810 and later in several enlarged editions. It gave a detailed description of the literature that was worth collecting, paying special attention to Latin and French books and including the particularly valuable and rare books from incunabula to books of the 18th century. Historical information was provided for each book, also a list of the prices that had been paid for it at auction. The influence of Brunet's handbook was very great; collectors paid more attention to early books and became interested in the history of the various books as they had passed from one owner to another. They also developed an appreciation for first editions of classical literary works, including those of the great English and German authors. Because Brunet's work was regarded as a sort of standard catalog, it gave French collections a rather uniform character and caused a rise in the prices of the items that all collectors had to have.

Others in this field included Charles Nodier, who was like Dibdin in his passion for books, albeit more brilliant and sensitive. One of his best-known writings was the tale of "Le bibliomane," told with charming irony. Like Brunet, Nodier was one of the first to stress the historical approach to book collecting. This became the dominant trend in France for many years and has had permanent influence in other countries as well. One specific manifestation of this approach was an appreciation for the history of binding. It had been accepted practice to remove an old binding and replace it with a new one, but collectors came to understand the value of the original binding and to realize that even a worn and broken binding, as long as it was contemporary with the book, was more appropriate than a modern binding. Grolier bindings and other fine bindings of earlier periods were much in demand, and the study of ex libris and super ex libris aided in tracing the provenance of books.

Others with the same approach as Nodier were Paul Lacroix
(better known as "bibliophile Jacob"); the bibliographer G. Peignot;
the playwright G. de Pixerécourt, who founded the French bibliophile society; the bookdealer Joseph Téchener, who began publishing
the "Bulletin du bibliophile" in 1834; and Count de la Bédoyère,
whose collection of over 100,000 items on the French Revolution is
now in the Bibliothèque Nationale.

Some of the best hunting grounds for these bibliophiles were
the book stalls of the bouquinists. The first half of the 19th century became the golden age of the outdoor book trade, which included
among its members even the learned Latin scholar Achaintre. It
was by no means unusual to find books of great rarity in these dealers' stocks. Nodier came upon a copy of Hypnerotomachia on one
occasion and purchased this masterpiece of Renaissance woodcut art
for 30 centimes. The romantic aspects of such an experience make
it easy to understand why these daily trips along the quays of the
Seine would appeal to a poet like Nodier.

The Romantic movement, with its interest in the Middle Ages,
characterized the intellectual life of this period and provided the
background for the historical interests of bibliophiles. In the Napoleonic period neo-classicism was still predominant and it found expression in a predilection for decorative features of the art of the
Roman Empire. This is shown in the bindings that were produced,
even though Napoleon's own binders, the two Bozérian brothers, used
these features to a limited extent and often let the Emperor's coat-
of-arms constitute the principle element of the decoration. With the
fall of Napoleon, however, the Empire style declined and the gothic
of the Middle Ages became the style to imitate. Architects built
"gothic" castles and villas, craftsmen made gothic furniture, and
bookbinders used gothic motifs for their decoration, sometimes to
such a degree that the entire cover of the book was filled with adaptations of pointed arches and other elements from the church architecture of the Middle Ages. This style has quite properly been
called "à la cathédrale." It was used a great deal by Joseph Thouvenin, a first-rate craftsman and Nodier's favorite binder. The
decoration was applied by panel-stamping (French: gaufrure) in the

96. Red morocco binding with
lace design in corners, made by
the younger of the Bozérian brothers, who worked for Napoleon
and other collectors.

97. Green morocco binding
in the cathedral style, made in
the 1820's by Joseph Thouvenin,
a pupil of the Bozérian brothers.

same manner as in the 16th century, the design being engraved on
a metal plate. Thouvenin's panel stamps were executed with great
virtuosity, and the German-born binders Purgold and Simier also
used the method with considerable skill.

      The Empire style continued to be used alongside the cathedral
style and the growing appreciation of earlier bindings led to imitations of the Grolier, fanfare, Gascon and other styles, often executed with considerable artistry. For a time this historical interest
involved a high regard for the rococo style; a "neo-rococo" appeared
in the 1840's on many books in France as well as elsewhere. Especially in Germany and the Scandinavian countries large rococo ornaments were displayed on the covers of books and on the smooth,
loose spines that had gradually become common because they were
easier to decorate than the rigid spines, and because they made the
books easier to open. Bookbinding of the 19th century was thus
largely characterized by imitation and by mixture of styles and only
in exceptional instances was there a personal contribution by the

binder.   Antoine Bauzonnet introduced a style of binding in which
the entire decoration consisted of a framework of a few parallel
lines stamped with great precision on leather of the most select
quality prepared with the greatest possible care.   Another binder
who used this style was G. Trautz; he reintroduced the rigid spine,
and in gilding and treatment of the leather almost surpassed his
master Bauzonnet.

This concern for the styles of earlier periods led bookbinders
back to mosaic and plastic work in leather; these methods came into fashion increasingly after the 1870's and were used to produce
picturesque effects on book covers.   Two French masters of plastic
leather work were Marius Michel and Léon Gruel; in Denmark there
were H. C. Lerche, D. L. Clément, and later Immanuel Petersen
and J. L. Flyge.   A special variation within this style was the so-
called "narrative binding" (la reliure parlante) which made its appearance in France toward 1880; the intention--often rather forced
in its execution--was to have the picture on the cover tell something
about the contents of the book.   This style was imitated in other
countries but quite often, especially in Germany, the results were
poor.   Its most famous representatives in France were Cuzin,
Charles Meunier and René Kieffer.   England's most outstanding bookbinders in the second half of the 19th century were Joseph Zaehns-
dorf and his son Joseph William.

Technological Advances in Bookmaking

One of the most striking phenomena of the 19th-century book
world was the great expansion in literary productivity.   In Germany,
for instance, the annual production of printed books around 1800 was
about 3,300 titles; at the middle of the century this figure had risen
to 10,000 and at its close was nearly 25,000.   An increase of this
order required considerable advance in the technical aspects of bookmaking and use of machines.   The beginning of this development
came with the invention of the papermaking machine by Louis Robert
in 1799 and the invention of the power press by Friedrich König
around 1810.   The power press soon replaced the old hand presses
and made it possible to turn out large editions in a very short time.

Another significant development was the composing machine. The
earliest experiments with mechanical typesetting were made by a
Dane, Christian Sørensen, but the machine that became successful
was the "linotype" that the German watchmaker Ottmar Mergenthaler
invented in the 1880's. Like the various other composing machines
developed later (monotype, intertype, etc.) the linotype casts the
type ready for printing; the actual composing is done by striking
keys similar to those of a typewriter. Machine composition can be
done much faster than hand composition, and the combination of the
composing machine and the high-speed press gradually effected a
revolution in the printing trade.

These technological developments were of special importance
in the printing of the periodical literature that had grown so profusely since the 1820's. Newspapers as well as the numerous popular weekly papers, magazines, etc., benefited by the rapid rate at
which they could be produced, especially after the rotary press
came into use and paper was available in rolls. Of equal importance was the introduction of new methods of pictorial reproduction,
by which the tedious wood-carving and lithographic processes were
replaced by photographic etchings. These could be made in a matter of days or even hours. Before this, the illustrated press had
always been the best field of xylographers; papers like the Illustrated London News, L'Illustration, and Illustrierte Zeitung, all
founded in the 1840's, had published many excellent woodcuts along
with more ephemeral illustrative material.

Reaction Against Technology

These technological advances did reduce the quality of books
produced. The increased speed of the processes was detrimental
and discouraging to the esthetic aspects of bookmaking. In the 1880's
and 1890's a violent reaction set in against this trend, originating
from a small group of English artists of the Pre-Raphaelite brotherhood led by the painters Burne-Jones and D. G. Rosetti. One of the
most active members of this group was William Morris, who was a
painter, architect, poet and socialistic agitator. His versatility and
unflagging energy made him the spiritual and practical leader of the

Pre-Raphaelites' counterattack against technology. It was their aim to revive original methods and to recreate the purity of style that characterized the best craftsmanship of earlier periods. This was another manifestation of Romanticism, with its preference for the art of the Middle Ages and the Renaissance.

Morris and his co-workers made furniture, wall coverings, woven material, glass paintings and other things for the home, using the methods of the old hand-craftsmen. Their decorative style, like that of the French and German romantic artists, was inspired by the gothic form. Morris did not turn to bookmaking until he was well advanced in years. He first supervised the printing of several books at the Chiswick Press, one of the best in London, which was owned by the publisher and antiquarian William Pickering. In 1891 Morris established his own press, the famous Klemscott Press, at his country estate, Kelmscott Manor. From then to his death in 1896 he printed about 50 books, all in small editions and now very much sought by collectors. In his printing as in his other work he went back to the great models of the past; the types that he designed and had cut in collaboration with Emery Walker included a roman (Golden type) in the style of Nicolaus Jenson, and two black-letter gothic types (Chaucer and Troy) based on those of the earliest printers. The ornamentation with which he so lavishly decorated his pages was derived from the same sources. The woodcut initials and borders of vine branches that he designed for his roman-type books were clearly inspired by Venetian woodcut art of the Ratdolt and Aldus period. One of Morris' chief works was a large Chaucer edition with illustrations by Edward Burne-Jones. Another illustrator who worked with Morris was Walter Crane, who also took Italian Renaissance woodcuts as his models. Morris' books produced a powerful effect with their heavy type and profuse ornamentation. In spite of the close relationship of his work to that of earlier periods it was not purely imitative.

Long before Morris began printing there were signs of a reaction against the spindly and insipid typefaces of the time. Caslon's roman was revived by the Chiswick Press, where Charles Wittingham was the guiding spirit, and Bishop Fell's 17th-century Dutch

98.   Page from William Morris' edition of Chaucer (1893)
with illustration by Burne-Jones and the characteristic Morris initials
and vine-branch borders.

well-doing,' with the spirit & clear aims of a Man. He
has discovered that the Ideal Workshop he so panted
for is even this same Actual ill-furnished Workshop
he has so long been stumbling in. He can say to himself: 'Tools? Thou hast no Tools? Why, there is not
'a Man, or a Thing, now alive but has tools. The
'basest of created animalcules, the Spider itself, has a

99.   Emery Walker's roman, designed from Nicolaus Jenson's
type.

type had been rediscovered by C. H. O. Daniel, an instructor at Oxford.   After Morris founded his press a considerable number of other private presses sprang up to produce books in an antique and
artistic style.   However different the type used by Charles Ricketts
at his Vale Press, by John Hornby at the Ashendene Press or by
Cobden-Sanderson and Emery Walker at the Doves Press--to name
only four of the better known printers--they all had in common a re-
version to the type forms used by the great printers of the Renaissance, and they were all influenced by Morris' basic principles for
the artistic effect of the printed page.   Although these private
presses, for the most part, covered only a brief span of years, they
produced a definite effect on typographical art in England.
      Another member of Morris' circle was the former lawyer,
T. J. Cobden-Sanderson, who was the founder of the Doves Press.
He was not only concerned with printing but also won special fame
for the artistic bindings that he made at the Doves Bindery in Ham-
mersmith near London.   For decorative effect he relied on the same
elements used by the old masters, and Cobden-Sanderson's importance in English bookbinding was similar to that of Morris in printing.   He believed that the binding should be adapted to the contents
of the book.
      The English also were responsible for bringing typography to
America.   In the 1630's, Jose Glover, a pastor, and Stephen Daye,

a locksmith, founded a press at Cambridge, Massachusetts. Here
in 1640 they issued the now very scarce Bay Psalm Book, which
brought $151,000 at an auction in 1947; another famous work from
the same press was John Eliot's translation of the Bible into the
language of the Indians. One of the best-known printers in 18th-cen-
tury America was Benjamin Franklin, who had learned the trade in
England and then worked in Philadelphia for many years as printer,
publisher and newspaper editor. However, it is only in recent times
that American typography has attained independent importance.

      The movement inaugurated by Morris soon spread to the Con-
tinent. Its influence can be traced in Belgium and France and especially in Germany, where it was introduced by the Belgian architect Henry van de Velde. He was one of the most enthusiastic ex-
ponents of the Jugent style, so-called from the periodical Jugend.
In this style of ornamentation the effect was produced by line designs in geometric patterns combined with animal figures and flowers.
At the close of the 19th century and the beginning of the 20th the
Jugend style had considerable influence in German and, to some extent, Scandinavian bookmaking, but it did not attain, nor did it deserve, a position of lasting importance.

Renaissance of Scandinavian
Book Crafts

      The books made in Denmark in the first decades of the 19th
century showed the effects of the country's economic crisis that began in 1807. There was a considerable use of paper bindings, many
of which were quite attractive, and the tradition of mirror binding
was almost completely forgotten. The days of the great book collectors were past, the role of the nobility had declined, and bookbinders found employment scarce.

      Denmark also experienced the revival of old book culture un-
der the influence of William Morris and his circle. Simon Bern-
steen, who founded a small press in Copenhagen in 1882, had become acquainted with Morris during a stay in England and thereafter
began using a hand press to print books designed in accordance with
Morris' artistic principles, some of them in black-letter type. Bern-

steen's work was an inspiration to the artist and wood-carver K.
Kongstad, who operated a printing business in the years 1903-20.
He obtained his types from England, Holland and Italy and produced
over 40 books printed by himself and embellished with his own effective woodcuts.

The guiding spirit in this new Danish renaissance in book
craftsmanship was F. Hendriksen, who in the 1870's had attained the
ranking position among the many competent wood-carvers in Denmark.   In his weekly publication Ude og Hjemme (1877-84) he had,
in collaboration with other outstanding artists, shown how high the
art of shading in woodcuts could be carried.   From 1884 on he devoted all his energies to the task of raising the Danish book craft
out of its decadence and starting it along paths like those that Morris blazed.   This movement found a rallying point in Forening for
Boghaandvarek, an association that Hendriksen founded in 1888 and
directed for a generation; later a school was established for practitioners of the art of bookmaking.

Bookbinders also felt the new spirit.   Hendriksen had strongly attacked the publisher's bindings of the period--fancy cloth bindings often overloaded with gilded decoration--and defended the superi-
ority of the plain English cloth bindings.   In addition he brought
about the collaboration between bookbinders and artists that has continued to the present day as a characteristic feature of Scandinavian
bookmaking.

Expansion of the Book Trade

The fight against censorship and unauthorized reprinting had
been carried on by the book trade during the greater part of the 18th
century, especially in Germany where conditions had been disrupted
and uncoordinated for a long time.   Not until the end of the century
did the situation begin to improve.   In the beginning of the 19th century a cooperative effort was made to establish the special German
conditional sale system, whereby the retail bookdealer could obtain
a certain number of copies of any book from the publisher with the
privilege of returning those remaining unsold after a certain length
of time.   The adoption of this system and the fight against censor-

ship and the abuses of reprinting were greatly aided by the founding
in 1825 of a central organization for the German book trade, the
Börsenverein der deutschen Buchhändler, which excluded from mem-
bership anyone engaged in reprinting. In the ensuing decades this
association became increasingly influential. In 1848 censorship was
abolished, and in 1870 uniform laws were established throughout
the country protecting literary ownership rights for thirty years after the author's death. After a struggle of some years the Börsenverein also set up effective trade agreements between publishers and
dealers; these agreements provided a fixed retail price and established rules for publisher's discounts to dealers. Giving discounts
to retail purchasers was prohibited--it was this that had made the
fixed bookstore price meaningless in the past.

The Börsenverein had its headquarters in Leipzig, the leading book center in the country. This was also the home of the
board that controlled the relations between publishers and dealers,
and Leipzig also had a great book trade fair every spring, as in
earlier times. The Börsenverein published the chief organ of the
book trade, Börsenblatt, which had a weekly list of new books.
Many of the leading German publishing houses were in Leipzig.
These included: Hinrichs, Brockhaus, J. A. Barth, Göschen, Rec-
lam, Tauchnitz, B. G. Teubner, Velhagen & Klasing, etc. There
were important publishers in other towns as well: Gustav Fischer
in Jena, Walter de Gruyter & Co., Julius Springer and S. Fischer
in Berlin, and Julius Perthes in Gotha. A German publisher of recent times who has been greatly interested in Scandinavian literature
is Eugen Diederichs; he came under the influence of William Morris
and has produced books of very high quality.

One peculiarly German phenomenon is the so-called Barsortiment, a wholesale bookstore that keeps a stock of all current German literature, usually bound, and sells it at the regular discount
to retail dealers, who can thus concentrate the major part of their
purchases in one place. The largest business of this type is Koehler & Volckmar in Leipzig, whose complete trade catalog is a very
useful tool.

While the book trade in Germany is scattered throughout the

100.   Beowulf in combat with Grendel's mother.   Drawing by
Niels Skovgaard in Thora Konstantin-Hansen's adaptation of <u>Beowulf</u>
for children, 1914.

entire country, in France and England it is concentrated to a much
greater degree in the capital cities.   Paris has been the home of
many large publishing houses, some still in existence: Panckoucke
fils, Renouard, Otto Lorenz (known for his <u>Catalogue de la librairie</u>);
Hetzel, Hachette, Lemerre, Firmin Didot, Plon, Calman-Lévy, La-
rousse (world-famous for its dictionaries), and Armand Colin.   The
last specializes in popular scientific literature; this is also a specialty of Les Presses Universitaires, along with university textbooks.
The German conditional sale system is not used in France.   Publishers deliver most books only on regular order but there is a

"système du dépot" which has some similarity to the German system.   A special French phenomenon are the so-called "dépositaires,"
which have a monopoly on the delivery of certain publishers' books
to retail dealers.   In France and in England fixed retail prices were
not established until quite recently; before that many dealers gave
their customers considerable discounts and the prices marked on the
books became meaningless.   As a counteraction English publishers
in 1901 reduced their discount to dealers (the net system).

Nearly all English publishers are located in London; here we
find firms like Longmans, Green & Co. (England's oldest publishing
house), John Murray, George Allen & Unwin, William Heinemann
and Macmillan & Co. , and here we also have the Stationers' Company, the oldest bookdealers' association in the world.   The conditional sales system is not used in England either--English publishers
work on a short-range plan and deliver books only on regular order.
If a book does not become a success immediately after publication,
only a minimum sale can usually be expected; the publisher will
then put the remainder of the edition up at auction or throw it on the
market at a greatly reduced price.   Ever since James Lackington
in the late 18th century there has been a special type of bookdealer
in London, the remainder dealer, who buys up remainders and sells
them at bargain prices.   An important role has also until recently
been played by the great English circulating libraries; publishers
could always count on disposing of a certain number of copies to
them.

The situation in the United States is similar to that in England.   Here bookselling is carried on in stores of quite miscellaneous character, and books are also sold by traveling agents.   There
are important publishing firms in Boston, Philadelphia, and other
cities, but by far the greater number of the large publishing houses,
as well as the largest bookstores, are located in New York.

In the Scandinavian countries the book trade is organized
along the same lines as in Germany, with fixed retail prices, prohi-
bition against customer discounts, and the conditional sale system.
In 1837 Boghandlerforeningen (now Den danske Forlaeggerforening)
was formed on the German pattern; retail bookdealers have had their

own organization since the 1890's. As in Germany, the publishers
determined whether a retail dealer was entitled to receive a discount; this discount was usually between 25 and 30% of the selling price, depending on the nature of the book. The practice of
"prenumeration," which had originally come from England, was also
taken over from Germany as early as the 18th century; this was the
privilege granted to the cash customer of having his name printed
in the books he purchased. The practice continued far into the 19th
century but was gradually superseded by the subscription system and
has now given way to installment buying.

Trade in second-hand books had been carried on by bookbinders in the 16th century but in the course of the 17th century
many dealers in new books also took up this business. Dealers in
second-hand books alone, however, did not appear until the latter
half of the 18th century, arising first in Germany as a consequence
of the conditional sale system. The oldest German used-book business was founded in 1785 in Frankfurt by Joseph Baer. In England
at about the same time the great "Temple of the Muses" of James
Lackington, with its hundreds of thousands of books, was for a long
time the largest second-hand bookstore in the country. Half a century later Bernard Quaritch attained world renown as the greatest
and best informed second-hand dealer of his time. He and other
firms like H. G. Bohn, H. Sotheran, Maggs Brothers, Francis Ed-
wards, E. P. Goldschmidt, and Robinson have made London one of
the most important cities in the international second-hand book trade.

Until recent times Germany has also been the home of a
large number of flourishing used-book enterprises, especially in
Leipzig and Berlin. Names like Gustav Fock, K. F. Koehler, Otto
Harrassowitz and Karl W. Hiersemann were known everywhere in
scholarly circles. The German second-hand trade mainly concerned
itself with technical literature, not with collectors' books as other
European dealers did. Exceptions, however, were Martin Breslau
and Jacques Rosenthal (now moved to London and New York), who
dealt mostly in manuscripts, old and rare printed books, woodcut
books and fine bindings, both historical and modern. To this category of second-hand dealers belongs Martinus Nijhoff of the Hague,

who also operates one of Holland's largest publishing firms and retail book stores; also Menno Hertzberger in Amsterdam, L'art an-
cien in Zurich, Nic. Rauch in Geneva, Ulrico Hoepli in Milan, Leo
S. Olschki in Florence and C.E. Rappaport in Rome. In America
the second-hand trade in fine and rare books has prospered because
of the many wealthy collectors; of particular fame is A.S.W. Ros-
enbach, who like another great New York second-hand dealer, H.P.
Kraus, was born in Germany. Other important firms are Lathrop
C. Harper and James F. Drake in New York and Goodspeed's in
Boston.

In France, where the second-hand book trade had its golden
age in the period following the Revolution, and where G. F. Debure
in the middle of the 18th century published some of the earliest
catalogs designed for bibliophiles, Paris was the home of many
great second-hand dealers throughout the 19th century and down to
our time. Among the best known of the older ones are A. A. Renouard and J. Téchener, and of the more recent, E. Rahir, Maisonneuve & Cie. and De Nobele. Many of the European and American second-hand dealers have issued catalogs that contain detailed
descriptions, historical information and facsimile pages of the books
offered for sale. Like the great auction catalogs they have been
valuable for bibliographical and historical purposes.

Growth of Libraries

The enormous increase in literary production during the last
150 years stems in part from the growth of scientific research
which has given rise to numerous scientific and technical journals.
Increased interest in reading and desire for information by the public at large, as a consequence of the spread of democracy, has been
another factor in the tremendous growth of libraries during this period.

This growth is manifested in the new spirit that began to
permeate the activities of libraries along toward the middle of the
last century. An entirely new concept of the library's obligations as
a public institution gradually evolved. One of the pioneers in this
movement was Antonio Panizzi, who drew up a program for the Brit-

ish Museum, in which he emphasized that the aim should be to create a center for the spread of knowledge and culture. He antici-
pated the present-day concept of library service, in which the primary concern is usefulness.

One of Panizzi's greatest projects was the printing, in collaboration with Richard Garnett, of the catalog of the British Museum library. This gigantic bibliographical task resulted in over a hundred folio volumes. Another of Panizzi's memorable accomplish-
ments was the construction of a new reading room, circular in shape
and covered by a large glass dome, with several hundred seats and
an impressive reference collection. Around the outside of the reading room were the book stacks, so arranged as to make best possible use of the space and to provide convenient access to the books.
The stacks had adjustable shelves and the top shelf could be reached
without a ladder. These stacks, which were built in 1854-57, represented a break with the tradition of a large library hall, and they
were soon adopted in other new library buildings throughout the
world.

Unfortunately the stack system had not yet reached Denmark
when the new University Library building was erected in 1857-61 at
the University of Copenhagen, after the old library quarters in the
loft of Trinity Church became overcrowded. The system was adopted in the new building for the Royal Library in Copenhagen, which
was opened in 1906, and in the Statsbibliotek at Aarhus, built in
1898-1902, the University Library of Oslo, 1907-13, Lund University Library, 1907, and in several other Scandinavian library buildings.

France had a first-rate library architect in Henri Labrouste.
In the middle of the 19th century he designed a new building for the
Bibliothèque Sainte-Geneviève that was fully adapted to its purpose.
With a reading room containing 700 seats and a reference collection
of over 100,000 volumes, this library is the most used of any in
Paris, the average number of visitors per day reaching some 4,000.
In 1864-68 Labrouste introduced modern stacks in France in his re-
modeling of the Bibliothèque Nationale; on that occasion the library
also acquired its monumental reading room, lighted through nine

domes. In the French national library there were still hundreds
of thousands of volumes from the period of the Revolution that had
not been organized or cataloged. In 1874 Leopold Delisle, a man
of wide knowledge and great administrative ability, became director
of the library. In the course of the next twenty years Delisle ac-
complished the extraordinary feat of cataloging this enormous collection. In 1897 he was able to begin the printing of an author catalog of the library.

In Germany the library at Göttingen had long been a model.
Here and there throughout the country some steps were being taken
toward reorganization, but the majority of German libraries were
still marked by neglect. There was no appreciation of the special
qualifications required for library work and the management of a library was not even considered a full-time task; usually it was en-
trusted to a member of the university faculty as a secondary assign-
ment. While a number of these professor-librarians, like Robert
von Mohl in Tübingen, did outstanding work, the arrangement
hindered library development. Not till the 1870's was there a change
in this situation, when the state governments, especially that of
Prussia under the leadership of Fr. Althoff, began to recognize their
obligations toward libraries and demonstrated this recognition in the
form of increased appropriations and in the development of a separate library profession and the provision of special education for library work.

Panizzi's stack system was first used in Germany when a
new building was erected for the University library at Halle in 1878-
80. Throughout Germany the various state and university libraries
now began to be reorganized. In 1914, just before the outbreak of
the first World War, the country's largest library, the Royal Library
in Berlin, finally acquired a new building, one distinguished rather
by its extraordinary size than by its practical design. A much better result was attained shortly thereafter when a building was erected for the Deutsche Bücherei in Leipzig, a library that had been
founded in 1912 by the German bookdealers' trade association in an
effort to build up a national library and a center for German bibliography. Among other cooperative library projects in Germany dur-

ing this period were a number of centralized or union catalogs. Especially noteworthy was the great Gesamtkatalog. It began to appear in 1929 but soon proved impractical to complete. Of great importance for the growing interlibrary loan program was the information office at the Royal Library in Berlin (Auskunftbüro), which also facilitated loans between German and foreign libraries.

Each German state pursued its own course, though there were certain common features in the methods and procedures of German scholarly libraries. German library practice, as reflected in the distinguished journal Zentralblatt für Bibliothekswesen which began publication in 1881, has been of great importance for the development of scholarly librarianship in the Scandinavian countries. In the 20th century, the influence of the Anglo-Saxon library world came to Denmark, particularly under the inspiring leadership of H. O. Lange.

English, American and Scandinavian Public Libraries

The development of free public libraries in the English-speaking countries has surpassed that in all others and is one of the great cultural contributions made by the Anglo-Saxon world.

In England and the United States the development began around the middle of the 19th century when laws were adopted giving governmental units the right to assess a special tax for the establishment of public libraries. In England the beginning was made at Manchester, and the free public library of this great manufacturing town is still one of the largest and most active in England. It has an annual circulation of 5.5 million volumes. In the United States the first significant steps were taken in Boston, and American free public libraries have become even more important and influential than those of England.

Enormous sums have been and are being spent on libraries in the United States, not only by the states and cities but also by individuals. Andrew Carnegie, the greatest patron of libraries, provided funds for the erection of almost two thousand library buildings.

American appreciation of the importance of public libraries

has also found expression in the formation of organizations (Friends of the Library) to provide financial support for libraries, and in the fact that many of the country's large book collectors have made their own libraries accessible to the public or have donated them to public libraries.

One of the greatest of these collectors was the financier John Pierpont Morgan, who, with some justification, has been compared to the Medici in Florence. At his death in 1913 his private library was valued at around 10 million dollars. Among his 20,000 printed books were many with bindings of historical interest. Of the 1,300 manuscripts a large number were illuminated manuscripts from the Middle Ages, but Morgan had also bought most of the Coptic manuscripts from the 9-10th centuries that the Arabs found buried in a monastery ruin near Faijum in 1910. Morgan's library is now a public one and is housed in a marble building in New York; additions are still being made to it. Still greater in size and value is the collection that the railroad magnate Henry E. Huntington brought together in a palatial library building on his estate in San Marino, near Los Angeles, and which is now owned by the State of California. Huntington did not begin collecting until he was along in years, but he had a good knowledge of books and often bought entire private libraries in order to pick out the best items; his fantastic purchases contributed in a considerable degree to raising the prices of rare books. The Huntington Library is, like the Morgan Library, still being added to. Some 20 years ago it had a quarter million volumes, including 5,000 incunabula, besides thousands of maps and also manuscripts and letters of famous authors.

Among the auctions at which Huntington made extensive purchases were those held in 1911-12 in London to dispose of the library left by the English banker Henry Huth, whom we have already mentioned, and also the New York auction of the library of the American bibliophile Robert Hoe, who owned the world's leading factory for the manufacture of rotary presses. Hoe had brought together a library in the true collector's tradition; he was also the founder of the famous association of bibliophiles, the Grolier Club, in New York, and like Morgan he was especially interested in historical bindings. The auction of his books brought in almost 3 million dollars for about 15,000 items. At the Huth and Hoe auctions many other American collectors appeared as buyers, among them the young and wealthy Harry Elkins Widener. On his way home from London with his purchases from the Huth auction Widener drowned in the shipwreck of the Titanic, and the books were lost. His own library, which was distinguished by its many Stevenson and Dickens items, was donated to Harvard University. Like Widener, other American bibliophiles have given special attention to particular authors or certain fields of literature. Prof. D.W. Fiske, for instance, was especially interested in Icelandic literature and in Dante and Petrarch; he presented his books to Cornell University, except for a collection of chess literature that went to the library at Reykjavik. Henry Clay Folger's unique library of Shakespeare editions and material from the Shakespearean period was presented to Amherst College and now contains about 200,000 volumes; it is housed in a monumental building in Washington, D.C., alongside the Library of Congress.

Many collectors in the United States naturally gave preference to early American printed books, as well as to books about the colonization of America, the Indians, and the later history of the country, so that the prices of rare Americana have gradually risen to fantastic heights. There are many private collections of great national importance in this field. Among the older collectors of Americana were James Lenox, whose collection is now in the New York Public Library, and John Carter Brown, who presented his books to Brown University in Rhode Island. The Newberry Library in Chicago contains a large portion of the books collected by Edward E. Ayer; besides ornithology his field was literature on the Indians and about Mexico and Central America. The University of Michigan Library acquired the collection of William Lawrence Clements, an exceptional fund of material on the Revolutionary War and the Wars with the Indians.

The greatest of the libraries of the United States is the Library of Congress in Washington, D.C., whose millions of printed volumes and enormous special collections of manuscripts, maps, and

101.   The palatial Henry E. Huntington Library in San Marino, California.

music make it one of the largest libraries in the world.   It was
founded in 1800 as a reference library for the members of Congress,
but in the second half of the 19th century, mainly under the direction of A.R. Spofford and later Herbert Putnam, it developed into
the national library of the United States.   The first of the group of
buildings of the Library of Congress was dedicated in 1897.   It is
one of Washington's most striking government buildings and, like the
British Museum, it has a large domed reading room.

     Another of the very large libraries in the United States is the
New York Public Library, which came into being in 1848 when John
Jacob Astor presented the city with a book collection to form the
nation's first public library.   The main library structure on Fifth
Avenue is a huge cultural center that is visited annually by some 3
to 4 million persons.   It offers exhibits, lectures, concerts, film
showings, and entertainment for children, and its many reading

102. Interior of the circular domed reading room of the
Library of Congress.

rooms provide material for research as well as general information.
The New York Public Library is both a scholarly and a popular library, and it is financed mainly by private funds. In both these respects it is typical of many similar cultural institutions in large
American cities. In this variegated American library picture an
important place is held by the technical and research libraries of
universities and other institutions of learning. Among the largest
university libraries are those of Harvard, Chicago, Columbia,
Princeton, Illinois, Yale and California.

One requirement for an enterprise of the proportions represented by American library service is highly developed library technique. In the arrangement and the equipment of library buildings,
the cataloging and classification process, the recording of loans and
in the expansion of the libraries' effective range to out-of-the way
localities, modern technology has been extensively applied, resulting
in the development of practical procedures that are used throughout
the country and have helped give the many thousands of separate institutions a generally uniform character.

It was from the United States that several European countries, especially the Scandinavian, derived the impulses for the
growth of their public libraries in the last generation. Most of the
small reading circles and parish libraries that, like the diocesan libraries, had been established throughout Denmark during the time
of the Enlightenment had died out. The Danish government did begin in the 1880's to grant small sums for popular libraries but these
did not attain any real significance. At the turn of the century a
new movement, with English and American public libraries as
models, laid the foundation for the modern development of Danish libraries; the chief person in this movement was Andreas Schack
Steenberg. Norway's largest public library, the Deichmanske Bibliotek in Oslo, was thoroughly reorganized about 1898 on the American
pattern, with Hakon Nyhuus as the motivating force. In Sweden,
American influence became effective through a program proposed by
Valfrid Palmgren in 1911, which resulted in a complete reorganization of the Swedish public library system.

Chapter 7. The Period Since 1914

The period since 1914 is still so close to us that it cannot
be treated historically in the same manner as earlier periods. But
with this reservation an attempt will be made to present a picture
of the developments in our field during this unsettled and confused
era, however hazy and uncertain this picture may be. To some extent it will be necessary to discuss persons and events belonging to
the very beginning of the century in order to illustrate, among other
things, a continuity which has not been entirely severed by the destruction and upheavals brought on by two world wars. On the other hand, names and events of the most recent years will be mentioned only to a very limited extent.

Book Production and Book Arts

The advance of technology has been just as remarkable in
this field as in other fields. The bookmaking craft has become the
graphic arts industry, but the earlier methods have not been entirely superseded. Even though by far the bulk of modern book printing is done on composing machines and power presses, there is still
some work that requires hand setting; while binderies make extensive use of machinery, there is still a demand for fine binding that
can be done only by hand. But new technical methods will nevertheless continue to be adopted. For printing very large editions, especially of illustrated magazines, an intaglio (photogravure) process is
now used. The text and illustrations are etched into a copper plate
from which the impressions are taken; a modern rotogravure press
can make 20,000 or more impressions per hour. Another method of
printing large editions, offset printing, has been used increasingly.
In this process the impression is transferred from a zinc plate to a
rubber blanket from which the impression is made.

Both the gravure and the offset method can be used for color

242

printing and pictures in color are also produced by a three- or four-color process using separate relief plates. High quality of color reproduction is obtained with the collotype process, in which the printing surface is a specially treated glass plate. This method is best suited to small editions and is used mainly for facsimiles; the accuracy of reproduction is so great that it is almost impossible to tell the original from the printed copy. These various mechanical processes have superseded the printing of illustrations from woodcuts and copperplate engravings. Recently, however, woodcuts have again come into use in special fields. In various countries there are a number of modern artists making woodcuts for book illustrations. They work in the style of the illustrations in the earliest printed books rather than in the manner introduced by Bewick, but with a much greater personal quality. Some of these artists also work with etching and lithography, although these processes are so fundamentally different from book printing that homogeneous results are difficult to obtain.

Machine composition is now in general use for textual matter, and beautiful books can, in fact, be composed by machine. The determining factor is the typeface itself and the way it is used to produce harmonious and readable pages but care is required in the inking and press operation. Many modern types designed for machine composition are based on the models of the great type designers of earlier periods; Jenson, Garamond, Caslon, Bodoni, Baskerville and several others are represented in today's composing rooms. Alongside these an entirely new series of types has been created, including some that are close to the historical forms, others of a calligraphic character, and still others in which the striving for originality has produced a result that is often more outré than pleasing and which have consequently been short-lived.

Increasing emphasis is being placed on the importance of adapting the typography and the other external features to the nature of the book. This has given rise to a new category of personnel in the graphic arts field: book consultants who design and supervise the various steps in the production of a book. Their work involves the choice of format and selection of paper and the most suitable typeface, in the best size and with the correct amount of leading, as well as decisions regarding the placing of illustrations in the text and the design of the title page. The principles on which these decisions are based have gradually evolved in the substantial literature dealing with the history, esthetic and technical aspects of paper, printing and illustration. These same topics are taught in schools of graphic art that can now be found in most countries. One current practice that helps to maintain interest in the quality of book production is the annual selection of well-made books in several countries --an idea that originated in the United States.

As in earlier periods, changing styles and fashions in art have influenced book arts. An example of this occurred in the years between the two world wars when functionalism appeared in Russia and Germany: its principle that whatever is practical is also esthetically correct led to the creation of functional or elemental typography. The basic functional type became the so-called grotesque, or gothic (Fig. 106), originally an English type from about 1815, in which all the lines are the same thickness. Another characteristic of functionalism was the division of the text into irregular sections and an unsymmetrical arrangement of the title page. This was intended to emphasize the important matter and to attain the greatest effect through extreme simplicity. One of the most enthusiastic proponents of the movement was Jan Tschichold, who was born in Germany but lived in Switzerland; he also influenced bookmaking in the Scandinavian countries. Later, he decided that this elemental typography was better suited to commercial printing than to books. By 1946, when he undertook to redesign the inexpensive English Penguin Books, he had gone back to traditional typography. Although elemental typography is no longer used to any extent for books, it performed a useful service in freeing book printing from the earlier dependence on traditional typefaces and the heavy ornamentation that William Morris made fashionable in the first decade of this century.

In general, England and the United States lead in typography today. English private presses continue their role of keeping up interest in high quality, and England has first-rate type and book designers who, in contrast to Morris, have fully accepted modern

THE PERPETUA TYPE

CUT FROM THE DESIGNS MADE BY

ERIC GILL

FOR THE LANSTON MONOTYPE CORPORATION

LONDON

The following founts only have been made to date; it is projected to cut the usual sizes for book and display work

103.   Eric Gill's Perpetua type.

technology.   Names like Eric Gill, Stanley Morison, Oliver Simon and Francis Meynell have become known throughout the world.   Another great name is Edward Johnston, whose book Writing, Illumination and Lettering issued in 1906 attained great influence both in England and in Germany; his pupil Anna Simons has inspired many German type designers.   The periodical The Fleuron, issued by Stanley Morison and Oliver Simon from 1923 to 1930, was devoted to serious discussions of the esthetic problems of book printing. Several new typefaces have made their appearance, among them Perpetua (Fig. 103) designed by Eric Gill.   This is one of the best book types of our day.   As consultant to the Monotype Corporation, Morison brought out Garamond, Baskerville and Caslon type in forms suitable for machine composition; for the London Times he also created the first really good newspaper type, the very readable "Times roman," which has also been adapted for use in book printing.   Among the best-printed English books of the present day are those issued by the two university presses, Oxford and Cambridge, which date back to the 16th century; the clear, quiet effect of their books is typically English.

Several organizations have been established in the United States for producing fine printed books in limited editions, and a number of private and university presses have been set up on the English pattern.   The outstanding typographer, Daniel Berkeley Updike, was active at one of these private presses, The Riverside

THE

HOLY BIBLE

Containing the Old and New
Testaments : Translated out
of the Original Tongues and
with the former Translations
diligently compared and revised by His Majesty's special
Command

Appointed to be read in Churches

OXFORD
Printed at the University Press
1935

104.   Title page of the Oxford Lectern Bible, printed by
Bruce Rogers with his Centaur type in 1935.

Press, in the 1880's, and in 1893 he set up his own press, The
Merrymount Press. He was well versed in the history of the craft,
and his book Printing Types is an authoritative work in the history
of this subject. Updike was a printer, but two of the other great
men in modern American typography, Bruce Rogers and Frederic W.
Goudy, were primarily type designers. Rogers, like William Morris, started with Nicolaus Jenson's roman type and from it he designed a new series of types. In Centaur he created a completely
original modern typeface; one of the best works printed with it is
the monumental Oxford Lectern Bible. Goudy, who owned The Village Press, designed some 100 typefaces, inspired by historical
forms all the way from old Roman inscriptions to black-letter missal types of the 15th century; his Kennerly roman has been of great
importance in modern printing in the United States.

     In Germany there was a time in the 1880's when printers
went back to the models of the 15th century and attempted to give
their books an old-German appearance by extensive use of Schwabacher type. The Jugend style came later but when it died out,
shortly after the turn of the century, the influences from England
and America began to be felt. Count Harry Kessler of the Insel-
Verlag, founded in 1899, had established contact with Emery Walker,
Eric Gill and other leading English type designers. When Carl
Ernst Poeschel, who had studied his craft in the United States, returned to Leipzig he and typefounder Karl Klingspor became pioneers
in modern German typography, working closely with a number of
outstanding type designers. Poeschel founded a private press (Janus
Presse) in company with the type designer Walter Tiemann. Most
of the new types that Germany experimented with in the 1920's were
roman types, but many fraktur types were also designed, such as
Koch's Deutsche Schrift. Fraktur type came into vogue during the
first World War, and in the 1930's the Nazis enforced its use as the
national type. Not until after 1945 did roman type again become
prevalent in Germany.

     Modern German book illustrators include three artists who
deserve special mention: Max Slevogt, Hans Meid and Alfred Kubin.
Slevogt's impressionistic pictures are particularly effective and in-

Angst ist nahe + denn es ist hie kein Helfer. + Große Farren haben mich umgeben + gewaltige Stiere haben mich um= ringet + ihren Rachen sperren sie auf wider mich + wie ein brüllender und reißender Löwe. +Ich bin ausgeschüttet wie Wasser + alle meine Gebeine haben sich zertrennet; mein Herz ist in meinem Leibe wie zerschmolzen Wachs. + Meine Kräfte sind vertrocknet wie eine Scherbe + und meine Zunge klebt an meinem Gaumen, und du legest mich in des Todes Staub. +Denn Hunde haben mich umgeben + und der Bösen Rotte hat mich umringt + sie haben meine Hände und Füße durchgraben. + Ich kann alle meine Gebeine zählen. + Sie

105.   Rudolf Koch's Deutsche Schrift.

Es hat wenig Sinn, über die Zukunft der Schriftentwicklung nachzudenken. Mag die Schrift der kommenden Zeit den Charakter der Groteskschriften behalten oder zu den Schriften der älteren Antiqua zurückkehren: jedenfalls haben wir heute den historischen Vorbildern gegenüber eine innere Freiheit wiederge- wonnen, mit der wir auf diesem neuen Anfang weiterbauen können.

106.   "Grotesque" type designed by Rudolf Koch.

clude more than 500 illustrations that he drew for Faust.

In France the printing types of the Empire period were domi- nant for a long time.   Recently types have been designed from earli- er models such as the rococo-like Cochin (Fig. 110) and Garamond, in addition to types of original modern design.   It is not so much in the field of typography that present-day France lives up to her earli- er traditions, but rather in the field of book illustration, where she still holds the lead.   There was a period of decline in the latter part of the last century, but with the 70 or so books that Edouard Pelletan issued between 1896 and 1912 French illustrative art again came into its own.   First-rank artists, working with competent wood-carvers, created pictures that harmonized with the text of the

107.   Woodcut by Aristide Maillol for Longus' Les Pastorales,
ou Daphnis et Chloe, 1937.

books and Pelletan saw to it that the typography in each book was
suited to its contents.   One of his contemporaries, Ambroise Vol-
lard, published a number of fine books in small editions, illustrated
with original drawings by such outstanding artists and sculptors as
Pierre Bonnard, Aristide Maillol, Henri Matisse, Pablo Picasso,
Auguste Rodin, Georges Rouault and André Dunoyer de Segonzac.

Other publishers have also made a point of issuing books with original drawings in the form of woodcuts, lithographs and etchings, and
have given a large number of "peintres-illustrateurs" an opportunity
to put their personal stamp on modern French book art. Many of
these luxury books--most of them editions of contemporary writers--
are of high artistic quality and represent the work of numerous great
artists. Taken together they constitute just as strong a manifestation of the French spirit as did the work of the great illustrators of
the rococo period. Unfortunately, as was the case then, there have
also been produced "bibliophile" books whose handsome exterior cannot hide the fact they they represent primarily a speculative appeal
to the dubious taste of a wealthy parvenu clientele.

Woodcuts received special attention in Bewick's homeland,
England. In the periodical The Dial artists like Charles Ricketts,
Charles Shannon and Lucien Pissarro had a chance to express themselves. Pissarro's private press, the Eragny Press, issued a series of books with colored illustrations made by transferring woodcuts
to lithographic stone. William Nicholson and Gordon Craig also used
colored woodcuts. Other modern English book artists, besides Eric
Gill, are Paul Nash, Hughes-Stanton and Clifford Webb.

Woodcuts have had considerable use in Belgium in recent
times; the vigorous and dramatic pictures by Frans Masereel are
among the best in this field. In Poland, Czechoslovakia, Hungary
and Russia woodcut illustration is also important. Russian children's
books with illustrations by Wladimir Lebedew and Konstantin W.
Kusnezow have attracted particular attention in a period when the
Soviet government's demand for a realistic and directly intelligible
art has limited artistic freedom of expression in the field of book
illustration.

The Scandinavian countries, especially Sweden and Denmark,
have kept abreast of foreign developments in typography in the period since 1914. After the introduction of sturdy types and close-set
text pages by F. Hendriksen, Denmark had gradually adopted more
varied typography. Architects like Knud V. Engelhardt and Gunnar
Billmann Petersen have had considerable influence as type experts
and have designed books of great esthetic appeal, as have Steen Ei-

Betragtninger over anbringelse
af illustrationer i bøger

Af Ejnar Philip

BEMÆRKNINGER OM DANSK BIBLIOPHILIS OPGAVER

Af H. O. LANGE

Aaret 1891 udkom i Forening for Bog-
haandværks Aarsskrift EMIL HANNOVERS
Afhandling: Om at samle paa Bøger. Det
var vel nok den første Vejledning for danske Bibliophiler, og ved sine klóge og kyn-
dige Anvisninger til Indkjøb, Indbinding og Ordning
af Bøger har denne Afhandling sikkert havt en ikke
ringe Betydning for begyndende Bogsamlere, sparet
dem Penge og Ærgrelser og særlig de Græmmelser,
som principielle og methodiske Fejltagelser og Mis-
greb i Begyndelsen forvolde den Bogven, der først
efterhaanden bliver klar over sine Maal og erhværver
dybere Indsigt og videre Kundskaber.
Siden den Tid er Samlerlysten og Interessen for
den gode, den smukke, den sjældne Bog mangedoblet
i vort Folk. Bibliophili er ikke, som det synes for
mange, en overflødig Luxus, en Udvæxt paa Kultu-
ren, en Udvendiggjørelse af indre, aandelige Værdier;
Bibliophilien er i Virkeligheden et selvfølgeligt Ud-
slag af Aandskulturen, en af de ædle Passioner, der
kun slaa Rod i Kultursamfund, som have naaet en vis
Grad af Modenhed, et nødvendigt og naturligt Ud-
slag af historisk Sans og Følelse for Sammenhængen

Der findes naturligvis elementære regler, som enhver sætterlærling
faar banket ind i hovedet i løbet af sin uddannelse, og som gør det
muligt for ham at gaa i lag med alle almindelige opgaver, der i sig
selv ikke rummer særlige problemer. De findes aftrykt i de fleste
lærebøger om typografi, f. eks. i „Selmars Typografi", og bl. a.
Jan Tschichold har behandlet de lidt mere komplicerede problemer, som anbringelse af billeder i plancheværker frembyder; de
er gengivet i Grafisk Teknik nr. 2, juni 1946.
   I snart adskillige aar har vi arbejdet med friere titelopbygninger,
som, selvom langt fra alle de eksempler, vi har set, har virket
overbevisende, dog har været en gevinst for typografien, fordi de
har frigjort os for vaneforestillinger, og navnlig fordi de har
bidraget til, at hele bogens typografi blev genstand for større
interesse. Paa samme maade kan det være nyttigt at anskue
problemet billedanbringelse fra andre end tilvante synsvinkler.
Det maa heller ikke glemmes, at de faste regler ofte forflygtiges
i omgangen med reklametypografien, som i kataloger, brochurer,
annoncer og ugeblade arbejder med andre og mere direkte virke-
midler, der ikke ubetinget kan bringes i overensstemmelse med
bogens typografi, selvom de ofte kan virke forfriskende og
inspirerende.
   For den læge læser kan det forekomme pedantisk at ville hævde,
at det ikke er ligegyldigt, hvordan man anbringer billederne i en
bog, men den, der har beskæftiget sig med tingene, vil vide, at

108. Page from first issue
of Aarbog for Bogvenner (Year-
book for Bibliophiles) printed in
1917 by C. Christensen with
Scandinavian roman type. Greatly reduced.

109. Page from Bogvennen,
1955, set in Garamond by F. E.
Bording.

ler Rasmussen, Vilhelm Wanscher and Kai Friis Møller. Among

the most active professional book designers are Viggo Naae and

Erik Ellegaard Frederiksen.

   Danish pen-and-ink artists have been active in book illustra-

tion. The pioneers in this group were Valdemar Andersen and Axel

Nygaard, both gifted artists. A number of highly individualistic

painters also have devoted themselves to book illustration. Of par-

ticular interest has been the work of the painter Aksel Jørgensen,

who did the woodcut illustrations for the monumental edition of the

first part of Oehlenschläger's Gods of the North. He also founded

a school of graphic art at the Danish Art Academy in 1920, where

a number of important woodcut artists have been trained. Jørgen-

sen's most gifted pupil in this field was Povl Christensen, whose il-

lustrations for Blicher's and H. C. Andersen's works show his great

UR SVENSKA AKADEMIENS
ARKIV

✻

SVENSKA AKADEMIENS

DAGBOK

1 7 8 6 • 1 7 8 9

UTGIFVEN

AF

HENRIK SCHÜCK

STOCKHOLM

P. A. NORSTEDT & SÖNERS FÖRLAG

110.   Title page designed by Akke Kumlien in the Cochin
style, a modern imitation of the work of the 18th-century French
book artist.   The type used here was produced at the end of the
19th century under the name of Cochin roman by the Peignot type-
foundry in France; it was designed from one of Pierre Simon Fournier's 18th-century types.

imaginative powers and his craftsmanship.

Typography development in Norway and Finland proceeded

somewhat slowly, but in Sweden it has been quite rapid.   A notable

advance was made there in 1916 when Akke Kumlien became artistic

advisor to the Norstedt publishing firm and completely changed the

character of its books.   He reacted against the heavy tone of the

previous period and gave the books a less formal appearance.   He

was aided by artists like Yngve Berg, whose illustrations for Bell-

man's works represent a fine adaptation of the Gustavian style,

and by Bertil Lybeck, whose work still has a tendency toward the

grandiose.   At this time typefaces like Garamond and Bodoni began

to take their place in Swedish printing, and in the 1930's the consultant to the great Nordisk Rotogravyr press, Anders Billow, became a spokesman for elemental typography, which was accepted
even by Hugo Lagerström. In our day Swedish printing has been influenced by modern British typography through such men as Carl Z.
Häggström, who directs the great press of Almqvist & Wiksell in
Uppsala; English and American typefaces are now as much used in
Sweden as they are in Denmark. One modern type designer of considerable significance is Karl-Erik Forsberg who is known for his
Berling roman among other things.

Various modern fashions have also set their mark on the decoration of bookbindings. A very special development in recent English binding is represented by T. J. Cobden-Sanderson and his pupil
Douglas Cockerell. At Cobden-Sanderson's Doves Bindery, which he
operated from 1900 to 1916, he himself bound the books and decorated the covers with his own designs, consisting of small conventional flowers and leaves arranged in groups framed by straight
lines. The title was combined with the decoration of the binding to
form an artistic unit. Of special importance are also the Danish
bindings that Anker Kyster and others made from designs by the
architect Thorvald Bindesbøll (Fig. 111).

Bindesbøll might be considered a precursor of cubism, which
played such a great role in art during the years that preceded the
first World War and which was also frequently evident in bookbindings. Functionalism, which flourished between the two World Wars,
likewise had an influence on the art of bookbinding by encouraging
the greatest possible simplicity in decoration. This influence has
continued, and many of the best bindings of today produce their effect by the high quality and treatment of the materials and by the
proper combination of colors.

Some bindings still make use of excessive gilding or elaborate symbolism. Many modern French bindings are characterized
by overdeveloped "reliure parlante." Like the original "narrative
bindings" these attempt to indicate the content of the book, and in
many instances the decoration continues as a unit over both the back
and the sides. Rather than direct representation of the contents of

111. Binding in dark green
morocco by Anker Kyster, with
decoration by Thorvald Bindesbøll.

112. Binding in reddish-
brown morocco, designed and
executed by August Sandgren.

the book, the attempt is to produce an idealized expression of its
essence through abstract designs and the use of color.

Surrealist tendencies have appeared in book decoration in
France and other countries. One of the most important French
binders of our day, along with René Kieffer and Léon Gruel, is Pierre Legrain, who has made extensive use of geometric designs as
decorative elements. Others who deserve to be mentioned are
Georges Cretté, Paul Bonet, Pierre Martin and women like Jeanne
Langrand and Rose Adler; a numer of these draw their own designs
while others use designs made by other artists.

In Germany, both the Jugend style and cubism have been
much in vogue. The leading German bookbinders of the recent period include Paul Adam and Paul Kersten, later also Ignaz Wiemeler
and Otto Dorfner. The work of the last two exhibits extreme simplicity in decoration; on many of Dorfner's bindings the title is also
used very effectively as a decorative feature of the front cover.

The dominant figures in Swedish bookbinding have been Gustav
Hedberg, who died in 1920, and his brother Arvid. Their work is

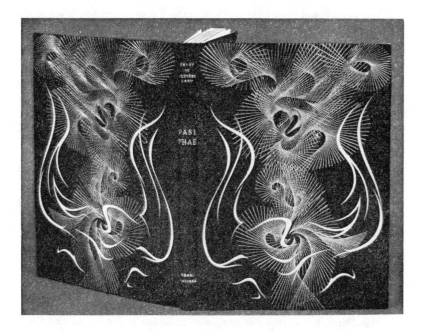

113.   Binding by Paul Bonet in black morocco with white
leather mosaic work and gold-tooled lines.

in many styles, and they show the influence of Cobden-Sanderson.
Nils Linde in Gothenburg, with his faultless taste and daring imagination, has effected a revival in modern Swedish binding.

Even though artistic bindings are usually done entirely in
leather, half-leather bindings are far more numerous. In these only
the spine and the corners are of leather, the rest being covered
with paper, cloth or other material.   There are many kinds of paper
available to bookbinders and very attractive bindings can be made
entirely of paper.   This is done to some extent in current publishers' bindings, but aside from these and the sturdy English cloth
bindings that usually have no decoration other than the title on the
spine, publishers' bindings are frequently in half-leather.   There has
been a clearly detectable improvement in trade bindings; nearly all
countries produce each year a number of publishers' bindings that

are simply and artistically decorated. These are made of good materials with pleasing color combinations and are more durable than
those made in the past.

No one country can be singled out as the recognized leader
in bookbinding today, nor can we speak of definite national style. In
general, however, we can probably say that the reform movement
instigated by William Morris--including the Jugend offshoot--has had
its greatest influence on English, American, German, Dutch and
Scandinavian bookbinding. The fine bindings produced in France present the same variegated appearance that we see in modern French
illustrative art, which is generally inclined toward the picturesque.
Bookbinding in the southern European countries follows the historical
tradition more closely. There is no common or uniform style for
all countries and for all aspects of book art, as there was in the
baroque and the rococo periods and even during the Empire. It is
questionable whether any such uniformity, in spite of the greater
communication among nations, could develop today, when artistic
considerations must often give way to demands for speed and life itself is seldom distinguished by any balance or harmony.

The Book Trade

During the first World War the book trade and the publishing
business had a prosperous period in the neutral countries. In the
countries at war publishers were beset by great difficulties, although
they did issue a steady stream of small propaganda items in large
editions. The German book trade was particularly hard hit, and its
fixed retail price and conditional sale system was disrupted for a
long time. Its extensive export business also dropped to a minimum. After the Nazis came to power the Börsenverein was incorporated into the so-called Reichskultur office, in 1933, and publishing was brought completely under state control. In May of 1935 a
large number of "undesirable" books were confiscated and burned;
many authors, publishers, and bookdealers to whom the government
objected for racial or political reasons left the country. Some of
them started business anew in other countries, including the United
States.

The second World War was disastrous for the German book trade. Millions of books in publishers' and bookdealers' stocks were destroyed by aerial bombardment. When Germany collapsed in 1945 its greatly diminished literary production dropped to almost nothing for a time. The book trade was split up between East and West Germany; the Börsenverein was divided into separate organizations in Frankfurt and in Leipzig, and the large Barsortiment of Koehler & Volckmar was similarly divided. Within West Germany the division into zones created further difficulties, while dealers and publishers in East Germany became subject to state control. Under these conditions a number of large scientific works that had previously been published in Germany were now issued in America or England, and many German authors had their works published in Holland and Switzerland. For a time it appeared that Switzerland might become the center of publishing on the continent, but in recent years the German book business has revived and has shown that it is capable of handling projects of considerable size. German second-hand dealers, however, have not as yet recovered their former position.

In France and England, in spite of the disruption and destruction caused by the two wars, the book trade suffered less, even though the aerial bombardment of the second World War caused great losses to London book stocks, and the headquarters of the English bookdealers' association, Stationer's Hall, was destroyed. In England the fight for the adoption of a fixed retail price continued down into the 1920's, but it has now been won to the extent that no books marked "net" may be sold at a price below that printed on them. The disposal of remainder stocks is still a characteristic feature of the English book trade, although there have been signs that publishers eventually will adopt the practice of making annual price reductions, as is commonly done in the Scandinavian countries.

As mentioned earlier, most of the larger American publishing firms are located in New York, where the larger bookdealers are also found. One of the most important modern publishers is Doubleday & Co., which also operates a score of book stores in various cities and several book clubs with a total of over 2 million

members.   These clubs bear witness to the widespread interest in
reading as do the inexpensive Pocket Books editions which, like the
Penguin Books issued in England since 1935, make popular scientific
works and classical literature available to large sections of the population.   An important part is played by the presses operated by the
larger American universities on the pattern of those at Oxford and
Cambridge, and a number of book clubs also engage in the publication of limited editions of fine books.   American publishers every
year print enormous editions of "best-sellers," which are distributed
in large quantities in other English-speaking countries.   Direct can-
vassing by agents is carried on to a greater extent in the United
States than in Europe.   It is an important factor in the book business and is an economic necessity for some publishing firms; many
encyclopedias, reference books, and collected works of literary
writers would be difficult to publish without this method of distribution.

The United States has not subscribed to the Berne Convention,
which was adopted in 1886 by the majority of European countries for
the mutual protection of literary and artistic property rights (since
1948 rights are effective for 50 years after the death of the author).
The United States has its own Copyright Act, adopted in 1909, which
in general protects an author's rights for 28 years after publication
if the book carries a notice of copyright.   Each book is entered on
a list issued by the Library of Congress; it is also required that
two copies of the book be deposited in the Library.   In 1952 a
World Copyright Union was established in Geneva but it did not go
as far as the Berne Convention, which is still in force.

The Soviet Union is also outside the Berne Convention, and
hence foreign books can be published there without remuneration to
the author.   However, many works of foreign authors are not ac-
ceptable for publication in Soviet countries or in the countries under
Soviet domination, since all publishing is under the control of the
State and books that do not agree with its ideology are rejected.
There is a great need for books in Russia today, and even though
book production figures have been up in the millions in recent years
it is still far from adequate.   Besides the great Russian and foreign

classics, literature on questions of national economy and on technical subjects is very much in demand, and there is also an unusually good market for children's books.

Libraries

The period from 1914 to the present has been one of the
strangest in the history of libraries.   While public libraries have
achieved a stronger position than ever before and have experienced
an extraordinary growth in both their internal and external functions,
this period has also witnessed the greatest destruction of books and
libraries that the world has known since the days of the barbarian
invasions.

In the first World War book losses were relatively small;
the only library that was completely destroyed was that of the University of Louvain, which was burned when German troops captured
the town.   German libraries felt the effects of the war and the subsequent period of inflation.   Between 1920 and 1930, the Notgemeinschaft der deutschen Wissenschaft, which had been organized after
the war, provided considerable financial aid, but when this came to
an end, the situation again deteriorated.   In 1933 the Göttingen library, for example, had to discontinue all its periodical subscriptions and other difficulties arose when the Nazi government came to
power.   The Nazis' plan of bringing the entire German library system together in a single unit made libraries a political instrument,
subject to the ideology of the party.   All book purchases were controlled by a central purchasing office in Cologne.   Long lists were
compiled of prohibited books that were to be removed from libraries,
and Jews were denied the use of public libraries.   At the same time
a special library was established in Frankfort for the study of international Jewry.

Some of the books added to this library had been seized by
the Germans in the countries that they occupied during the first period of the second World War.   Like Napoleon's armies of an earlier
day, the German troops were accompanied by experts who picked
out the most valuable parts of the confiscated libraries.   This was
done extensively in the Balkans and even more so in Poland; here

the books that were not taken back to Germany were in large part
collected at the Krasinski Library in Warsaw, and shortly before
the German troops had to leave the city in 1944 they set fire to
this library as well as to the municipal library. Many Polish public libraries were also burned, at least the Polish parts of their
collections. Similar action was taken against bookdealers' and publishers' stocks and numerous private collections, all for the purpose
of destroying Poland's national culture. Fortunately the old Jagellon
Library in Krakow was saved--its book treasures as well as its magnificent new building.

Other countries also had their libraries plundered and destroyed by the Nazis. A frightful nemesis was to visit German libraries when aerial warfare began in earnest. It has been calculated
that German libraries lost about a third of the more than 75 million
volumes that they had before the war. At the outbreak of the war
the most valuable portions of the collections had been moved to the
library cellars, and it was not till very late in the war that they
were evacuated to castles, churches, monasteries and mines, where
some of the material was destroyed by dampness or fire. Before
this evacuation took place bombs had already partly or wholly destroyed a large number of library buildings. The two most magnificent German libraries, the Preussische Staatsbibliothek in Berlin
and the Bayerische Staatsbibliothek in Munich, were largely in ruins
at the end of the war. The buildings of the following libraries were
totally or almost totally destroyed: the university libraries of Bonn,
Breslau, Frankfort, Giessen, Hamburg, Münster and Würzburg, and
the regional libraries in Dresden, Darmstadt, Karlsruhe, Kassel and
Stuttgart. Several of the old city libraries and a number of technical and special libraries were also destroyed. Many other libraries
were heavily damaged, and several lost their entire catalog or parts
of it.

This catastrophe had serious effects in the years immediately following the war, for German culture and science had suffered
an almost inconceivable and irreplaceable loss. The Preussische
Staatsbibliothek alone had lost a million and a half printed books, almost 6,000 incunabula, and about 6,700 manuscripts, or more than

the entire contents of the Royal Library in Copenhagen. Most of
what remained was taken to Marburg, where it was to form the
basis for a new West German central library. Many of the ruined
libraries found temporary, though often very unsuitable, quarters.
Only slight assistance was provided by the Deutsche Froschungsge-
meinschaft, a revival of the earlier Notgemeinschaft, or by gifts
from abroad. But the ability of the German people to rally in an
apparently hopeless situation, as well as their organizational ability,
asserted itself also in the field of library activity. At various
places throughout the country regional union catalogs were compiled,
and liberal loan arrangements were instituted among the individual
libraries. To replace the Deutsche Bücherei, which now operates
only in East Germany, a new library was established in Frankfort
in 1946; here all new German books are collected and a current German bibliography is being compiled. In spite of all these efforts,
however, the great libraries of Germany will always carry the marks
of the second World War and will always be limited in their ability
to maintain the cultural contacts with the past that are of special
importance in this day of rapid advances in technology.

One ray of hope for German popular libraries appeared in
1954, when the Americans gave West Berlin a great Berliner Zen-
tralbibliothek, built and arranged on the pattern of an American public library. In it Germany had for the first time a completely modern public library, which will certainly be imitated in other cities
of West Germany. An encouraging event for the scholarly library
system was the reappearance of Milkau's great Handbuch der Bibliothekswissenschaft, originally published in 1931-42. Publication of
the new and greatly expanded edition began in 1952 under the direction of the former head of the University Library in Tübingen,
Georg Leyh.

Germany was not the only country that was damaged by aerial bombardment, although nowhere else was the damage nearly so
great. In Bulgaria the National Library in Sofia was completely destroyed. In Yugoslavia the national library in Belgrade was extensively damaged. Libraries in Czechoslovakia lost over 3 million
volumes, mainly in the Sudeten area. In Austria and Hungary, and

presumably also in Russia, the damage was less serious; the same was true of Holland and Belgium, but the Louvain University Library was destroyed a second time. In France the university libraries of Caen and Strasbourg were destroyed, as were the municipal libraries of Caen, Douai, Cambrai and Tours. In Beauvais, Brest, Chartres, Dunkerque, Lorient, St. Malo, Vitry-le-françois, Metz and others the libraries were partially destroyed. In all, French libraries lost over 2 million volumes, but none of the large collections in Paris was affected. Neither did Italy fare as badly as might have been expected, although part of the Monte Cassino monastery was hit and the libraries in Bologna, Messina, Milan, Naples, Parma, Pisa and Turin suffered considerable losses. The most important library treasures from Monte Cassino and other monasteries and churches and from the various state libraries had been taken to the Vatican Library which, like the other libraries of Rome, escaped damage. In England, libraries in Liverpool, Bristol, Plymouth, Portsmouth and other towns were hit. The University College Library in London was destroyed, and at the British Museum Annex outside the city a bomb did away with a great part of the collection of English provincial newspapers. At the National Central Library more than 100,000 volumes were lost.

Challenges of the Twentieth Century

The great increase in the world's literary productivity has made it more important than ever that libraries be assured of adequate financial support, and also that careful decisions be made regarding book purchases and periodical subscriptions. The selection of books has always been the most difficult of the librarian's tasks, and in the present age of intensive specialization the difficulty as well as the importance of making the proper choice from the large number of possibilities is even greater. Here, as in the case of so many other library problems, the proper course is to establish cooperative arrangements, so that the purchase of unnecessary duplicates can be avoided and a greater number of different titles and periodicals can be acquired by the cooperating libraries. Examples are the division of subjects that was adopted in 1927 by Danish re-

114. Left, library interior with alcoves in the old section of
the Bodleian Library at Oxford; reading desks in each alcove. Right,
steel bookstacks with adjustable shelves in the new section of the
same library.

search libraries, and the commission that was appointed some years
ago to coordinate the book purchasing of the larger libraries of Paris. Under the so-called "Farmington plan," the various fields of literature have been distributed among a number of the leading American libraries; a large-scale cooperative purchasing program insures
the acquisition of a copy of every foreign book that could conceivably
be of interest to Americans by at least one American library. West
German libraries have had to adopt a similar distribution of fields
because of their limited funds. The international exchange of the
publications of scientific societies and institutions and of official government documents has also been important to libraries.

Another feature of library cooperation has been the establishment of union catalogs, such as the one that was set up in the Royal
Library at The Hague for about 50 Dutch libraries, or the one compiled at the Bibliothèque Nationale to cover the foreign book holdings
of some 400 French libraries. German union catalogs have already
been mentioned, and in Great Britain the National Central Library is

performing a function similar to that of the Library of Congress in
the United States.   The Library of Congress also issues printed
catalog cards of its accessions and distributes them to other libraries.

Microfilming is being used to meet the problem of space, especially for large collections of newspapers; it also protects items
from damage by frequent handling.   Similarly, microfilming can be
used to preserve copies of manuscripts and rare or irreplaceable
books should the originals be destroyed, and for acquiring copies of
books and manuscripts from other libraries.   For example, American libraries have been engaged in filming all European source material for American history that is not already available in the
United States.

The many problems arising from today's intensive library ac-
tivity--of which only a few have been mentioned here--are continual-
ly being discussed in library periodicals and at library meetings.
There is great interest in the training of librarians; in some cases
this is done at special schools while in other cases library training
is offered by universities or by courses at the libraries themselves.
Great progress has been made in teaching the technical skills involved; the weak point, especially from the standpoint of scholarly
libraries, is knowledge of books and of their history, and in this
respect most librarians cannot measure up to the scholarly librarians
of earlier times.   This situation has caused considerable difficulty,
particularly in the United States, since large quantities of manuscripts and rare old books have found their way to American libraries.

In most other respects, however, the Americans are the
leaders in the library world today.   Throughout the United States
and Canada libraries of all types and sizes have either recently built
or are planning new buildings.   The American Library Association
has a permanent architectural committee to aid librarians in arriv-
ing at the most practical building designs to meet their needs.   The
catalog now occupies a dominant location, reading desks have been
provided even in the stacks, and buildings are designed so that in-
teriors can be rearranged whenever a new distribution of space is

115. Iowa State University Library building, erected in 1951.

required. Deposit libraries or warehouses have been built in Boston and in Chicago; in these, libraries within the area can store
their little-used books, conserving their own limited space.

In the Soviet Union, the library movement started its modern
development after the revolution. The largest library in the Soviet
Union, the Lenin Library in Moscow, is now said to contain 15 million volumes, besides large collections of manuscripts, incunabula
and oriental material. Like the New York Public Library it is a
great cultural center in addition to being a combination of research
library and popular library. The capitals of the various Soviet republics have state libraries, many of them rich in manuscript and
printed material for the study of the history of the country. These
function as centers for the network of popular libraries that now
covers the entire Soviet Union. They also send traveling book collections to out-of-the-way places by bus, sleigh, motorboat and air-
plane--a rural service similar to that provided by English regional

libraries or the Scandinavian central libraries.

In Italy and France centralization has gradually been achieved; in France it became still more effective when a unified administration was established, in 1951, for all the libraries of the country. In England the situation has been exactly the opposite; here the individual libraries are largely independent and the initiative for cooperative projects comes from the British Library Association rather than from the government. Switzerland's division into cantons has hindered uniform development, though the founding of the Landesbibliothek in Berne in 1895 did provide a national library for the entire country, and the Schweizerische Volksbibliothek, founded in 1920, functions as a central agency for popular libraries. In Italy and Spain popular libraries are still lagging and the same can in general be said of Holland and Belgium, where strong religious opposition has hindered their growth; Antwerp is the only Netherlands city with a modern system of public libraries. On the other hand the influence from England and the United States has been very effective in the Scandinavian countries. In 1920 Denmark became the first of them to adopt public library legislation, with state support based on local contribution. Since then Danish popular libraries have had a rapid development; those of the other Scandinavian countries have followed somewhat more slowly.

Research libraries in both America and Europe no longer profit so much from the work of private collectors as they did in earlier times. Nevertheless, the collections of David Simonsen and Lazarus Goldschmidt have made the Royal Library in Copenhagen a center for Jewish studies, and the University Library in Uppsala has received from Erik Waller his internationally famous collection on the history of medicine. Other Scandinavian library patrons of the present time are the Danes V.R. Christiansen and A. Jurisch and the Swedes Gustaf Bernström and Thore Virgin.

The stream of books going to the United States from Europe is not so great now as formerly; in Switzerland, for example, Martin Bodmer in Coligny near Geneva has built up a collection of manuscripts, incunabula and first editions that can compete with the Huntington Library in California.

In Asiatic as well as in eastern European countries, where illiteracy still creates enormous difficulties, modern public library systems are just beginning to develop. There is no doubt that other countries that are gradually freeing themselves from European control and developing their own national culture will recognize the importance of public libraries.

From time to time, pessimistic voices predict that books will be displaced by newspapers and magazines, motion pictures, radio and television. It cannot, of course, be denied that many persons' reading does not go beyond daily newspapers, picture magazines, and comic books, or that much of their free time is devoted to motion pictures, radio and television. The amount of this free time will increase as the standard of living rises, but no one can say whether this will mean greater use of books. New technical discoveries in the field of mass communication will be competing with books to an even greater degree than at present, and hence no comforting parallels can be drawn from earlier periods.

In spite of all this there is reason to believe that the history of the book will not end with the end of the 20th century. It is no accident that illiteracy is being combatted so vigorously wherever it still exists, and that books play an important role in the program of UNESCO. There will continue to be a place for the book as a practical means of communication, since it has a significant advantage over more transitory and ephemeral means: the book is an enduring repository for the thoughts, knowledge, emotions and imagination of mankind, ever ready to serve each new reader.

Bibliography

Books and the History of Books in General

Das alte Buch und seine Ausstattung vom 15-19. Jahrhundert. Hrsg.
    von M. Gerlach. Wien [1915]. (Die Quelle. Mappe XIII).
Otto Andersen. Boghaandvaerket. 3. udg. Kbh. 1954.
J. Christian Bay. The Fortune of Books. Essays, Memories and
    Prophecies of a Librarian. Chic. 1941.
André Blum. Les origines du papier, de l'imprimerie et de la
    gravure. Paris 1935.
En Bog om Bogen. Under Redaktion af Aage Marcus. Kbh. 1950.
Bogen. En Haandbog for Boghandlere og Bogvenner. Udg. af Otto
    Andersen og Aleks. Frøland. Kbh. 1925.
Hans Bohatta. Einführung in die Buchkunde. Wien 1928.
Bokvandringar. Uppstatser om böcker och samlare under red. av
    J. Viktor Johansson. Sthlm. 1945.
F. Calot, L. M. Michon et P. Angoulvent. L'art du livre en France
    des origines à nos jours. Paris 1931.
Albert Cim. Le livre. Historique, fabrication, achat, classement,
    usage et entretien. Tome 1-5. Paris 1905-08.
D. W. Davies. The World of the Elzeviers, 1580-1712. Haag 1954.
K. Fleischhack. Wege zum Wissen. Buch, Buchhandel, Bibliothe-
    ken. 2. erweit. Aufl. Würzburg 1940.
Eric de Grolier. Histoire du livre. Paris 1954.
Haandbog i Bibliotekskundskab. Udg. af Svend Dahl. 3. forøgede
    udgave. Bd. 1-2. Kbh. 1924-27. Svensk udgave ved Samuel
    E. Bring. Bd. 1-2. Sthlm. 1924-31.
Handbuch der Bibliothekswissenschaft. 2. Aufl. hrsg. von George
    Leyh. Bd I: Buch und Schrift. Wiesbaden 1952. Bd. 3:
    Geschichte der Bibliotheken. Sst. 1955 ff. (endnu ikke afs-
    luttet).
J. Viktor Johannson. Från Gutenbergbiblen till Gösta Berlings Saga.
    Vandringar i Bibliotheca Quarnforsiana. Sthlm. 1952.
Wilhelm H. Lange. Das Buch im Wandel der Zeiten. 6. Aufl.
    Wiesbaden 1951.
Hellmut Lehmann-Haupt. A History of the Making and Selling of
    Books in the United States. 2. ed. New York 1951.
Lexikon des Buchwesens. Hrsg. von Joachim Kirchner. Bd. 1-4.
    Stuttg. 1952-56.
F. C. Lonchamp. Manuel du bibliophile français (1470-1920). Tome
    1-2. Paris 1927.
Wilhelm Munthe. Boknåm. Essays for bokvenner. Oslo 1943.
Bert Möller. Svensk bokhistoria. Sthlm. 1931.
Lauritz Nielsen. Den danske Bog. Forsøg til en dansk Boghistorie
    fra de aeldste Tider til Nutiden. Kbh. 1941.

Bibliography 269

Nordisk Leksikon for Bogvaesen. Red. af Esli Dansten, Lauritz
  Nielsen og Palle Birkelund. Bd. 1 ff. Kbh. 1949. ff (endnu
  ikke afsluttet).
Leo S. Olschki. Le livre italien à travers les âges. Florence
  1914.
W. Dana Orcutt. The Book in Italy During the 15th and 16th Cen-
  tury. London 1928.
Johs. Pedersen. Den arabiske Bog. Kbh. 1946.
K. F. Plesner. Bøger. Kbh. 1942.
---- Mellem reoler. Kbh. 1947.
G. J. Poršnev. Das Buchwesen in der U.S.S.R. Ein kurzer Abriss.
  Berlin 1927.
Karl Schottenloher. Bücher bewegen die Welt. Eine Kulturgeschich-
  te des Buches. Bd. 1-2. Stuttg. 1951-52.
---- Das alte Buch. 3. Aufl. Braunschweig 1956.
Albert Schramm. Das Schreib- und Buchwesen einst und jetzt. Lpz.
  1928.
Henrik Schück. Bidrag till svensk bokhistoria. Sthlm. 1900.
O. Weise. Schrift- und Buchwesen in alter und neuer Zeit. 3.
  Aufl. Lpz. 1910.

Papyrus and Paper

En bok om papper tillägnad. Upps. 1944.
Ch. M. Briquet. Les filigranes. Dictionnaire historique des mar-
  ques du papier 1282-1600. Tome 1-4. Genève 1907. (Nytryk
  Lpz. 1925).
W. A. Churchill. Watermarks in Paper in Holland, England, France
  etc. in the XVII and XVIII Centuries. Amst. 1935.
Dard Hunter. Papermaking. The History and Technique of an An-
  cient Craft. 2. ed. New York 1947.
Karl Preisendanz. Papyrusfunde und Papyrusforschung. Lpz. 1935.
Armin Renker. Das Buch vom Papier. 4. Ausg. Lpz. 1951.
Wilhelm Schubart. Einführung in die Papyruskunde. Berlin 1918.

Writing, Manuscripts and Illumination

P. d'Ancona. Le miniature italienne du 10e au 16e siecle. Paris
  et Brux. 1925.
P. d'Ancona et E. Aeschlimann. Dictionnaire des miniaturistes.
  2. éd. Milano 1949.
Erich Bethe. Buch und Schrift im Altertum. Lpz. u. Wien 1945.
---- Buch und Bild im Altertum. Lpz. u. Wien 1945.
Theodor Birt. Das antike Buchwesen. Berlin 1882.
P. Blanchon-Lasserve. Ecriture et enluminure des manuscrits du
  9e au 12e siècle. Paris 1926-31.
A. Blum et Ph. Lauer. La miniature française aux 15e et 16e
  siècles. Paris et Brux. 1930.
A. W. Byvanck. La miniature dans les Pays-Bas septentrionaux.
  Paris 1937.
Albert Boeckler. Abendländische Miniaturen bis zum Ausgang der

romanischen Zeit. Berlin u. Lpz. 1930.
L. Coellen. Die Stilentwicklung der Schrift im christlichen Abend-
lande. Ü. st. 1922.
E. Crous und J. Kirchner. Die gotischen Schriftarten. Berlin
1928.
H. Delitsch. Geschichte der abendländischen Schreibschriftformen.
Lpz. 1928.
Karl Dziatzko. Untersuchungen über ausgewählte Kapitel des antiken
Buchwesens. Lpz. 1900.
J. G. Fevrier. Histoire de l'écriture. Paris 1948.
A. Goldschmidt. Die deutsche Buchmalerei. Bd. 1-2. Firenze u.
München 1928.
Greek and Latin Illuminated Manuscripts in Danisch Collections.
Kbh. 1921.
Gyldne bøger. Illuminerede middelalderlige håndskrifter i Danmark
og Sverige (Nationalmuseet). (Katalog of Kåre Olsen og Carl
Nordenfalk. Indledn. af Carl Nordenfalk). Kbh. 1952. Svensk
udg. Sthlm. 1952.
J. A. Herbert. Illuminated Manuscripts. 2. ed. London 1912.
H. Hermannsson. Icelandic Illuminated Manuscripts of the Middle
Ages. Copenh. 1935.
Hermann Hieber. Die Miniaturen des frühen Mittelalters. München
1912.
Carsten Høeg. Skrift og Bog i den klassiske Oldtid. Kbh. 1942.
M. Rh. James. The Wanderings and Homes of Manuscripts. Cambr.
1928.
H. Jensen. Die Schrift in Vergangenheit und Gegenwart. Glückstadt
u. Hamburg 1935.
F. G. Kenyon. Ancient Books and Modern Discoveries. Oxford
1927.
---- Books and Readers in Ancient Greece and Rome. 2. ed. Ox-
ford 1951.
Karl Löffler. Einführung in die Handschriftenkunde. Lpz. 1929.
F. Madan. Books in Manuscript. London 1893.
H. Martin. Les miniaturistes français. Paris 1906.
---- La miniature française du 13e au 15e siècle. 2. éd. Paris
et Brux. 1924.
W. A. Mason. A History of the Art of Writing. New York 1920.
E. G. Millar. La miniature anglaise. Paris et Brux. 1926-28.
Lauritz Nielsen. Danmarks middelalderlige Haandskrifter. En
sammenfattende boghistorisk Oversigt. Kbh. 1937.
H. L. Pinner. The World of Books in Classical Antiquity. Leiden
1948.
M. Salmi. Italian Miniatures. New York 1956.
O. Elfrida Saunders. English Illumination. Vol. 1-2. Firenze
and Paris 1928.
Wilhelm Schubart. Das Buch bei den Griechen und Römern. Berl.
u. Lpz. 1921.
Franz Steffens. Lateinische Palãographie. 125 Tafeln in Lichtdruck
mit einer systematischen Darstellung der Entwicklung der la-
teinischen Schrift. Trier 1909.
E. M. Thompson. An Introduction in Greek and Latin Palaeography.

Oxford 1912.
W. Wattenbach. Das Schriftwesen im Mittelalter. 3. verm. Aufl.
Lpz. 1896.
F. Winkler. Die flämische Buchmalerei des 15. u. 16. Jahrhunderts. Lpz. 1925.

The Art of Printing and Bookmaking

Harry G. Aldis. The Printed Book. Cambr. 1916.
H. Barge. Geschichte der Buchdruckerkunst von ihrn Anfängen bis zur Gegenwart. Lpz. 1940.
Konrad F. Bauer. Aventur und Kunst. Eine Chronik des Buchdruckgewerbes. Frankf. a. M. 1940.
Carl Björkbom. Gutenberg. Upps. 1951.
G. A. E. Bogeng. Geschichte der Buchdruckerkunst. Bd. 1-2. Lpz. u. Berlin 1930-41.
Bogtrykkerbogen. Laerebog ved Mesterprøven. Red. af O. Hassing og C. Volmer Nordlunde. Kbh. 1946. (Ny udg. under udgivelse).
Der Buchdruck des 15. Jehrhunderts. Eine bibliographische Uber~ sicht hrsg. von der Wiegendruckgesellschaft. Berlin 1929-36.
Isak Collijn. Svensk boktryckerehistoria under 14- och 1500-talen. Sthlm. 1947.
~~~~ Svensk typografisk atlas. 1400- och 1500-talen. Sthlm. 1952.
Svend Dahl og Thomas Døssing. Bogtrykkerkunsten. Kbh. 1940.
Dansk Boghaandvaerk gennem Tiderne. 1482-1948. Kbh. 1949.
Deutscher Buchdruck im Jahrhundert Gutenbergs. Hrsg. von der Preussischen Staatsbibliothek und der Gesellschaft für Typenkunde des 15. Jahrhunderts. Berlin 1940.
E. Gordon Duff. Early Printed Books. London 1893.
~~~~ Fifteenth Century English Books. Oxford 1917.
F. H. Ehmcke. Die historische Entwicklung der abendländischen Schriftformen. Ravensburg 1927.
E. P. Goldschmidt. The Printed Book of the Renaissance. Cambridge 1950.
Grafiska yrken. Red. av Bror Zachrisson. Bd. 1-2. Sthlm. 1956.
Henry Guppy. Stepping Stones to the Art of Typography. London 1928.
A History of the Printed Book. Ed. by L. C. Wroth. New York 1938.
Konrad Haebler. Handbuch der Inkunabelkunde. Lpz. 1925.
D. C. McMurtrie. The Book. The Story of Printing and Bookmaking. 3. revised ed. London 1943.
H. Meisner und J. Luther. Die Erfindung der Buchdruckerkunst. Bielefeld u. Lpz. 1900.
Stanley Morison. Four Centuries of Fine Printing. 2. revised ed. London 1949.
Lauritz Nielsen. Boghistoriske Studier til dansk Bibliografi 1500-1600. Kbh. 1923.
~~~~ Dansk typografisk Atlas 1482-1600. Kbh. 1934.
C. Volmer Nordlunde. Bogskrifter og Bogtrykkere. Kbh. 1945.
Nils Nordqvist. Berömda boktryckare. Sthlm. 1954.

J. C. Oswald.   A History of Printing.   Its Development Through 500
    Years.   London 1928.
Ejnar Philip og C. Volmer Nordlunde.   Bogtrykkets fortid og nutid.
    (Kalligrafi og bogskrift.   Fra Kelmscott Press til Penguin
    Books).   Kbh. 1952.
H. R. Plomer.   A Short History of English Printing 1476-1900.
    London 1927.
Alfred W. Pollard.   Fine Books.   London 1912.
Printing.   A History of the Art.   Ed. by R. A. Peddie.   London
    1927.
W. Ransom.   Private Presses and the Books They Have Given Us.
    London 1929.
Paul Renner.   Die Kunst der Typographie.   2. Aufl.   Berlin 1948.
Volmer Rosenkilde.   Europaeiske bibeltryk.   Omkring den Rosen-
    dahlske bibelsamling.   Esbjerg 1952.
Aloys Ruppel.   Johannes Gutenberg.   Sein Leben und sein Werk.
    2. Aufl.   Berlin 1947.
F. A. Schmidt-Künsemüller.   Die Erfinderung des Buchdrucks als
    techniches Phänomen.   Mainz 1951.
Oliver Simon and Julius Rodenberg.   Printing of To-day.   An Illus-
    trated Survey of Postwar Typography in Europe and the United
    States.   London 1928.
S. H. Steinberg.   Five Hundred Years of Printing.   Penguin Books
    1955.
Jan Tschichold.   Geschichte der Schrift in Bildern.   Hamburg 1941.
Daniel Berkeley Updike.   Printing Types, Their History, Forms
    and Use.   Vol. 1-2.   Cambr., Mass. 1922.
Harold Williams.   History of Book Clubs and Printing Societies in
    Great Britain and Ireland.   (First Edition Club).   London 1929.
E. Vouillième.   Die deutschen Drucker des 15. Jahrhunderts.   2.
    Aufl.   Berlin 1922.

Book Illustration

Anthologie du livre illustré par les peintres et sculpteurs de l'école
    de Paris.   Avant-propos de Claude Roger-Marx.   Genève 1946.
D. Bland.   The Illustration of Books.   London 1951.
A. Blum.   Les origines du livre à gravure en France.   Paris 1928.
Lothar Brieger.   Das goldene Zeitalter der französischen Illustra-
    tion.   München 1924.
R. Brun.   Le livre illustré en France au XVIe siècle.   Paris 1930.
Henri Cohen.   Guide de l'amateur de livres à gravure du 18. siècle.
    6. éd.   Paris 1912.   [Nytryk af 4. éd. Lpz. 1924].
Walter Crane.   On the Decorative Illustration of Books.   3. ed.
    London 1921.
A. J. J. Delen.   Histoire de la gravure dans les anciens Pays-Bas
    et dans les provinces belges des origines jusqu'à la fin du
    XVIIIe siècle.   Tome 1-2.   Paris 1924-34.
Raymond Hesse.   Le livre d'art du XIXe siècle à nos jours.   Paris
    n. d.
Arthur M. Hind.   History of Engraving and Etching.   3. ed.   London
    1923.

Bibliography 273

Arthur M. Hind. An Introduction to a History of Woodcut. Vol. 1-2. London 1935.
Philip James. English Book Illustration 1800-1900. Harmondsworth, 1947.
Niels J. Johnsen. Døler og troll. Fra norsk illustrasjonskunsts historie. Oslo 1935.
Paul Kristeller. Kupferstich und Holzschnitt in vier Jahrhunderten. 4. Auf. Berlin 1922.
Th. Kutschmann. Geschichte der deutschen Illustration vom ersten Auftreten des Holzschnitts bis auf die Gegenwart. Bd. 1-2. Goslar u. Berlin 1896-99.
Karl Madsen. Franske Illustratorer fra det XVIII Aarhundrede. Kbh. 1929.
Theodor Musper. Der Holzschnitt in fünf Jahrhunderten. Stuttg. 1944.
R. Muther. Die deutsche Buchillustration der Gotik und Frührenaissance. Bd. 1-2. München 1884.
B. H. Newdigate. The Art of the Book. (Studio. Special Number). London 1938.
Alfred W. Pollard. Early Illustrated Books. A History of the Decoration and Illustration of Books in the 15th and 16th Centuries. London 1917.
Felix Poppenberg. Buchkunst. (Die Kunst Bd. 57-58). Berlin 1908.
H. P. Rohde. Dansk Bogillustration 1800-1890. Kbh. 1949.
Arthur Rümann. Das illustrierte Buch des 19. Jahrhunderts in England, Frankreich und Deutschland. Lpz. 1930.
---- Das deutsche illustrierte Buch des achtzehnten Jahrhunderts. Stuttg. 1931.
Max Sander. Die illustrierten französischen Bücher des 18. Jahrhunderts. Stuttg. 1926.
---- Le livre à figures italien. Milan 1942.
Albert Schramm. Der Bilderschmuck der Frühdrucke. Bd. 1-23. Lpz. 1922-43.
W. L. Schreiber. Der Buchholzschnitt im 15. Jahrhundert. München 1929.
Walter Schwartz. Dansk Illustrationskunst fra Valdemar Andersen til Ib Andersen. Kbh. 1949.
Jørgen Sthyr. Dansk Grafik 1500-1800. Kbh. 1943. --1800-1910. Kbh. 1949.
Georg Svensson. Modern svensk bokkonst. Sthlm. 1953.
F. Weitenkampf. The Illustrated Book. Cambr., Mass. 1938.

Bookbinding

Paul Adam. Der Bucheinband. Lpz. 1890.
William Barkell. Från papyrusrulle till partiband. Sthlm. 1950.
H. Béraldi. La reliure du 19e siècle. Tome 1-4. Paris 1895-97.
G. A. E. Bogeng. Der Bucheinband. Halle a. S. 1950.
W. S. Brassington. A History of the Art of Bookbinding. London 1894.
H. O. Bøggild-Andersen og Edward C. J. Wolf. Bogbindets His-

torie. Kbh. 1945.

Douglas B. Cockerell. Bookbinding and the Care of Books. New ed. London 1948.

Danish Eighteenth Century Bindings 1730-1780. 102 Plates. With an Introduction by Sofus Larsen and Anker Kyster. Kbh. 1930.

E. Déville. La reliure française. Tome 1-2. Paris 1930-31.

Edith Diehl. Bookbinding, Its Background and Technique. Vol. 1-2. New York 1946.

Carl Elberling. Breve fra en Bogelsker. Kbh. 1909.

Ernst Fischer. Bokbandets historia. Sthlm. 1922.

W. Fletcher. Bookbinding in England and France. Vol. 1-2. London 1905.

E. P. Goldschmidt. Gothic and Renaissance Bookbindings. Vol. 1-2. London 1928.

Léon Gruel. Manuel historique et bibliographique de l'amateur des reliures. Paris 1887.

G. D. Hobson. Maioli, Canevari and others. London 1926.

---- Bindings in Cambridge Libraries. London 1929.

---- English Binding Before 1500. London 1929.

---- Les reliures à la fanfare. London 1935.

Herbert P. Horne. The Binding of Books. An Essay in the History of Gold-tooled Bindings. London 1894.

Kunstfaerdige gamle Bogbind indtil 1850. Det danske Kunstindustri-museums Udstilling 1906. Med en Indledning af Emil Hannover. Kbh. 1907.

E. Kyriss. Verzierte gotische Einbände im alten deutschen Sprach-gebiet. Stuttg. 1951.

Anker Kyster. Om Indbinding af Bøger. Holstebro 1920-35.

Hans Loubier. Der Bucheinband von seinen Anfängen bis zum Ende des 18. Jahrhunderts. 2. Aufl. Lpz. 1926.

Ch. Meunier. La reliure française ancienne et moderne. Paris 1910.

Marius Michel. La reliure française. Paris 1880.

Louis Marie Michon. La reliure française. Paris 1951.

Carl P. Nielsen og. R. Berg. Danmarks Bogbindere gennem 400 Aar. Kbh. 1926.

Axel Nilsson. Bokbandsdekorens stilutveckling. Göteborg 1922.

Sarah T. Prideaux. An Historical Sketch of Bookbinding. London 1893.

Ch. Ramsen. French Bookbinders 1789-1848. London 1950.

---- London Bookbinders 1780-1940. London 1956. --Bookbinders of the United Kingdom (outside London) 1780-1940. London 1954.

J. Rudbeck. Svenska bokband under nyare tiden. Bidrag till svensk bokbinderhistoria. Bd. 1-3. Sthlm. 1910-14.

Heinrich Schreiber. Einführung in die Einbandkunde. Lpz. 1932.

The Book Trade

Aus Wissenschaft und Antiquariat. Festschrift zum 50-jährigen Bestehen der Buchhandlung Gustav Fock. Lpz. 1929.

Der Buchhandel der Welt. Aufbau, Verkehrswesen, Anschriften des Buchhandels in Europa und U.S.A. Hrsg. von A. Drucken-

müller. Stuttg. 1935.
Ed. Frommann. Aufsätze zur Geschichte des Buchhandels. Hft.
1-2. Jena 1881.
Friedrich Kapp und Joh. Goldfriedrich. Geschichte des deutschen
Buchhandels. Bd. 1-4. Lpz. 1886-1913.
Henrik Koppel. Spredte Traek af Boghandelens Historie. Kbh.
1932.
Walter Krieg. Materialien zu einer Entwicklungsgeschichte der
Bücherpreise und des Autoren-Honorars von 15. bis zum 20.
Jahrhundert. Wien 1953.
Gerhard Menz. Deutsche Buchhändler. 24 Lebensbilder führender
Männer des Buchhandels. Lpz. u. München 1925.
---- Der deutsche Buchhandel. 2. Aufl. Gotha 1942.
F. A. Mumby. The Romance of Bookselling. 2. ed. London 1930.
Jean-Alexis Néret. Histoire illustrée de la librairie et du livre
français des origines à nos jours. Paris 1953.
Camillus Nyrop. Bidrag til den danske Boghandels Historie. Del
1-2. Kbh. 1870.
W. Olbrich. Einführung in die Verlagskunde. 3. Aufl. Lpz. 1956.
M. Paschke und Philipp Rath. Lehrbuch des deutschen Buchhandels.
Bd. 1-2. 6. Aufl. Lpz. 1922.
Marjorie Plant. The English Book Trade. An Economic History.
London 1939.
Volmer Rosenkilde. Af Antikvarens Historie. (Saertr. af: Men-
nesker og Bøger). Kbh. 1945.
Henrik Schück. Den svenska förlagsbokhandelns historia. Bd. 1-2.
Sthlm. 1923.
V. Sønstevold og Harald L. Tveteras. Den norske bokhandelns his-
torie. Bd. 1 ff. Oslo 1936 ff.
Friedrich Uhlig. Geschichte des Buches und des Buchhandels.
Stuttg. 1953.

Libraries and Librarianship,
Book Collecting and Ex Libris

Ester Aarup Hansen. Exlibriskunstens Udvikling i Danmark. Kbh.
1944.
Jørgen Banke. Folkebibliotekernes Historie i Danmark indtil Aar
1920 i Omrids. Kbh. 1929.
G. A. E. Bogeng. "Die grossen Bibliophilen." Geschichte der
Büchersammler und ihrer Sammlungen. Bd. 1-3. Lps. 1922.
---- Einführung in die Bibliophilie. Lpz. 1931.
Arthur E. Bostwick. The American Public Library. 4. ed. New
York 1929.
Henri Bouchot. Les ex-libris et les marques de possession du
livre. Paris 1891.
Margaret Burton. Famous Libraries of the World. Their History,
Collections and Administration. London 1937.
G. H. Bushwell. The World's Earliest Libraries. London 1931.
Christian Callmer. Antike Bibliotheken. (Opuscula archaeologica.
3). Lund 1944 (Skrifter utg. av Svenska institutet i Rom. 10).

Carl L. Cannon. American Book Collectors and Collecting from Colonial Times to the Present. New York 1941.

C. M. Carlander. Svenska bibliotek och ex-libris. 2. uppl., bd. 1-4. Sthlm. 1896-1903.

J. Cerný. Paper and Books in Ancient Egypt. London 1952.

J. W. Clark. The Care of Books. London 1901.

Ch. J. Elton and Mary A. Elton. The Great Book Collectors. London 1893.

Arundell Esdaile. National Libraries of the World. London 1934.

William Younger Fletcher. English Book Collectors. London 1902.

Theodor Gottlieb. Ueber mittelalterliche Bibliotheken. Lpz. 1890.

Joannis Guigard. Nouvel armorial du bibliophile. Tome 1-2. Nouv. éd. Paris 1899.

W. J. Hardy. Bookplates. London 1893.

Arthur G. Hassø. Danske Exlibris. Kbh. 1942.

Alfred Hessel. History of Libraries, trans. with supplementary material by Reuben Peiss. ed. 2. New York, 1955.

Hugo Høgdahl. Norske exlibris og andre bokeiermerker. Oslo 1946.

Clément Janin. Essai sur la bibliophilie contemporaine de 1900 à 1928. Tome 1-2. Paris 1931.

A. Jörgensen. Bokägermärken i Finland. Helsingfors 1916.

Preben Kirkegaard. Folkebibliotekerne i Danmark. Kbh. 1948.

Kl. Löffler. Deutsche Klosterbibliotheken. 2 stark verm. Aufl. Bonn und Lpz. 1922.

F. S. Merryweather. Bibliomania in the Middle Ages. Revised ed. London 1933.

F. Milkau. Die Bibliotheken. (Kultur der Gegenwart Teil 1, Abt. 1). 2. Aufl. Lpz. 1912.

Otto Mühlbrecht. Die Bücherliebhaberei in ihrer Entwicklung bis zum Ende des 19. Jahrhunderts. 2. Aufl. Bielefeld und Lpz. 1898.

Lauritz Nielsen. Danske Privatbiblioteker gennem Tiderne. I, Indtil Udgangen af det 17. Aarhundrede. Kbh. 1946.

Carl S. Petersen. Afhandlinger til dansk Bog- og Bibliotekshistorie. Kbh. 1949.

Popular Libraries of the World. Ed. by Arthur E. Bostwick. (American Library Association). New York 1933.

Saymour de Ricci. English Collectors of Books and Manuscripts (1530-1930). Cambr. 1930.

Ernest A. Savage. The Story of Libraries and Book-Collecting. New York, n. d.

W. Schürmeyer. Bibliotheksräume aus fünf Jahrhunderten. n. p., n. d.

G. Seyler. Illustriertes Handbuch der Exlibris-Kunde. Berlin 1895.

Arthur Sjögren. Svenska kungliga och furstliga bokägaremärken. Sthlm. 1915.

A. Stalhane. Finska ex-libris. Helsingfors 1940.

J. W. Thompson. The Medieval Library. Cambr. 1939.

Svenska bibliotek. Under red. av J. Viktor Johansson. I. Sthlm. 1946.

O. Walde. Storhetstidens litterära krigsbyten. En kultur-historisk-bibliografisk studie. I-II. Upps. og Sthlm. 1916-20.

M. Weitemeyer. Babylonske og assyriske arkiver og biblioteker. Kbh. 1955. (Studier fra Sprog- og Oldtidsforskning. 227).

W. von Zur Westen. Exlibris (Bucheignerzeichen). 3. Aufl. Bielefeld 1925.

Index

Byzantine (cont.)
  55, 56, 60, 78
Byzantine libraries 38
Byzantium 38, 39 (see also Constantinople)

Caen 262
Caesar 23, 31, 163
Caesarea library 37
Cairo 22, 40
calamus 9
California 237, 239, 240, 266
Caliph Harun-al-Raschid 39, 40
calligraphy 15, 21, 28, 45, 47,
  117, 119, 207, 243 (see also
  handwriting)
Callimachus 19, 21
Calman-Lévy 230
Calvin 163
Cambrai 262
Cambridge 67, 115, 152, 193,
  196, 227, 245, 258
cameo bindings 125, 129
Campe 195
Canada 264
Canevari, Demetrio 125
"canon" see "missal"
Canterbury 43, 52, 64
Canterbury Tales 106
capitalis quadrata 33
capitalis rustica 33, 34
capsa 21
"Caractèrès de civilité" 149
cardboard 123
Carnegie, Andrew 236
Caroline style, (see Carolingian)
Carolingian 54-6, 57, 60, 62,
  77, 102
Carolingian Minuscule 77, 102
Carthusians 76
cartography 166-7
cartouche 155, 192
Caslon, William 207
Caslon's type 208, 224, 243
Cassidorus 41
castigatores 113
casting (type) 87-8, 90, 92, 158,
  222
catalog(s) 17, 19, 58, 65, 70,
  80, 83, 120, 136, 168, 180,
  211, 219, 229, 233, 235, 260,

261, 263
catalog card 264
cataloging process 240
Catalogue la librairie 230
Cathedral style (binding) 220, 221
Catherine de Medici 147
Catholic Church 39, 42, 135,
  136, 137, 139, 176, 211
Catholicon 96, 97
Caxton, William 105, 114, 115,
  193
Celsus Library 32
Celtic 50, 53
Centaur type 246
Champfleury 146, 148
Charlemagne 54
Charles, Earl of Sunderland 214
Charles, 3rd Earl of Stanhope
  196
Charles V (the Wise) 70
Charles IX 149
Charles X 177, 189
Charles XI 178
Charles Gustavus 177
Charles the Bald 70
charta 18, 22
charta pergamena 24
chartres 18
Chartres 262
Chaucer 106, 225
Chaucer type 224
Chevalier, Étienne 72
Chicago 238, 240, 265
children's books 195, 250, 259
China 13, 33-4, 84, 85, 116
Chiswick Press 224
Chodowiecki, Daniel 196, 198,
  218
Choffard, Pierre Philippe 186
Christ 48, 60, 70, 85, 86, 97,
  141
Christensen, C. 251
Christensen, Povl 251
Christian III 138, 139, 141, 144
Christian IV 178, 181
Christian(s) 23, 26, 37, 38, 41,
  43, 56, 85, 98
Christian Egyptians (see Coptic)
Christiansen, V.R. 266
Christina (Queen) 169, 177
chronicles 106, 112
Church Fathers 58
church libraries 37, 41

Church of Rome (see Catholic
Church)
Cicero 29, 35, 77, 78
"civilité" type 146
clasps 63, 64, 81
Classical antiquity (see antiquity)
Classics (see antiquity, Greek,
Latin)
Clemens, Johan Frederik 205
Clément, D. L. 222
Clements, William Lawrence 238
cloth bindings 228, 255
Cluniac 64
coat(s) of arms 97, 114, 143,
146, 151, 152, 157, 171, 192,
220
Cobden-Sanderson, T. J. 226,
253, 255
Cochin, Charles Nicolas 186,
205, 248, 253
Cochin roman (type) 253
Cockerell, Douglas 253
codex (codices) 24-27, 33, 39,
50, 52, 67, 77, 80, 93, 178
Codex Argenteus 50, 178
Codex Sinaiticus 39
Colbert 168
Colin, Armand 230
Colines, Simon de 146
collector(s) and collection(s) 17-
23, 30, 31, 37, 39, 40, 42,
56-8, 64-8, 70, 75, 76-7, 78-
83, 125, 138, 139, 144, 147,
152, 153, 161, 165, 168-9,
177-9, 187-9, 192-3, 197, 200,
202-3, 207, 211, 213, 214,
219-22, 227, 232, 237, 238,
239, 260-2, 264, 265, 266
(see also book collectors)
collotype process 243
Cologne 87, 90, 106, 112, 135,
259
Cologne Bible 99, 105
Colonna, Francesco 122, 124
colophon 47, 97
color printing 242-3
colporteurs 112, 113
Columban 43
Columbia University 240
composing machines 223, 242,
243
Condé Museum 56
conditional sale system 229, 230,

231, 256
Conrad, Zacharias 195
Constantine the Great 38
Constantinople 38, 51, 78, 81
"contra-roll" 26
Copenhagen 22, 34, 51, 57, 59,
66, 74, 76, 79, 98, 105, 108,
110, 111, 116, 131, 139, 140,
150, 157, 165, 168, 176, 178,
180, 181, 199, 210, 227, 266
(see also Denmark)
copper engraving 131, 154, 157,
158, 160-1, 162, 164, 176,
181, 183, 185, 186, 187, 188,
189, 196, 198, 199, 205, 218,
242, 243
Coptic 27, 28, 37, 62, 117,
168, 237
Copyright Act 196, 258
Corbie 43, 44, 75
Cordova 40, 81
Corneille 163, 187
Cornell University 238
"Corvinians" 82, 117, 118, 119
Corvinus, Matthias 82, 111,
117
Cosimo de Medici 78, 80
Cosimo III 179
Coster, Heinrich 115
Coster, Laurens Janszoon 87
cottage bindings 173
Cotton, Bruce 192
Count Adolph 88
Count de la Bédoyère 220
Count Harry Kessler 247
Count Heinrich von Brühl 194
Count Karl Heinrich von Hoym
189
Count Otto Heinrich 143
Count Palatine 144
Count Philip 74
Court Library 170, 213
Coyet, Peter Julius 178
cradle books (see incunabula)
Craig, Gordon 250
Cramer, Peter 197
Cranach, Lucas 133, 135, 136,
143
Crane, Walter 224
Crawford, Earl of 215
crescent-shaped tool 198
Cretté, Georges 254
Crusades 133

283

engraving(s) (cont.)
197, 201, 205, 215, 216, 218, 242, 243, 250 (see also copper engraving, decorations, illustrations, woodcuts, etc.)
enlightenment 195, 241
Enschedé, Izaak 165
en-tetes 183
Eragny Press 250
Erasmus 130, 131, 146
Escorial Library 169, 213
Étienne, Henri 147
Étienne, Robert 146-7, 153
Etymologiae 42
Eumenes II 23
evangeliaries 47
Evans 214
Eve, Nicolas 149
ex bibliotheca 192
ex libris 190-2, 200, 208, 219
ex museo 192
"explicit" 47
"explicitus est" 47
Eyb, Baron Albrecht von 82

fables 98, 112, 186, 196
Fabri, Johannes 108
facsimile editions 233, 243
fairy tales 218
Fallitur hora legendo (reading passes the time) 192
fanfare style 149, 151, 152, 171, 221
Farmington plan 263
Farnese 125
Fatimite 40
Faust 248
Fell, John (Bishop) 163, 224
Ferrari, Gabriel de 126
Ferreolus, Tonantius 42
fers à la dentelle (lacework pattern) 190
fers azurés (shaded stamps) 125
fers pointillés (dotted lines) 171
Feuerabend, Sigismund 134, 154
Finland 252
Fischer, Gustav 229
Fischer, S. 229
Fiske, D. W. 238
fixed retail prices 228, 231, 256, 257
flaps 117, 118

flat printing 218
Flatey Book 58
Flemish 72, 104, 185, 187
fleur-de-lis bindings 146, 149
Fleuron, The 245
fleurons (headpieces) 183
Flora Danica 181
Florence 80, 82, 126, 127, 160, 179, 233, 237
Flyge, J. L. 222
Fock, Gustav 232
Fogel, Johann 115
Folger, Henry Clay 238
foliation 27
folium (sheet) 27
fonts (see types)
foolscap 69, 71
Forening for Boghaandvaerk 228
format(s) 26, 69, 70, 72, 106, 119, 120, 123, 161, 166, 183, 185, 194, 243
Forsburg, Karl-Erik 253
42-line Bible 93, 95, 115
Fouquet, Jean 72, 74
Fournier, Pierre Simon 188, 252
fraktur type 132, 133, 134, 135, 157, 197, 208, 209, 247
France and French, 43, 44, 56, 57, 69, 70, 75, 82, 94, 106, 108, 115, 124, 126, 135, 137, 144-52, 168, 171, 172, 175, 185-92, 197, 203, 205, 207, 209-11, 216, 219, 220, 221, 222, 230, 233, 234, 248, 249, 253, 256, 257, 262, 266
Francis I 82, 147, 171
Franciscan(s) 64, 65
Franklin, Benjamin 227
Franks 42
Frederick II 70
Frederick III 180
Frederick the Great 194, 213, 217, 218
Frederick William 179
Frederiksen, Erik Ellegaard 251
French Encyklopaedi 195
French Revolution 183, 209-11, 213, 219, 220, 235
French Royal Library 189
friezes 56, 122
Froben, Johan 130, 146
frontispieces 160, 161, 162,

Luther Martin 135, 137, 138
Luther's catechism 136, 141
Lützelburger, Hans 130
Luxdorph, Bolle 197, 204
Luxeuil 43, 45
Lybeck, Bertil 252
Lyman, Andreas 200
Lyons 106, 120, 130, 135, 144, 146

machine composition 222, 243, 245
Macmillan 231
Madrid 169, 213
Mads Uingaard 157
Maerne, Samuel 173
magazines 223, 242, 267 (see also periodicals)
Maggliabecchi, Antonio 179
Maggs Brothers 232
Magnus family 165, 173
Mahieu, Thomas 125, 128
Maillol, Aristide 249
Mainz 87, 88, 89, 91, 94, 102, 108, 135
Mainz Psalter 97, 104
Maiolu 125
Maisonneuve & Cie 233
majuscules 44
Malermis 104
Mansion, Colard 105, 106
Manuel du libraire 219
manuscript(s) 13, 20, 21, 24-8, 34, 35, 38, 39, 43, 47, 56-60, 75, 77-80, 109, 111, 113, 118, 123, 137,139, 140, 178, 192, 211, 213, 214, 232, 237, 260, 264, 266
manuscript decoration 47-50
Manutius, Aldus Pius 119-23
maps 166, 237, 239
Marburg 138, 261
Marciana 80
Marillier, Pierre Clément 187, 205
marine charts 166
"maroquin" 123
Marquis of Blanford 214
Marquis of Paulmy 189
Martin, Pierre 254
Martzan, Melchior 180, 181
Masereel, Franz 250

Matisse, Henri 249
matrices 90, 92
Maugérard, Jean Baptiste 213
mauresques 117
Maurus, Hrabanus 54
Maximilian I, 82, 130, 133, 176
Mazarin, (Cardinal) 94, 168, 172
Mazarin Bible 94
Mearne, Samuel 173
measuring type 205
Medici, The 78-83, 125, 147
Medicine, Book of 57
Meid, Hans 247
Melanchthon 141, 143
Mendicants 64
Menzel, Adolf von 217, 218
Mergenthaler, Ottmar 223
Merian, Matthäus 161
Merovingian 44, 46, 48, 54
Merrymount Press 247
Mesopotamia 14, 15, 18
Meunier, Charles 222
Meuser, Caspar 144
Meynell, Francis 245
Michel, Marius 222
Michelangelo 80
microfilming 264
Middle Ages 37-83, 84-158, 216, 218, 220, 224, 237
Milkau 261
"miniator" 48
miniatures 48, 52, 58, 60, 70, 77, 117
minuscules 44, 46, 54, 55, 77, 102
mirror bindings 200, 202
Missale Slesvicense 108
missal(s) 106, 108, 133, 137
missal script 55, 57
missal type 94, 108, 247
Møller, Kai Friis 251
Møller, Nicolaus 197
Moltke, Joachim 181
monasteries 37, 38, 39, 41-8, 50, 54, 56, 57, 58, 62, 64, 65, 73, 75, 80, 102, 111, 137, 138, 169, 177, 211, 213, 260, 262
monograms 147, 175
monotype 223, 245
Monte Cassino 44, 64, 75, 262
Montefeltro, Federigo da 82
Montesquieu 187

Oxenstierna, Axel 177
Oxenstierna, Erik 177
Oxford 22, 64, 65, 67, 138, 263
Oxford, Earl of 193
Oxford Lectern Bible 246, 247
Oxford University Press 163, 245, 258

Padeloup, Antoine 190
paintings 47, 50, 51, 56, 70, 71, 73, 93, 98, 99, 117, 121, 155, 160, 161, 185, 187, 203, 224, 251
Palatinate 143
Palatine library 31
Palatine Hill 31
paleotypes 113
Palestine 37
palimpsests 24, 35
Palladius, Peter 140
Palmgren, Valfrid 241
Pamphilos 37
pamphlets 157, 193
Panckoucke fils 230
panel-stamped bindings 114-6, 141, 143, 152, 172, 175, 200, 202, 221, 222
Panizzi, Antonio 233, 234,
Pannartz, Arnold 102
Papal Library 34
paper 33, 34, 36, 40, 68-70, 116, 118, 135, 137, 154, 157, 171, 218, 222, 243, 244
paper bindings 227, 255
paper inlay 144
papermaking machine 222
Papillon, J.B. 216
papyrus 7-11, 18-22, 25, 26, 33, 47
parchment 24-28, 33, 35, 62, 141, 143
Parentucelli, Tommaso 80
Paris 65, 66, 72, 75, 106, 112, 123, 135, 146, 147, 153, 185, 189, 194, 195, 205, 211, 213, 216, 230, 233, 234, 262, 263
parish libraries 241
Parliament 192
Pascal 163
Paul III 125
Paulli, Simon 181

Payne, Roger 208, 209, 215
Peace of Vienna 213
Peder Paars 197
Pedersen, Christiern 141, 157
Peignot, G. 220
Peignot foundry 252
"peintres-illustrateurs" 250
Peiresc, Nicolas Claude de 168, 172
Pelletan, Edouard 248
pen-and-ink artists 251
pencil 46
pen(s) 9, 13, 20, 28, 48 (see also brushes)
Penguin Books 258
Pergamum 23, 24
periodicals 223, 228, 245, 259, 262 (see also journals and magazines)
Perpetua type 245
Persians 17, 24, 40, 117, 118
Petersen, Gunnar 250
Petersen, Immanuel 222
"petites heures" 106
Petrarch 77, 78, 80, 82, 102, 238
Pfister, Albrecht 98, 99
Philadelphia 227, 231
Philip, Count 74
Philip, Duke 185
Philip II 156
Philip the Good 70
Phillips, Sir Thomas 214
Philobiblon 75
philologist 82
Philosophical Transactions 195
Phoenician 17
Photius 39
photographic etchings 218, 223
photogravure 242
Picasso, Pablo 249
Pickering, William 224
pictorial reproduction 223
picture books 185
picture-rolls 22
picture(s) (see decoration, illustration, ornamentation)
pilgrim book 127
pinhead binding 171
Pisos collection 31
Pissarro, Lucien 250
Pixerécourt, G. de 220
plano printing 218

293

Salerno 65
sales systems 228, 230
Samarkand 40
San Lorenzo 80
San Marco 80
Sandgren, August 254
Sans-Souci 194
Savanarola 126
Saxo Grammaticus 139
Saxon 44
Saxony 65, 143, 194
Saxo 141
Scandinavian 56-8, 69, 73, 81,
143, 179, 195, 200-3, 221,
227, 228, 229, 231, 234, 241,
244, 250-3, 254, 256, 266
Schedel, Hartman 100, 101, 127
Schellhorn Bible 94
Schneidler, Kristoffer 203
Schöffer, Peter 89, 94, 100,
112
Schøning, Gerhard 203
Schönsperger, Hans 133
Schwabacher type 133, 134, 135,
247
Schwind, Moritz von 217
scientific journals 195, 233
scientific works 208, 230, 257,
258
Scotland 42, 196
scribes 9, 11, 15, 21, 25, 40,
47, 48, 54, 65, 73, 80, 82,
89, 139
script 21, 27, 33, 37, 43, 44,
45, 53, 54, 55, 57 (see also
calligraphy and handwriting)
Scriptores rerum Danicarum 197
scriptorium 58
scriptuarius 58
second-hand book trade 231-3
Seefeldt, Jørgen 178
Seelengärtlein 135
Sefavids 40
Segonzac, André Dunoyer de 249
Seguier 172
Seneca 31
Senefelder, Alois 218
Serapeion 19
ser-i-lauh 117
servi literati 29
Shakespeare 238
Shannon, Charles 250
Shihaungti, Emperor 13

Sibylla, Maria 161
Sidonius Apollinaris 42
signatures 26
Simon, Oliver 245
Simons, Anna 245
Simonsen, David 266
Sinaiticus (Codex) 39
Sixtus IV 81
Skov, Lavrids 197
Shovgaard, Niels 230
Simier 221
Sir Thomas Phillips 214
Slesvig 57
Slevogt, Max 247
Sloane, Hans 192
Sorbona, Robert de 65
Sorbonne 65
Sørensen, Christian 223
Sorø 57, 181
Sosii brothers 30
Sotheran, H. 232
Soviet Union (see Russia)
spacing 92, 94, 114, 116, 117
Spain 39, 40, 41, 42, 44, 50,
69, 117, 126, 156, 171, 266
special libraries 260
Speculum humanae salvationis
85, 97
Speier 135
Spencer, Lord 214
Speyer 102, 104
Spofford, A. R. 239
Springer, Julius 229
Staatliche Museum 22
stacks (library) 234, 235, 263
Stadbibliotheken 137
stamps and stamping 62, 64,
68, 87, 114, 125, 157, 171,
172, 173, 175, 198, 200, 220
(see also blind-stamped,
panel-stamped, roller stamps)
Stanhope, Lord 196
state libraries 266
stationarii 65
Stationers' Company 231, 257
Statsbibliotek 234
Stavanger 58
steel engraving 215
Steenberg, Andreas 241
Steffens, Franz 35, 46, 47, 54,
55
Stephanius, Stephan 177
stereotyping 196, 205

296